The $100 Hamburger

SM

A Pilots' Guide
2022

by

John Purner

ISBN: 9798546067731

For quantity discounts on volume orders please contact
John Purner
Chicago, IL
Email: jpurner@100dollarhamburger.com

Internet: www.100dollarhamburger.com

First Printing: August 2022

ABOUT the AUTHOR

John Purner is the editor and publisher of the **$100 Hamburger** *(www.100dollarhamburger.com)* website which has been the most popular website for recreational flyers for a quarter of a century.

The following is a list of other books by John Purner that you might enjoy. They are available at Amazon.com, pilot shops and bookstores across the world.

$100 Hamburger – A Pilots' Guide 2022
The $100 Hamburger Guide to Buying & Selling Aircraft
The Chickenfried Café
02 GOLF
$100 Hamburger – A Pilots' Guide 2019
Electric Car Buyers' Guide – 2018
The $100 Hamburger – A Pilots' Guide
The $100 Hamburger – 2014/15
6 Weeks to Winning Weekend Golf
BUYcycle: The Best Kept Secrets ….
15 BEST Airport Restaurants plus 2,347 Runner-Ups!
101 Best Aviation Attractions
The $500 Round of Golf: A Guide to …..
The $100 Hamburger – …..Editions 1, 2 & 3

Foreword

Thank you for purchasing this copy of the **$100 Hamburger - A Pilots' Guide 2022**. Like all travel guides it is an incomplete work. The information it contains is constantly being updated for subsequent printings. The latest information we have is available on our subscription-based website – *100dollarhamburger.com*. Should you find any errors or have any suggestions please reach out to me – *jpurner@100dollarhamburger.com*.

In addition to updating the restaurant and airport information I am constantly on the lookout for ways to improve the book. Only restaurants that are actually **ON** an airport are included in this book. Burger flights are usually about flying away for a meal not a weekend getaway, which makes covering only **ON** airport venues exclusively in keeping with this book's mission. A few **ON** airport flyin museums, golf courses, campgrounds, resorts and hotels are included.

All of the reviews in this book come directly from my personal experiences or from PIREPs that have come in from subscribers to my website *100dollarhamburger.com*. The star rating system I use is driven by six factors: ambiance, cleanliness, service, food, price and attitude. The first five are easy to quantify. The last one, attitude, is summed up with the answer to a simple question. Do I feel welcome? By the way, I go to each restaurant as you do – *privately*. No one at the restaurant knows who I am, even the ones that I frequent. I sit at the same tables you will, am served by the same waitstaff, eat the same food and pay the same price always with cash as a credit card would give me away.

What does it take to get five stars? Simple – ***something very, very special***. This can point to a restaurant that rivals New York and Chicago's finest. It doesn't mean that the restaurant is necessarily upscale and pricey, rather that it is off the charts in each of the six measurement areas I value. Each of you will have a wonderful experience at any of the restaurants that has earned five stars.

Four stars are given to really good restaurants that are a little off base in one of the six areas, but it can't be attitude. You must **ALWAYS** feel welcome. Maybe the ambiance isn't all that it could be or maybe the food is just a cut below best in class.

Three stars is our average. A seriously good place that measures up to all of the other good places that you expect to find at an airport but there is nothing about it that hits the outstanding button. It is good in all six areas and neither excellent nor awful in any of them.

Two stars restaurants are troubled but adequate. You can get a meal that you'll be **OK** with and service that isn't offensive though it may be slow and sometimes really slow. The lower quality is **ALWAYS** reflected in *attitude*. You may feel welcome or you may feel that you are a bother, but you'll never feel special.

One star is my way of saying – **AVOID**. It is on an airport so we include it but I certainly don't support it and neither should you unless you're really in a pinch.

A word about COVID. It changed our world in many ways and none of them for the better except maybe that we all pay more attention to washing our hand and/or using hand sanitizers. I think that's good. Doctors learned during the American Civil War that not washing their hands between operations such as amputations spread disease from patient to patient. Handwashing keeps you healthy. So that's a good thing that the COVID lockdowns reminded us of.

Everything else about COVID was bad. Everything. Many airport restaurants closed during the past two years, some forever. Mostly the ones that closed have been replaced by a new restaurant. American Optimism was not diminished by COVID and there are plenty of entrepreneurs who feel they can make an airport restaurant their life or at least an important part of it. When you can give these folks a vote of confidence by dropping in to see how they're doing.

One final thought. Please use this book as an information resource only and not as your be all and end all. Email addresses, website URLs and phone numbers are included wherever possible. Check out the place you're about to visit before you launch. Flying is expensive. A mistaken destination is costly. Restaurants come and go, hours and menus change. I ALWAYS call first and ask, *"what are your hours and do you still have the best corned beef sandwich in the state?"* Asking about a specific menu item gives you a clue about changes.

Finally, I appreciate feedback, good and bad. Please let me hear from you via email to **jpurner@100dollarhamburger.com**. I personally answer every note that comes my way.

Fly someplace today. You've earned it!

Table of Contents

Legend

Star Ratings

*	**Needs Improvement**
**	**Adequate**
***	**Average**
****	**Well Above Average**
*****	**Outstandin**

John Purner

FlyIn Alabama

ANDALUSIA/OPP, AL (SOUTH ALABAMA RGNL - 79J)
Aprt Mgr: MISTY JONES **PH:** (334) 222-6598
Field Elevation: 310 **CTAF:** 119.550 **FUEL:** 100LLA+
Runway: 11/29 **Length:** 6000 **Width:** 100 **Surface:** ASPH-G

*** Blade 'n' Wing Café – (334) 222-0638
Open: Depends
PIREP:
The food here is classic Alabama *'Meat and 3'* steam table fair. Simple and lip smackin' good. Here's the thing. It is open at different times for different folks.

The **General Public** can come for Lunch
Monday - Friday (Holidays Excluded) 10:00 a.m. - 2:00 p.m.

The **Flying Public** (Military & Civilian Pilots who Fly-In)
Monday-Friday 7:30 a.m. - 11:30 p.m.

Here's the deal, the cost:
Adults $10.50 for 30 minutes.

BESSEMER, AL (BESSEMER - EKY)
Aprt Mgr: MIKE COLLINS **PH:** 205-428-9292
Field Elevation: 700 **CTAF:** 123.000 **FUEL:** 100LLA+
Runway: 05/23 **Length:** 6007 **Width:** 100 **Surface:** ASPH-F

*** The Hangar – (205) 434-2121
Open:
Mon -Thur: 11:30 - 10 Fri 11:30 - Midnight Sat. 2 - Midnight
PIREP:
It's right on the ramp and there's never a fee to land at EKY and eat at The Hangar. I always order the Cheeseburger basket with onion rings and I have them throw a Slaw Dog on my plate for good measure. I love Slaw Dogs! Oh almost forgot, they have terrific live music call ahead to see who's appearing. It's a fun spot!

FLORALA, AL (FLORALA MUNI - 0J4)
Aprt Mgr: FLORALA AIRPORT AUTHORITY **PH:** 334-858-6173
Field Elevation: 314 **CTAF:** 123.000 **FUEL:**
Runway: 04/22 **Length:** 3197 **Width:** 75 **Surface:** ASPH-G

*** Sunshine Aero Industries - (334) 858-6720

Open:

Daily: Lunch

Restaurant Website: www.sunshineaero.com

Restaurant Email: ddavis@gtcom.net

Restaurant Email: sunshineaero0j4@yahoo.com

PIREP:

The FBO has a buffet loaded with BBQ, dogs and burgers. Dave smokes the pork right at the airport.

Watch out for military choppers, these guys flock to this place for lunch and fuel. It's open seven days a week, year around. They're really setup to cater to the military choppers (they hot fuel on site, fun to watch), and the Navy trainers out of Pensacola. It's a very friendly bunch and GA is always welcome.

MONROEVILLE, AL (MONROE COUNTY - MVC)

Aprt Mgr: ANDY HARHAI **PH:** 251-575-4235

Field Elevation: 419 **CTAF:** 123.000 **FUEL:** 100LLA+

Runway: 03/21 **Length:** 6028 **Width:** 100 **Surface:** ASPH-F

*** Monroeville Aviation – (251) 575-4235

Open:

Mon - Fri: Lunch

PIREP:

They offer **'complimentary'** home cooked meals to fuel customers Monday-Friday, with the minimum purchase of ten gallons of fuel. You'll meet plenty of flight students from Naval Air Station Pensacola when you stop here.

FlyIn ALASKA

BETHEL, AK (BETHEL - BET)
Aprt Mgr: DAVID CUMMINGS PH: 907-543-2495
Field Elevation: 126 **CTAF:** 118.700 **FUEL:** 100LLA1+ B
Runway: 01L/19R **Length:** 6400 **Width:** 150 **Surface:** ASPH-F
Runway: 01R/19L **Length:** 4000 **Width:** 75 **Surface:** ASPH-G
Runway: 12/30 **Length:** 1860 **Width:** 75 **Surface:** GRVL-G

*** Bethel Airport Restaurant - (907) 692-5111
Open:
>Daily: Breakfast, Lunch & Dinner

PIREP:
The **BEST** view in Bethel

Located directly above the Alaska Airlines counter. Great breakfasts with a taste of local cuisine (reindeer sausage!)

Despite being directly on the ramp, getting to the restaurant from GA Transient Parking on Juliet Ramp requires some walking. There's no pedestrian gate through the security fence – go to vehicle gate 31 and press the OPEN button, on your right as you face the fence. Then write down the Alaska DOT number on the keypad outside. Call them (907-545-4670) for the code to get back in. If no cell reception *(AT&T doesn't work)* – ask the restaurant for a phone. Follow the road to your right to a 4-wheeler trail that cuts across the tundra to the main terminal.

Go in where you see the Alaska Airlines counter. 1st floor has some interesting information on the Yukon-Kuskokwim Delta, one of the richest waterfowl nesting areas in the world.

Restaurant is on the 2nd floor.

BETTLES, AK (BETTLES - BTT)
Aprt Mgr: JEREMY WORRALL **PH:** 907-451-5230
Field Elevation: 647 **CTAF:** 122.900 **FUEL:** 100LLA1+ B
Runway: 01/19 **Length:** 5190 **Width:** 150 **Surface:** TURF-GRVL-G

*** Bettles Lodge - (907) 692-5111
Proprietor: Dan and Lynda Klaes
Open:
>Daily: Breakfast, Lunch & Dinner

Restaurant Website: www.bettleslodge.com

Restaurant Email: info@bettleslodge.com
PIREP:
One of the best places to get a burger above the Arctic Circle is in the fly-in only community of Bettles, Alaska (50 residents) in the foothills of the Brooks Range (180 nm north of Fairbanks). The airstrip officially enjoys the most clear weather days out of anywhere in the State and is a well-maintained 5,200 foot gravel strip with nearby 5,000 foot float pond. A historic lodge acts as a pilot roadhouse and has a full service kitchen with many hamburgers on the menu. Stay overnight for the Midnight Sun in the summer or spend an afternoon exploring the unique and friendly community where everything (mail, fuel, food) is flown in daily. Visiting pilots enjoy talking with bush pilots and seeing the diverse amount of aircraft (from Cubs on tundra tires to DC-4 fuel carriers) that arrive daily. Pilots from as far away as Florida make the trip to Bettles annually.

BIG LAKE, AK (BIG LAKE - BGQ)
Aprt Mgr: NEAL HENSLEE **PH:** 907-745-2159
Field Elevation: 158 **CTAF:** 122.800 **FUEL:**
Runway: 07/25 **Length:** 2435 **Width:** 70 **Surface:** GRAVEL-G

*** The Hangar Lounge - (907) 892-9230
Proprietor: Cindy and Mark Riley
Open:
Daily: Breakfast, Lunch & Dinner
PIREP:
The 2,400-foot gravel runway is well maintained and has pilot controlled lighting at 122.8 There is no fuel for sale on the field but fuel is available at Wasilla approximately 10 miles west of BGQ. **The Hangar Lounge** is located across the street. It is a favorite with locals. The food is great and the service is friendly.

JUNEAU, AK (Juneau Harbor - 5Z1)
Field Elevation: 0 **CTAF:** 122.900 **FUEL:**
Waterlanding

*** The Hangar on the Wharf – (907) 586-5018
Open:
Daily: 11:00 AM – 10:00PM
PIREP:
Truth is, I've never been here. A subscriber to the $100 Hamburger website provided the following review. I hope you find it useful. While traveling in Alaska, I found a great $100 Hamburger spot.

John Purner

Great seafood, great views from the dockside restaurant. Lots of seaplane activity. The fish and chips were wonderful!

On a side note, I got to fly the co-pilot seat on three new planes for me while in Alaska and British Columbia. A Piper Navaho around the tip of Mt. McKinley, and two seaplanes, a DH Beaver and DH Otter. Good times and great views of some of the most beautiful places in our world!

SITKA, AK (SITKA ROCKY GUTIERREZ - SIT)
Aprt Mgr: DAVE LUCHINETTI **PH:** 907-966-2960
Field Elevation: 21 **CTAF:** 123.600 **FUEL:** 100 A1+
Runway: 11/29 **Length:** 6500 **Width:** 150 **Surface:** ASPH-G

****** Nugget Restaurant & Bakery - (907) 966-2480**
Proprietor: Patty Colton
Open:
        Mon – Sun: 8:00am - 8:00pm
Restaurant Website: www.facebook.com
Restaurant Email: nuggetsitkaak@yahoo.com
PIREP:
The Nugget is in the terminal. The ocean view is really nice. This place is famous for pie, so famous in fact that they have put in a vending machine to sell their pie slices quickly to airline passengers that must have a slice for their flight. Breakfast is also pretty good here but the service is spotty.

TOK, AK (TOK JUNCTION - 6K8)
Aprt Mgr: DENNIS BISHOP **PH:** 907-883-5128
Field Elevation: 1639 **CTAF:** 122.800 **FUEL:** 100LLA
Runway: 07/25 **Length:** 2509 **Width:** 50 **Surface:** ASPH-E

****** Fast Eddies - (907) 883-4411**
Proprietor: Ed Young
Open:
        Summer Hours: 6am – 11pm
        Winter Hours: 6am – 10pm
Restaurant Website: www.fasteddysrestaurant.com
Restaurant Email: edyoung@aptalaska.net
PIREP:
This is a nice, clean, well-decorated restaurant. The service is professional and food just one notch below excellent. I was lucky enough to be here when the Prime Rib Sandwich was the lunch special. It was really good.

6

FlyIn Arizona

CHANDLER, AZ (CHANDLER MUNI - CHD)
Aprt Mgr: CHRISTINE MACKAY PH: 480-782-3540
Field Elevation: 1243 CTAF: 126.100 FUEL: 100LLA
Runway: 04L/22R Length: 4401 Width: 75 Surface: ASPH-G
Runway: 04R/22L Length: 4870 Width: 75 Surface: ASPH-G

Chandler Air Service – 480-963-6420
FBO Website: www.aerobatics.com
Affiliate: UNK
Self Service: YES
Pilot Supplies: YES
Hours: 7 days 6 – 8

*** **Hangar Cafe – (480) 899-6965**
Proprietor: Lillian George
Open:
Mon – Sun: 7am - 2pm
PIREP:
The Hanger Cafe is more than your typical airport café. It is on the ramp with a good view. Their service was interrupted and irregular for a while due to the BIG V but as of July they're back at it. Well worth a stop.

ELOY, AZ (ELOY MUNI - E60)
Aprt Mgr: JOE BLANTON PH: 520-466-9201
Field Elevation: 1513 CTAF: 122.800 FUEL: 100LLA
Runway: 02/20 Length: 3900 Width: 75 Surface: ASPH-G

*** **Bent Prop Saloon & Cookery - (520) 466-9268**
Open:
Hours of operation vary according to season
Daily: breakfast, lunch & dinner
Restaurant Website: www.skydiveaz.com/skydiving-Facilities/food
Restaurant Email: jump@skydiveaz.com
PIREP:
The airfield is frequented primarily by both young and old but always energetic skydivers from around the world - to be sure. They are here because Skydive Arizona is here with its large fleet of jump planes: 7 Skyvans, 4 Super Twin Otters, and one each DC3, Beech 18 and Pilatus Porter. The Bent Prop is right in the central business square of this old west styled skydiving village. Eat inside *(cool A/C!)* or on the porch *(later in the winter)*. It is large, clean and fun. The service at the Bent

Prop restaurant was outstanding; decent burger bordering on unique, and a menu with a wide variety and very reasonable prices. Be careful! Skydive Arizona is extremely active most of the year. Approach from the west and do not overfly. Skydivers land on the east. Watch out for skydivers and skydiver aircraft neither follow the regular rules. Listen carefully to traffic advisories on the way in.

KINGMAN, AZ (KINGMAN - IGM)

Aprt Mgr: DAVID FRENCH **PH:** 928-757-2134
Field Elevation: 3449 **CTAF:** 122.800 **FUEL:** 100LLA
Runway: 17/35 **Length:** 6725 **Width:** 75 **Surface:** ASPH-G
Runway: 03/21 **Length:** 6827 **Width:** 150 **Surface:** ASPH-G

Air' Zona Aircraft Services – 928-757-7744

*** Kingman Airport Cafe - (928) 757-4420
General Manager: Breanna Malone
Open:
> Mon – Sun: 7AM to 2PM

Restaurant Website: www.kingmanairportcafe.com
PIREP:
Kingman Airport Café is by the pumps. The food is good and inexpensive. I've been here for breakfast and enjoyed it. Old WWII uniforms and photos dot the walls bringing you back to times gone by. The breakfast food is good, and the prices are cheap.

LAKE HAVASU CITY, AZ (LAKE HAVASU CITY - HII)

Aprt Mgr: STEVE JOHNSTON **PH:** 928-764-3330
Field Elevation: 783 **CTAF:** 122.700 **FUEL:** 100LLA
Runway: 14/32 **Length:** 8001 **Width:** 100 **Surface:** ASPH-G

**** Hangar 24 Brewery – **(928) 846-4447**
Proprietor: Ben Cook
Open:
> M-F 11am - 10pm
> Sat-Sun 7am - 10pm

Restaurant Website: hangar24brewing.com/taprooms/lake-havasu-city/

PIREP:
This is a brewery slash burger joint like so many other brewery slash burger joints but this one has the secret sauce it's on an airport and has a great view of the runway. So, if you like burgers and fly with a crew that likes beer this is a place for you. They make a GREAT root beer and amazing cheeseburgers.

MESA, AZ (FALCON FLD - FFZ)
Aprt Mgr: CORINNE NYSTROM **PH:** 480-644-2450
Field Elevation: 1394 **CTAF:** 124.600 **FUEL:** 100LLA
Runway: 04L/22R **Length:** 3799 **Width:** 75 **Surface:** ASPH-G
Runway: 04R/22L **Length:** 5101 **Width:** 100 **Surface:** ASPH-G

***** Steak and Stone of Mesa - (480) 830-6100
Open:
Mon-Sat 11AM-9PM, Sunday 4PM-9PM
Restaurant Website: www.steakandstone.com
PIREP:
This is a truly fabulous on airport steakhouse. The steaks are grilled to perfection and presented on a 500-degree stone. Keeps it sizzlin' fresh. My friend decided to accept the *Boulder* a 56-ounce Ribeye, which comes with a challenge. Eat it in 25 minutes and it's free. He paid!

NOGALES, AZ (NOGALES INTL - OLS)
Aprt Mgr: LAWRENCE TIFFIN **PH:** 520-287-9120
Field Elevation: 3955 **CTAF:** 122.800 **FUEL:** 100LLA
Runway: 03/21 **Length:** 7200 **Width:** 100 **Surface:** ASPH-G

Tiffin Aviation – 520-287-9120
FBO Website: www.tiffinaviation.com
Affiliate:
Self Service: No
Pilot Supplies: YES/Limited
Hours: 7 Days – 7AM – 7PM

*** Nogales Airport Café - (520) 287-9120
Proprietor: Jose Duran
Open:
Mon – Sun: 7:30am to 2:00pm
PIREP:
The Nogales Airport Café is in the Tiffin Aviation Services building. The airport, like most in Arizona, has a long runway to compensate for high-density altitude days. It features a pretty good downhill slope, and some rising terrain to the northeast, which will make your first arrival interesting. Don't make your first trip here at night. The food is strictly airport coffee shop fare; neither good nor bad.

PAYSON, AZ (PAYSON - PAN)
Aprt Mgr: BETH MYERS **PH:** 928-472-4748
Field Elevation: 5157 **CTAF:** 122.800 **FUEL:** 100LLA
Runway: 06/24 **Length:** 5500 **Width:** 75 **Surface:** ASPH-G

*** The Crosswinds Café - (928) 474-1613

Proprietor: Darla & Roger Annabel
Open:
>Mon - Tue: 6:00 am - 3:00 pm
>Wed - Sat: 6:00 am - 8:00 pm
>Sun - 6:00 am - 6:00 pm

Restaurant Website: www.facebook.com/crosswindsrest
PIREP:
The surrounding terrain is beautiful making this one of my favorite flights for scenic views. **The Crosswinds Café** is overrun by locals. They love the place. I love the pancakes and the friendly people.

Pies are baked fresh daily and you can take one home for less than 10 bucks.

PHOENIX, AZ (PHOENIX DEER VALLEY - DVT)
Aprt Mgr: ART FAIRBANKS **PH:** 623-869-0975
Field Elevation: 1478 **CTAF:** 118.400 **FUEL:** 100LLA
Runway: 07L/25R **Length:** 4508 **Width:** 75 **Surface:** ASPH-G
Runway: 07R/25L **Length:** 8197 **Width:** 100 **Surface:** ASPH-G

Cutter Aviation – 623-581-1444

Atlantic Aviation – 623-869-0866
FBO Website: www.atlanticaviation.com
Self Service: No
Pilot Supplies: YES
Hours: Mon – 24/ 7 days

Hertz – Atlantic Aviation – 623-869-0866

PRESCOTT, AZ (ERNEST A. LOVE FIELD - PRC)
Aprt Mgr: BENJAMIN D VARDIMAN **PH:** 928-777-1114
Field Elevation: 5045 **CTAF:** 125.300 **FUEL:** 100LLA
Runway: 12/30 **Length:** 4408 **Width:** 75 **Surface:** ASPH-G
Runway: 03L/21R **Length:** 4848 **Width:** 60 **Surface:** ASPH-G
Runway: 03R/21L **Length:** 7616 **Width:** 150 **Surface:** ASPH-G

Legend Aviation – 928-443-9333
Affiliate: Phillips
Self Service: YES
Pilot Supplies: YES
Hours: Mon – 7am – 8pm 7 days

Antelope Hills Golf – 928-776-7888
Golf Course Website: www.billycaspergolf.com

*** Susie's Skyway Restaurant - (928) 445-6971
Proprietor: Susan Sullivan
Open:

Mon – Sun: 7am – 3pm

PIREP:
Suzie's has a great view of the airport and the mountains beyond. It offers the typical airport diner menu but executes it better than most. The atmosphere is warm and friendly. The décor is straight out of the fifties.

SCOTTSDALE, AZ (SCOTTSDALE - SDL)
Aprt Mgr: GARY MASCARO **PH:** 480-312-7735
Field Elevation: 1510 **CTAF:** 119.900 **FUEL:** 100LLA
Runway: 03/21 **Length:** 8249 **Width:** 100 **Surface:** ASPH-G

**** Volanti - (480) 657-2426
Open:

Mon-Thu: 9am - 9pm
Fri-Sat: 9am - 10pm
Sun: 9am - 8pm

Restaurant Website: volantiscottsdale.com
PIREP:
Great food.
Farm to table with a familiar twist.
Amazing views of the Tarmac. Don't miss this one.

SEDONA, AZ (SEDONA - SEZ)
Aprt Mgr: EDWARD MC CALL **PH:** 928-282-4487
Field Elevation: 4830 **CTAF:** 123.000 **FUEL:** 100LLA
Runway: 03/21 **Length:** 5132 **Width:** 100 **Surface:** ASPH-G

Red Rock Aviation – 928-282-4487
Affiliate: Phillips
Self Service: NO
Pilot Supplies: NO
Hours: Mon – 6:30 - 5:30 7days

***** The Mesa Grill - 928-282-2400
Proprietor: Marc Battistini
Open:

Mon – Fri: 7am – 9pm
Sat – Sun: 7am – 9:30pm

Restaurant Website: www.mesagrillsedona.com
Restaurant Email: marc@mesagrillsedona.com
PIREP:

John Purner

The Sedona Airport is awesome. For that matter Sedona is awesome. This is a wonderful place to fly and watch your passengers press their noses against the window as they strain to get the best view possible. **The Mesa Grill** fits the locale. It too is perfect. Get this, it is even pet friendly so you can bring your furry flying buddies and sit outdoors on their patio. The ambiance is state of the art. The food? Some of the best you'll ever enjoy!

TUCSON, AZ (MARANA RGNL - AVQ)
Aprt Mgr: ORVILLE SALING **PH:** 520-437-6220
Field Elevation: 2031 **CTAF:** 123.000 **FUEL:** 100LLA
Runway: 03/21 **Length:** 3892 **Width:** 75 **Surface:** ASPH-G
Runway: 12/30 **Length:** 6901 **Width:** 100 **Surface:** ASPH-G

** Sky Rider Coffee Shop - (520) 682-3046
 Proprietor: Brenda Carter
Open:
        Mon – Sun: 6:30am – 2pm
Restaurant Website: www.maranaaz.gov/airport-services
Restaurant Email: jmangialardi@marana.com
PIREP:
I come here for one reason, the Chicken Fried Steak. They do a really good job with it. Other than that, it is a pretty standard airport restaurant.

FlyIn Arkansas

BENTONVILLE, AR (BENTONVILLE MUNI - VBT)

Aprt Mgr: DAVE POWELL **PH:** 479-254-0817
Field Elevation: 1298 **CTAF:** 122.800 **FUEL:** 100LLA
Runway: 18/36 **Length:** 4426 **Width:** 65 **Surface:** ASPH-F

**** Louise - 479-254-0817
Open:
> Tu - Fri: 11am - 8pm
> Sat: 9am - 8pm
> Sun: 9am - 3pm

Restaurant Website: www.iflysummit.com/thaden-fieldhouse
PIREP:
Louise is a restaurant and all-day cafe offering restaurant-quality cuisine with an airport diner experience.

Whether you're a local or you're flying in from out of town, you can enjoy made-to-order breakfast, brunch, lunch, and dinner items while overlooking Lake Bentonville and the unique operations of the Bentonville Airport.

Dig into a stack of made-from-scratch pancakes paired with "the best cup of airport coffee in the country" for breakfast or brunch or enjoy a classic "$100 Hamburger" for lunch or dinner as you watch airplanes and helicopters take off and land. It's an experience matched by few other restaurants in the worl

LAKEVIEW, AR (GASTONS - 3M0)

Aprt Mgr: JA GASTON **PH:** 870-431-5202
Field Elevation: 479 **CTAF:** 122.800 **FUEL:** 100LL
Runway: 06/24 **Length:** 3200 **Width:** 55 **Surface:** TURF-G

Gaston's – 870-431-5202
FBO Website: www.gastons.com
Affiliate: UNK
Self Service: NO
Pilot Supplies: NO
Hours: Mon – 8 - 9 7days

***** Gaston's Restaurant - (870) 431-5202
Proprietor: Jim Gaston
Open:

Daily: Breakfast, Lunch, Dinner
Restaurant Website: www.gastons.com
Restaurant Email: gastons@gastons.com
PIREP:
You come here to eat trout not steak and not breakfast. This is the house that trout built. My favorite is the Pan Seared Boneless Rainbow Trout. Guess where it comes from? I must mention that the approach and the landing strip are among my personal favorites. I love the sound that tires make as they kiss the grass.

***

***** Gaston's White River Resort - (870) 431-5202
Proprietor: Jim Gaston
Open:
Year-Round
Restaurant Website: www.gastons.com
Restaurant Email: gastons@gastons.com
PIREP:
If you are a pilot and a fisherman this should be on your bucket list. Certainly, there are better fishing holes in Canada and Alaska but this one is almost dead center in the middle of America. That means you can get here with a Cherokee from about anywhere in the USA. The landing strip is 3,200 feet of manicured turf with an easy approach. Once on the ground, you'll find everything you need including guides, boats, training and rental fishing gear. The plus factor is the setting, the cabins, the Lodge and the restaurant. Do this. You'll thank me a thousand times for recommending it.

LITTLE ROCK, AR (ADAMS FIELD - LIT)
Aprt Mgr: RON MATHIEU **PH:** 501-372-3439
Field Elevation: 266 **CTAF:** 0.000 **FUEL:** 100LLA
Runway: 18/36 **Length:** 6224 **Width:** 150 **Surface:** CONC-G
Runway: 04R/22L **Length:** 8251 **Width:** 150 **Surface:** CONC-G
Runway: 04L/22R **Length:** 8273 **Width:** 150 **Surface:** CONC-G

***

Avis Car Rental – (501) 376-9151
Sun 7:00 AM - 12:30 AM
Mon - Fri 5:45 AM - 12:30 AM
Sat 7:00 AM - 12:00 AM

***

*** Whole Hog BBQ - (501) 975-9315
Open:
Daily: 11am to 8pm
Restaurant Website: www.wholehogcafe.com
PIREP:
Whole Hog BBQ at Bill and Hillary Clinton/Adams Field (LIT) in Little Rock makes a great food stop. It is located inside the **Tac Air**

14

FBO building on the GA ramp. They have a full restaurant BBQ menu. The ambiance is clean and modern made better by large floor to ceiling windows overlooking a very active field. You will be very impressed by the service both on the ramp and in the restaurant – fast and friendly! The Whole Hog BBQ food is trucked in from another location in Little Rock. This was the decision of the new owners of Tac Air who bought out Central Flying Service FBO.

PINE BLUFF, AR (GRIDER FIELD - PBF)
Aprt Mgr: DOUG HALE **PH:** 870-534-4131
Field Elevation: 206 **CTAF:** 123.000 **FUEL:** 100LLA
Runway: 18/36 **Length:** 5998 **Width:** 150 **Surface:** ASPH-G

Pine Bluff Aviation– 870-534-4131
FBO Website: www.cityofpinebluff.com
Affiliate: UNK
Self Service: YES
Pilot Supplies: NO
Hours: Mon – 24/7

*** Grider Field Restaurant - (870) 534-4131
Proprietor: Doug Hale
Open:
   Mon - Fri: 11am - 2pm
Restaurant Website: www.pbf-airport.com/restaurant.html
Restaurant Email: doug.grider@yahoo.com
PIREP:
The Grider Field Restaurant is in the main terminal building. You can literally taxi up to the front door. The food, especially the fried chicken, is first rate. They offer a meat and three, buffet which I always enjoy. Everything is cooked from scratch according to the manager. Great airport; Great restaurant!! Give it a try. I'm glad I did.

SPRINGDALE, AR (SPRINGDALE MUNI - ASG)
Aprt Mgr: JAMES SMITH **PH:** 479-750-8585
Field Elevation: 1353 **CTAF:** 118.200 **FUEL:** 100LLA
Runway: 18/36 **Length:** 5302 **Width:** 76 **Surface:** ASPH-F

Summit Aviation – 479-751-4462
FBO Website: iflysummit.com
Affiliate: UNK
Self Service: YES
Pilot Supplies: YES
Hours:
   M-F 6:00am - 9:00pm
   Sat/Sun 7:00am - 7:00pm

Mon - Fri: 10:00 am - 2:00 pm
Sat: 10:00 am - 9:00 pm

WALNUT RIDGE, AR (WALNUT RIDGE RGNL - ARG)
Aprt Mgr: MITCH WHITMIRE **PH:** 870-886-5432
Field Elevation: 279 **CTAF:** 122.800 **FUEL:** 100LLA
Runway: 04/22 **Length:** 6001 **Width:** 150 **Surface:** ASPH-G
Runway: 18/36 **Length:** 5001 **Width:** 150 **Surface:** CONC-F
Runway: 13/31 **Length:** 5003 **Width:** 150 **Surface:** CONC-F

Pine Bluff Aviation– 870-534-4131
FBO Website: www.cityofpinebluff.com
Affiliate: UNK
Self Service: YES
Pilot Supplies: NO
Hours: Mon – 24/7

*** Wings of Honor Museum – (800) 584-5575
Proprietor: Donna Robertson
Open:

Mon - Sat: 9:00am - 5:00pm
Museum Website: www.wingsofhonor.org
Museum Email: harold@wingsofhonor.org
PIREP:
"The wings they wore…the wings that carried them to victory"
The Wings of Honor Museum is located across the road from the Walnut Ridge Regional Airport. It was established in 1999 to preserve the history of the Walnut Ridge Army Flying School, the Marine Corps Air Facility at Walnut Ridge, the War Assets Administration's Warbird Storage, Sales and Scrapping Facility, and the USAF 725th Radar Squadron; and to remember and honor those civilian and military personnel who served to maintain our freedom.

FlyIn California

ARCATA/EUREKA, CA (ARCATA - ACV)
　　Aprt Mgr: JACQUELYN HULSEY **PH:** 707-839-5401
　　Field Elevation: 222 **CTAF:** 123.000 **FUEL:** 100LLA
　　Runway: 01/19 **Length:** 4501 **Width:** 150 **Surface:** ASPH-G
　　Runway: 14/32 **Length:** 6046 **Width:** 150 **Surface:** ASPH-G

County Owned FBO – 707-839-5401
Affiliate: Unknown
Self Service: NO
Pilot Supplies: NO
Hours: 7 Days 4am – midnight

AUBURN, CA (AUBURN MUNI - AUN)
　　Aprt Mgr: MS. BERNIE SCHROEDER **PH:** 530-386-4211
　　Field Elevation: 1539 **CTAF:** 122.700 **FUEL:** 100LL80 A
　　Runway: 07/25 **Length:** 3700 **Width:** 75 **Surface:** ASPH-G

Threshold Aviation – 530-823-0744
FBO Website: www.flyiti.com
Affiliate: Unknown
Self Service: YES
Pilot Supplies: NO
Hours: 7 Days 8am – 5pm

**** Wings Grill & Espresso Bar - (530) 885-0428
Proprietor: Connie Horning
Open:
　　　　Mon – Sun: 7am – 2pm
PIREP:
Auburn is a very scenic airport best viewed from the deck of **Wings.**
The locals discovered this place many years ago so be prepared to wait;
it's worth it! I have been here twice for breakfast and once for lunch. At
breakfast, go with any omelet you like. They're all good and come with
a rasher of bacon (4 pieces) and a mountain of hash browns
(homemade). Be warned they are 'short staffed' so service maybe slow
and less than stellar.

AVALON, CA (CATALINA - AVX)
　　Aprt Mgr: PAUL MORITZ **PH:** 310-510-0143
　　Field Elevation: 1602 **CTAF:** 122.700
　　Runway: 04/22 **Length:** 3000 **Width:** 75 **Surface:** ASPH-F

**** Airport in the Sky Restaurant - (310) 510-2196
Proprietors: Megan Wright and sisters Natalie and Hayley
Campazzie
Open:
> Mon - Sun: 8:30 am - 4:00 pm

Restaurant Website: airportintheskyrestaurant.com
Restaurant Email:
PIREP:
On January 7, 2022, the torch was passed to new owners and a new name was given to this So Cal favorite. Megan Wright and sisters Natalie and Hayley Campazzie are the new owners.

This is the greatest getaway in SoCal! After a short flight from San Diego or LA you'll find yourself in another world. The landing is on a mountain ridge about 1,600 feet above the ocean. The burgers are made with Buffalo and the cookies with love. I really do like this place.

The views are incredible. Call the tower (310) 510-0143 for the shuttle to Two Harbors or Avalon. Not only is this a great Burger Run, there are campsites with running water and great trails to explore plus some of the best beaches in SoCal.

The U.S. Marine Corps resurfaced the runway a few years ago. It was long overdue, and we should all be grateful to the Marine Corps for stepping up and doing this.

Semper Fi!

Go for a great burger but never leave without a cookie.
I love the oatmeal raisin.

BIG BEAR CITY, CA (BIG BEAR CITY - L35)
Aprt Mgr: JAMES GWALTNEY **PH:** 909-585-3219
Field Elevation: 6752 **CTAF:** 122.725 **FUEL:** 100LLA
Runway: 08/26 **Length:** 5850 **Width:** 75 **Surface:** ASPH-G

Airport owned – 909-585-3219
Affiliate: Unknown
Self Service: YES
Pilot Supplies: NO
Hours: 24/7

*** Barnstormer - 909 585-9339
Proprietor: Renee Wagner
Open:
> Sun – Thur: 7am – 3pm

Fri – Sat: 5pm – 9pm
Restaurant Website:
www.bigbearcityairport.com/services-and-facilities/airport-restaurants/
Restaurant Email: reneew@Charter.net
PIREP:
The scenery up here is spectacular, especially after the first snowfall. Just be sure to watch that mixture! The altitude is 6,700' so count on eating up 1/3 to ½ of the 5,800' runway on takeoff especially in the summer. The restaurant is worth the trip so are the views of the mountains, the lake and the forest. On the weekends you can pretty much count on waiting in line behind the locals. Be patient, it's worth the wait.

BORREGO SPRINGS, CA (BORREGO VALLEY - L08)
Aprt Mgr: PETER DRINKWATER **PH:** 760-767-7415
Field Elevation: 520 **CTAF:** 122.800 **FUEL:** 100LL
Runway: 08/26 **Length:** 5011 **Width:** 75 **Surface:** ASPH-G
Airport Website: www.co.san-diego.ca.us/dpw/airports/borrego.html

Airport owned – 619-508-9171
Affiliate: Unknown
Self Service: YES
Pilot Supplies: NO
Hours: 24/7

CAMARILLO, CA (CAMARILLO - CMA)
Field Elevation: 77 **CTAF:** 128.200 **FUEL:** 100LLA
Runway: 08/26 **Length:** 6013 **Width:** 150 **Surface:** ASPH-CONC-G
Aprt Mgr: AARON WALSH **PH:** 805-388-4246

Channel Islands Aviation – 805-987-1301
FBO Website: www.flycia.com
Affiliate: Phillips 100LL/JetA
Self Service: NO
Pilot Supplies: YES
Hours: 7 Days 7am – 7pm

*** Waypoint Café – (805) 388-2535
Proprietor: Greg Hunter
Open:
Mon –Fri: 7am – 3pm
Sat: 7am- 4pm
Sun: 8am – 4pm
Restaurant Website: thewaypointcafe.com
PIREP:

Clean, pleasant efficient and friendly with food and service that rewards the effort it took to get there. Excellent tie downs adjacent to the restaurant.

The **Waypoint Café** is a nice place to go in the summer and enjoy the cool ocean breeze from the patio. I came here for breakfast and was intrigued by the Enchilada Omelet. It is made with one cheese enchilada buried in the omelet and one topside. It was really good.

CARLSBAD, CA (MC CLELLAN-PALOMAR - CRQ)
Aprt Mgr: WILLIE VASQUEZ **PH:** 760-966-3272
Field Elevation: 331 CTAF: 118.600 FUEL: 100LLA
Runway: 06/24 Length: 4897 **Width:** 150 **Surface:** ASPH-G

**** The Landings - (760) 929-0200
Open:
>   Mon – Sun: 7:30am – 8:00pm

Restaurant Website: www.carlsbadlandings.com
Restaurant Email: michele@carlsbadlandings.com
PIREP:
The Landings has a nice outside porch with a glass wall towards the apron. The runway is quite far away. This is a beautiful place decorated in a Land and Sea motif, it's an upscale eatery offering breakfast, lunch, happy-hour and dinner; with patio dining and live entertainment. The Landings at Carlsbad is a welcome addition to any SoCal $100 Hamburger scene.

CHINO, CA (CHINO - CNO)
Aprt Mgr: JAMES JENKINS **PH:** 909-597-3910
Field Elevation: 650 CTAF: 118.500 FUEL: 100LLA
Runway: 08L/26R Length: 4858 **Width:** 150 **Surface:** ASPH-G
Runway: 03/21 Length: 4919 **Width:** 150 **Surface:** ASPH-G
Runway: 08R/26L Length: 7000 **Width:** 150 **Surface:** ASPH-G

***** Flo's Airport Café – (909) 597-3416
Open:
>   5:00am - 7:00pm 7 days a week,

Restaurant Website: www.floscafes.com
PIREP:
Flo's is a true GA institution. I have been coming here forever. Its worth the trip just to meet and listen to the GA characters that show up. Mostly I go for breakfast, which is one bodacious omelet, or another followed by a freshly baked cinnamon roll. The pies are amazing, and I typically grab one or two as cargo.

Check it out. Flo's has been here since 1975 so they must be doing something right.

CHIRIACO SUMMIT, CA (CHIRIACO SUMMIT - L77)
Airport Website: skyvector.com/airport/L77/Chiriaco-Summit-Airport
Aprt Mgr: DARYL SHIPPY **PH:** 760-955-9722
Field Elevation: 1713 **CTAF:** 122.900 **FUEL:**
Runway: 06/24 **Length:** 4600 **Width:** 50 **Surface:** ASPH-P

**** Chiriaco Summit Café - 760-227-3227
Proprietor: Margit Chiriaco Rusche
Open:
> Mon – Sun: 6am -11pm

Restaurant Website: www.chiriacosummit.com
PIREP:
The word that comes to mind is eclectic. I came to visit the museum and have breakfast. Before leaving, I tried and liked the date shake. Tiedowns are at the west end of the field near the Patton Museum and the restaurant. If your takeoff is westbound, you'll have to taxi east on the runway. I was able to find some chains on the tiedown cables, but it would be a good idea to bring tie down ropes in case there are more than a couple of planes on the ramp. There's room for perhaps 10 planes. I was one of two. California Highway Patrol aircraft stop here often for meals. Overall this is an easy flight from the Los Angeles area with good food waiting at a very out-of-the-way, back-in-time diner.

*** General Patton Memorial Museum
Open:
> Mon – Sun: 9:30am - 4:30pm

Museum Website: www.generalpattonmuseum.com
Museum Email: gpmm@wildblue.net
PIREP:
This museum touches the west ramp of the airport. One million American soldiers were trained here for WWII at what was called the Desert Training Center. The spot was personally selected by "Old Blood and Guts" himself, General George Patton. Eventually it was set aside by the Bureau of Land Management as a spot to honor General Patton and the soldiers who followed him into battle against German General Rommel in North Africa. The museum opened November 11, 1988 at 11 in the morning. It would have been General Patton's one-hundredth birthday. A crowd of over 5000 attended the opening. Here you will see, explore and touch the tanks and other artifacts of that period. The museum includes a large tank yard with tanks ranging from World War II through the Vietnam War.

COALINGA, CA (HARRIS RANCH - 3O8)

Aprt Mgr: JACK BROWN **PH:** 559-935-0717
Field Elevation: 470 **CTAF:** 122.900 **FUEL:** 100LL
Runway: 14/32 **Length:** 2820 **Width:** 30 **Surface:** ASPH-G

Harris Ranch – 559-935-0717
FBO Website: www.harrisranch.com
Affiliate: UNK
Self Service: YES
Pilot Supplies: NO
Hours: 7 Days 9am – 5pm

***** Harris Ranch Restaurant - (599) 935-0717**
Chef: Erasmo Rodriguez
Open:
   7 days lunch and dinner
Restaurant Website: harrisranch.com/dine/#the-steakhouse-section
Restaurant Email: service@harrisranch.com
PIREP:
This is the place!

It does not get any better period! It's been here since 1937 so they've had plenty of time to get it right. They have used their time well. It is the best fly-in restaurant you will ever visit. The airstrip's large parking ramp is literally adjacent to the restaurant. The menu is overwhelming with beef choices from steaks and filets to pot roast (which is elegant). The service is superb, the decor compliments the menu, and the prices are very reasonable given the quality of the food. Worth the trip even if it is out of the way. I diverted 45 minutes from my flight path to come here the first time. Don't miss this one.

***** Harris Ranch Inn - (599) 935-0717**
Proprietor: The Harris Family
Open:
   Always
Restaurant Website: harrisranch.com
PIREP: service@harrisranch.com
The Inn claims to be of a "higher quality". It is. On the grounds you'll find a 25-meter Olympic style, heated pool and three spas. Once inside, your last visit to a Ritz-Carlton property will come to mind. It is premium class. Thankfully the rates aren't. My advice is to check-in enjoy your dinner paired with the wine or cocktail of your choice knowing that you won't be in the cockpit until you are rested and refreshed. The great restaurant and great hotel are made better by the Harris Ranch Store where you can buy beef to go! Leave passengers behind and fly home with steaks!!!

CONCORD, CA (BUCHANAN FIELD - CCR)
Aprt Mgr: KEITH FREITAS **PH:** 925-646-5722
Field Elevation: 26 **CTAF:** 119.700 **FUEL:** 100LLA1+
Runway: 14L/32R **Length:** 4602 **Width:** 150 **Surface:** ASPH-G
Runway: 01L/19R **Length:** 5001 **Width:** 150 **Surface:** ASPH-G
Runway: 01R/19L **Length:** 2770 **Width:** 75 **Surface:** ASPH-G
Runway: 14R/32L **Length:** 2799 **Width:** 75 **Surface:** ASPH-G

** Vineyards Restaurant Bar – (925) 521-3783
Open:
> Mon - Sun: 6:30 am - 11:00 pm

Restaurant Website: N/A
PIREP:
This is not a destination restaurant; this is an *"any 'port in a storm"* kinda' place.

There is a Crown Plaza Hotel at this airport with a restaurant named **The Vineyards Restaurant and Bar**. Use the pedestrian gate from the ramp to access the hotel. The restaurant is in the lobby by the indoor plants.

The great thing about airport hotels is they normally have restaurants that are open for breakfast lunch and dinner. The bad news is that chain hotels typically have lousy restaurants *(Marriott's excluded)*. This one follows the rule – the food and service are pretty bad but if you're hungry or thirsty – where's the risk?

CORONA, CA (CORONA MUNI - AJO)
Aprt Mgr: RICHARD BRODEUR **PH:** 951-736-2289
Field Elevation: 533 **CTAF:** 122.700 **FUEL:** 100LLA
Runway: 07/25 **Length:** 3200 **Width:** 60 **Surface:** ASPH-G

Corona Air Ventures – 951-737-1300
FBO Website: www.coronaairventures.com
Affiliate: UNK
Self Service: YES
Pilot Supplies: NO
Hours: 7 Days 7am – 4pm

*** Corona Airport Cafe - (951) 273-1643
Proprietor: Jorge Gomez
Open:
> Mon - Sun: 7:00 am - 3:00 pm

Restaurant Website: www.coronaairportcafe.com
PIREP:

This is a very basic airport restaurant that shows what a difference great service can make. On my recent visit the manager came out to say hello and no he didn't know whom we were, and we didn't tell him. Bet he'll treat you the same way, nice people are just nice people.

EL MONTE, CA (EL MONTE - EMT)
Aprt Mgr: CHRIS BROOKS **PH:** 626-448-6129
Field Elevation: 296 **CTAF:** 121.200 **FUEL:** 100LLA
Runway: 01/19 **Length:** 3995 **Width:** 75 **Surface:** ASPH-G

Billion Air Aviation – 888-818-8177
FBO Website: www.billionairaviation.com
Affiliate: UNK
Self Service: NO
Pilot Supplies: NO
Hours: Mon – Sat 8am – 4pm

American Airport Corp – 626-448-6129
FBO Website: www.americanairports.com
Affiliate: UNK
Self Service: YES
Pilot Supplies: NO
Hours: 24/7

*** Annia's Kitchen - (626) 401-2422
Proprietor: Flavio Bugarin
Open:
>Mon - Thu: 7:00 am - 8:00 pm
>Fri - Sat: 6:00 am - 8:00 pm
>Sun: 6:00 am - 3:00 pm

Restaurant Website: anniaskitchen.net
PIREP:
Right next to the ramp/transient parking. I came here to watch the sunset from the terrace while eating a burger and fries and enjoying the view. Great ambiance from this family run haven.

FRESNO, CA (FRESNO CHANDLER EXECUTIVE - FCH)
Aprt Mgr: RICK DUNCAN **PH:** 559-621-7677
Field Elevation: 279 **CTAF:** 123.000 **FUEL:** 100LLA
Runway: 12/30 **Length:** 3630 **Width:** 75 **Surface:** ASPH-G

** Flight Line Cafe – (559) 355-4186
Proprietor: Henry and Patty Wang
Open:
>Mon - Sat 6:30am to 2:30pm

PIREP:

The Flight Line Café menu features a variety of meal selections from traditional breakfast faire to Asian inspired lunch specials such as the Wang's well-known Kung Pao Chicken. It's worth the flight to see the inside of the terminal, which is vintage 1930. I have looked forward to my visits to for years. Now that the restaurant is guided by a truly gifted chef, I'll spend more time here.

FULLERTON, CA (FULLERTON MUNI - FUL)
Aprt Mgr: BRENDAN O'REILLY **PH:** 714-738-6323
Field Elevation: 96 **CTAF:** 119.100 **FUEL:** 100LLA
Runway: 06/24 **Length:** 3121 **Width:** 75 **Surface:** ASPH-G

***** Wings Cafe Fullerton Airport** – 714-735-8432
Proprietor: Brian and Sherri White
Open:
Mon.- Sun. 7am - 2pm
Restaurant Website: www.wingscafefullertonairport.com
PIREP:
It doesn't happen often, but it happened recently at the Fullerton Airport. A **NEW** restaurant has opened that isn't an under financed greasy spoon. This looks like a **GREAT** place that is destined to become a _**SoCal MUST STOP**_. That's the good news. Then came the pandemic. It looked like the kiss of death.
Thankfully it wasn't. They survived and are poised to thrive. Naturally, there is a great runway view and FREE WIFI.

HALF MOON BAY, CA (HALF MOON BAY - HAF)
Aprt Mgr: MARK LARSON **PH:** 650-573-3700
Field Elevation: 66 **CTAF:** 122.800 **FUEL:** 100LL
Runway: 12/30 **Length:** 5000 **Width:** 150 **Surface:** ASPH-CONC-G

**** Pilot Light** – (650) 627-4303

Proprietor:
Open:
    Mon – Fri: 8am – 2pm
    Sat – Sun: 7am – 3pm
Restaurant Website: N/A
PIREP:
Fog! Watch out for the fog. The marine layer rolls in quickly.

After 25 years or so **Three Zero** has closed. A new restaurant named **Pilot Light** will soon open up in the same space. It promises to be a real crowd pleaser following the same basic theme of **Three Zero** while adding a bakery vibe. I'll let you know, on www.100dollarhamburger.com, when I am certain that **Pilot Light** is ready for your first visit. It was not yet opened at the time of this book's publication.

HEMET, CA (HEMET-RYAN - HMT)
Aprt Mgr: DARYL SHIPPY **PH:** 951-955-9722
Field Elevation: 1512 **CTAF:** 123.000 **FUEL:** 100LLA
Runway: 04/22 **Length:** 2045 **Width:** 25 **Surface:** ASPH-G
Runway: 05/23 **Length:** 4314 **Width:** 100 **Surface:** ASPH-G

Hemet Ryan Aviation – 951-925-7618
FBO Website: www.billionairaviation.com
Affiliate: UNK
Self Service: YES
Pilot Supplies: NO
Hours: 7 Days 8am – 5pm

**** Hangar One Cafe - (951) 766-5460
Proprietor: Bambi Galloway
Open:
>Mon - Sat 6:30am - 2:30pm
>Sun: 7:30am - 2:30pm

PIREP:
You can taxi all the up and tiedown in front of the rear deck. The restaurant is very small, and the crowd can sometimes be large. The food and service is good. The big problem is that there is only one restroom; plan on standing in line to use it.

KERNVILLE, CA (KERN VALLEY - L05)
Aprt Mgr: RON BREWSTER **PH:** 661-391-1800
Field Elevation: 2614 **CTAF:** 122.800 **FUEL:**
Runway: 17/35 **Length:** 3500 **Width:** 50 **Surface:** ASPH-G

*** The Airport Café - (760) 376-2852
Open:
>Mon – Sun: 7am – 3pm

Restaurant Website: kernvalleyairport.com/airport-cafe.html
PIREP:
The restaurant is very rustic having a log cabin appearance. It is right on the ramp with two rows of parking available. Be warned that it slopes, and your plane can roll if not chocked and tied down. Also be aware that this airport can draw a crowd on the weekends. The scenery is excellent, and the airport is very laid back. You can listen to UNICOM on the patio. The old crusty local pilots will grade the landings and takeoffs. The food and service are more than adequate. You'll be happy but not overjoyed.

*** Kern Valley Airport Campground
Open:
Always
Camping Website: kernvalleyairport.com/campground.html
PIREP:
The campground is managed by the Airport Café. It is adjacent to the runway and has paved tie-downs for about 10 aircraft. The campground itself is a large grassy area shaded by many large trees. A picnic table and a fire pit are located at each camping space. Water is available from a spigot and a hose is provided for filling a black barrel above a shower enclosure for taking a *"solar shower."* The sanitary facility is only a portable potty, but it is adequate. Tie-down/space rental is $5 per day. It's a long walk from the campground to the café since the campground is at the north end of the runway and the café is at the south end, but it's only a short walk over to the Kern River which is the reason to camp here. The town of Kernville is within walking distance if you're in good shape. The airport has a beater car available to borrow.

LAKEPORT, CA (LAMPSON FIELD - 1O2)
Aprt Mgr: KURT ACKERMANN **PH:** 707-263-2341
Field Elevation: 1380 **CTAF:** 122.800 **FUEL:** 100LL
Runway: 10/28 **Length:** 3600 **Width:** 60 **Surface:** ASPH-G

***** Reds @ The Skyroom - 707-349-9812
Proprietor: Jer & Nicole
Open:
Mon - Sat 11:00 -9:00
Sun 10:00 – 9:00
Restaurant Website: www.redsskyroom.com
PIREP:
If the locals show up, you know it's good.

This is an out of the way gem that few know about. The food is simply amazing. The chicken sandwich that has to be seen to be believed *(1.5" thick chicken breast).* The **End of the World Burger** was truly out of this *world (1" of cooked meat and bacon and cheese).*

Single well-kept runway. A PBY Catalina is parked on the ramp.

Don't miss this one. It's a Purner Fave!

LANCASTER, CA (GENERAL WM J FOX AIRFIELD - WJF)
Aprt Mgr: STEVE IRVING **PH:** 661-940-1709
Field Elevation: 2351 **CTAF:** 120.300 **FUEL:** 100LLA
Runway: 06/24 **Length:** 7201 **Width:** 150 **Surface:** ASPH-G

John Purner

American Airport Service – 661-940-1709
Affiliate: UNK
Self Service: YES
Pilot Supplies: YES

** Foxy's Landing - (661) 949-2284
Proprietor: Joudi Alsady
Open:
>		Mon – Fri: 7am – 3pm
>		Sat – Sun: 7am – 4pm

PIREP:
It's an airport restaurant offering a good view of the runway. The food and service are spotty. Expect little and you won't be disappointed.

LA VERNE, CA (BRACKETT FIELD - POC)
>	**Aprt Mgr:** CYLE WOODRUFF **PH:** 909-593-1395
>	**Field Elevation:** 1014 **CTAF:** 118.200 **FUEL:** 100LLA
>	**Runway:** 08L/26R **Length:** 3661 **Width:** 75 **Surface:** ASPH-G
>	**Runway:** 08R/26L **Length:** 4841 **Width:** 75 **Surface:** ASPH-G

American Airport Service – 909-593-5224
Affiliate: UNK
Self Service: YES
Pilot Supplies: YES

*** Norm's Hangar - (909) 596-6675
Open:
>		Mon – Sun: 7am – 3pm

PIREP:
The view from the patio is awesome; ramp, taxiway, runway and mountains. You see them all in that order. This is a busy place on the weekends. Plan to come late, if not you'll wait to be seated and served and you'll be unhappy. Come later and you'll feel that you got the royal treatment complete with princely food.

LODI, CA (LODI - 1O3)
>	**Airport Website:** www.lodiairport.com
>	**Aprt Mgr:** ROBERT KUPKA **PH:** 209-369-9126
>	**Field Elevation:** 60 **CTAF:** 122.900 **FUEL:** 100LL80 A
>	**Runway:** 12/30 **Length:** 2073 **Width:** 26 **Surface:** ASPH-F
>	**Runway:** 08/26 **Length:** 3735 **Width:** 42 **Surface:** ASPH-F

**** Lodi Airport Café - (209) 369-6144
Proprietor: Joann Sturgeon
Open:

28

Mon – Sun: 7am – 2pm
Closed Tuesday
Restaurant Website: www.lodiairport.com
PIREP:
The cafe sits right on the flightline, which makes it easy to find. There is a good view of the flightline, but the real show is overhead. There is a skydiving operation here. Bring along some folding chairs. After your meal spend some time here and watch. It is very, very entertaining. It can get very, very crowded here on the weekend.

What about the food? The restaurant is chef owned and operated. She provides some of the best food I have every eaten. The ambiance is crisp and clean with appropriate decoration. On one wall hangs a piece of nose art apparently clipped from the bomber that once displayed it.

MOJAVE, CA (MOJAVE - MHV)
Airport Website: mojaveairport.com
Aprt Mgr: STU WITT **PH:** 661-824-2433
Field Elevation: 2801 **CTAF:** 127.600 **FUEL:** 100LLA
Runway: 12/30 **Length:** 12503 **Width:** 200 **Surface:** ASPH-E
Runway: 08/26 **Length:** 7049 **Width:** 100 **Surface:** ASPH-G
Runway: 04/22 **Length:** 3946 **Width:** 50 **Surface:** ASPH-P

*** Voyager Restaurant - (661) 824-2048
Proprietor: Joudi Alsaady
Open:
Mon – Fri: 7am – 3pm
Sat: 8am – 2pm
Sun: 8am – 2pm
Restaurant Website: mojaveairport.com
PIREP:
Mohave is a museum of the future, which celebrates the past.

The Voyager Restaurant is located on the flight line in the terminal under the old tower. After you land request taxi instruction to the old tower. Get a table next to the window. The runway before you is all about the history and the future of flight. Yesterday's record holders jumped off of this pavement just as tomorrow's dreams of private space flight are being launched today. The tower radio is piped to each table, so you'll know when to look. The food is good not special but good. The service is caring and friendly. Come here if you can. You'll leave happy to know that the best days of aviation are ahead of us. We can still dream of going where no man has gone before with the encouragement that we can be that man just as others have been before us. One day we can all be astronauts because of the men and women who call Mohave home.

MONTEREY, CA (MONTEREY PENINSULA - MRY)

Airport Website: www.montereyairport.com
Aprt Mgr: THOMAS E. GREER **PH:** 831-648-7000
Field Elevation: 257 **CTAF:** 118.400 **FUEL:** 100LLA
Runway: 10R/28L **Length:** 7616 **Width:** 150 **Surface:** ASPH
Runway: 10L/28R **Length:** 3513 **Width:** 60 **Surface:** ASPH-G

Avis Car Rental – (831) 647-7140
Sun – Fri 7:00 AM - 10:00 PM
Sat 7:00 AM - 8:00 PM

Del Monte Aviation – 800-452-6184
FBO Website: www.dcmetroaviation.com
Affiliate: UNK
Self Service: YES
Pilot Supplies: YES
Hours: 724/7

***** Woody's Restaurant and Bar - (831) 373-1232**
Proprietor: Chef Tim Wood
Open:
Mon – Sun: 9:30am – 9pm
Restaurant Website: www.woodysmontereyairport.com
PIREP:
Tim Woods of Carmel Valley Ranch fame has taken over the space formerly occupied by the **Golden Tee**. He's up the offering from Solid Gold to Pure Platinum. Be warned, don't miss this spot, it's a culinary oasis.

Located on the second floor of the terminal building, it offers great views of Monterey Bay and the airport. You'll watch takeoffs and landings if they're using Runway 10, and taxiing airplanes if they're using Runway 28. I come here for the **Sautéed Sand Dabs** and **Woody's Signature Wedge Salad** though the **Harris Ranch Burger** is a darn good bet!!!!

MURRIETA/TEMECULA, CA (FRENCH VALLEY - F70)

Aprt Mgr: DARYL SHIPPY **PH:** 951-955-9722
Field Elevation: 1350 **CTAF:** 122.800 **FUEL:** 100LLA
Runway: 18/36 **Length:** 6000 **Width:** 75 **Surface:** ASPH-G

*** French Valley Café – (951) 600-7396
Open:
Daily: Breakfast, Lunch & Dinner
Restaurant Website: frenchvalleycafe.eat24hour.com

PIREP:
The Chicken soup is worth flying in for. I have only been once and that was for lunch. It was filled with locals plus half a dozen transient pilots. Clearly, they're doing something. Pricing is a little on the high side, all and all it's a good stop.

Here's the thing. COVID has caused restaurants to react and modify their operation in curious ways. The French Valley Café has gone to a totally take-out model. Their website has been well modified to accommodate this change. I suspect it's a temporary thing. How long is temporary? No one seems to know for sure.

NAPA, CA (NAPA COUNTY - APC)
Aprt Mgr: MARTIN PEHL **PH:** 707-253-4300
Field Elevation: 35 **CTAF:** 118.700 **FUEL:** 100LLA
Runway: 18L/36R **Length:** 2510 **Width:** 75 **Surface:** ASPH-F
Runway: 06/24 **Length:** 5007 **Width:** 150 **Surface:** CONC-F
Runway: 18R/36L **Length:** 5930 **Width:** 150 **Surface:** CONC-G

**** The Runway by Patrick – 707-258-6115
Open:
Mon-Sat 11am-9pm
Restaurant Website: www.therunwaybypatrick.com
PIREP:
Very nice place, good food, good service, right on the runway. Fettuccini, Angus Burger, amazing steaks (priced accordingly!), great tomato soup. For dessert, go with the Bread Pudding, I like the Bourbon sauce. It is also available with a Vanilla or Carmel sauce. It replaced **Jonsey's**. I think it's twice as good.

OROVILLE, CA (OROVILLE MUNI - OVE)
Aprt Mgr: RICK WALLS **PH:** 530-538-2420
Field Elevation: 194 **CTAF:** 122.800 **FUEL:** 100LLA
Runway: 12/30 **Length:** 3540 **Width:** 100 **Surface:** ASPH-G
Runway: 01/19 **Length:** 6020 **Width:** 100 **Surface:** ASPH-G

*** The Restaurant at Table Mountain Golf Club - (530) 533-3922 ext. 101
Open:
Mon - Sun: 8am – 3pm
Sat – Sun: 6am – Sunset
Restaurant Website: www.tablemountaingolf.com/restaurant/
PIREP:
The restaurant is at the golf course, which adjoins the Oroville. The decor is typical golf club. Don't worry that the restaurant is on the

opposite side of the airport from the FBO as you can taxi right to the
golf club where there are tie-downs. They have sit-down service. The
food is good and the service enthusiastic.

*** Table Mountain Golf Club – (530) 533-3922 ext. 100
Open:
> Daily

Golf Club Website: www.tablemountaingolf.com
PIREP:
This is a very, very flat 18-hole course that is also a great flyin. You
can literally tie-down in their parking lot. The green fee with cart is
about fifty bucks. If you show up after 3PM they offer a $25 Twilight
Special.

PALO ALTO, CA (PALO ALTO ARPT OF SANTA CLARA CO - PAO)
Aprt Mgr: CHRIS NUCCI **PH:** 408-918-7700
Field Elevation: 7 **CTAF:** 118.600 **FUEL:** 100LLA
Runway: 13/31 **Length:** 2443 **Width:** 70 **Surface:** ASPH-G

*** Abundant Air Café – (650) 858-1003
Proprietors: Harpik Avetian & Dennis Mcknew
Open:
> Mon – Fri: 7:30am – 4pm

Restaurant Website: www.abundantair.com
PIREP:
This is a deli a very good deli but a deli. You stand in line to order and
pick up your food. They have really good Panini sandwiches. I have
enjoyed the Chipotle Roast Beef more than once. That and a lemon
drop smoothie and I'm good to go.

PASO ROBLES, CA (PASO ROBLES MUNI - PRB)
Aprt Mgr: ROGER OXBORROW **PH:** 805-237-3877
Field Elevation: 839 **CTAF:** 123.000 **FUEL:** 100LL
Runway: 13/31 **Length:** 4701 **Width:** 100 **Surface:** ASPH-G
Runway: 01/19 **Length:** 6008 **Width:** 150 **Surface:** ASPH-G

*** Joe's One-Niner Diner – (805) 238-3447
Proprietors: Joe Ontiveros
Open:
> 6AM - 2PM Monday thru Sunday

PIREP:
Joe has been a Paso Robles success story many years. His place
downtown is always packed and deservedly so. Here's the important
thing, Joe works as a line cook at his airport spot. The food is all Joe
and everything I love. Mexican food for breakfast prepared fresh for

each order by a man who grew up at his Mama's stove. I'll keep coming back and so should you.

PASO ROBLES, CA (HALTER RANCH AIRPORT - 89CA)
Aprt Mgr: BRYCE MULLINS **PH:** 949-310-0187
Field Elevation: 1488 **CTAF:** 0.000 **FUEL:**
Runway: 04/22 **Length:** 3353 **Width:** 25 **Surface:** ASPH

*** Halter Ranch Vineyard & Winery – 805-226-9455
Proprietors: Joe Ontiveros
Open:
> 10AM – 5PM Thursday to Monday

PIREP:
The Tasting Room at the Halter Ranch Vineyard & Winery is an excellent stop for lunch and a tasting.

Reservations are required

Private use. Permission required prior to landing

So phone ahead

PERRIS, CA (PERRIS VALLEY - L65)
Aprt Mgr: PAT CONATSER **PH:** 951-943-9673
Field Elevation: 1413 **CTAF:** 122.775 **FUEL:** 100LLA
Runway: 15/33 **Length:** 5100 **Width:** 50 **Surface:** ASPH-P

**** The Bombshelter Bar & Grill – (951) 943-4863
Proprietor: Ben Conatser
Open:
> Mon – Fri: 8am – 9pm
> Sat – Sun: 7am – 8pm

Restaurant Website: skydiveperris.com/other/bombshelter-bar-grill
Restaurant Email: bombshelter@skydiveperris.com
PIREP:
When you fly in, remain west of the field and call Unicom at least 5 miles out. The jump zone is east of the field and the ultralights remain generally south. The runway is in good condition and paved for at least 3,000 feet and then extends to 5,100 with smooth dirt. **The Bombshelter Bar & Grill** is on the **Skydive Perris** property. Typically I grab my grub and head for the outside patio and pull up a lounge chair by the pool. That's right they have a pool for their guest and yes you can use it. I can sit here for hours on a Saturday watching the Skydivers do their thing. This is probably the best skydive facility in the world. They have the usual planes in the fleet plus a DC-9 jet. By the way, this is the place to skydive if you're up for it because you

John Purner

don't have to jump from a plane. They have a terrific indoor skydive setup. It is way cool!

PETALUMA, CA (PETALUMA MUNI - O69)
Aprt Mgr: BOB PATTERSON **PH:** 707-778-4404
Field Elevation: 90 **CTAF:** 122.700 **FUEL:** 100LLA
Runway: 11/29 **Length:** 3601 **Width:** 75 **Surface:** ASPH-F

*** The Two Niner Diner - 707-765-2900
Proprietor: Joan Kelly
Open:
> Wed – Sun: 8am – 3pm

PIREP:
The restaurant is right on the ramp and offers indoor and outdoor dining. Stay outside if you can. The views of the hills and the runway are worth it. The food is a very good example of airport diner fare. I have been here for breakfast and had the Country Pilot which includes eggs, sausage and biscuits with gravy. It was very good.

PORTERVILLE, CA (PORTERVILLE MUNI - PTV)
Aprt Mgr: JIM MCDONALD **PH:** 559-782-7540
Field Elevation: 443 **CTAF:** 122.800 **FUEL:** 100LL80 A
Runway: 12/30 **Length:** 5960 **Width:** 150 **Surface:** ASPH-G

*** Airway Cafe - (559) 784-8208
Proprietor: Richard & Tami Chilcutt
Open:
> Wed – Mon: 8am – 2pm

Restaurant Website: facebook.com
Restaurant Email: rtchilcutt@aol.com
PIREP:
Transient parking is well marked and plentiful right in front of the terminal building. The restaurant is right inside. The terminal has some nice murals of vintage aircraft and firefighting planes. Overall, this is a good *"blue plate"* restaurant. The service is very efficient and friendly.

RED BLUFF, CA (RED BLUFF MUNI - RBL)
Aprt Mgr: MARTIN NICHOLS **PH:** 530-527-2605
Field Elevation: 352 **CTAF:** 123.000 **FUEL:** 100LLA
Runway: 15/33 **Length:** 5431 **Width:** 100 **Surface:** ASPH-G

*** Leigh & Val's Wings and Wheels – (530) 528-9198
Open:
> 7AM - 2PM Daily

PIREP:

Leigh & Val's *Wings and Wheels* restaurant is on the 1st floor of the terminal building. Breakfast is served until 2PM. An omelet for breakfast or lunch is a good way to go. Be warned- they are very large!

REDDING, CA (REDDING MUNI - RDD)
Aprt Mgr: ROD DINGER **PH:** 530-224-4321
Field Elevation: 505 **CTAF:** 119.800 **FUEL:** 100LLA
Runway: 12/30 **Length:** 5067 **Width:** 150 **Surface:** ASPH-G
Runway: 16/34 **Length:** 7003 **Width:** 150 **Surface:** ASPH-G

Avis Car Rental – (530) 221-2855
Sun 10:00 AM - 3:00 PM
Mon - Fri 8:00 AM - 6:00 PM
Sat 10:00 AM - 3:00 PM

*** Peter Chu's Skyroom - (530) 222-1364
Proprietor: Peter Chu
Open:
Mon - Sat: 11:00 am - 9:00 pm
Sun: 12:00 pm - 8:00 pm
Restaurant Website: www.peterchus.com
PIREP:
Peter Chu's Skyroom is upstairs above the terminal. It has huge windows so you can watch air operations and a nice, friendly atmosphere. The staff is efficient and courteous. The best part is the home style Chinese food. It offers a great escape from the usual burgers and fried things found at virtually every other airport restaurant.

RIVERSIDE, CA (RIVERSIDE MUNI - RAL)
Aprt Mgr: MARK RIPLEY **PH:** 951-351-6113
Field Elevation: 819 **CTAF:** 121.000 **FUEL:** 100LLA
Runway: 16/34 **Length:** 2850 **Width:** 50 **Surface:** ASPH-F
Runway: 09/27 **Length:** 5401 **Width:** 100 **Surface:** ASPH-G

Riverside Air Service – 951-352-2631
Affiliate: UNK
Self Service: YES
Pilot Supplies: YES
Hours: 7:00 - 5:00 M/F 8:00 - 5:00 Sat/Sun

*** D&D Airport Cafe - (951) 688-3337
Proprietor: Dave and Delmy
Open:
Mon-Sat: 6:30am-7:00pm
Sun: 6:30am – 4:00pm

John Purner

Restaurant Email: dndcafe@juno.com
PIREP:
This is a very standard airport restaurant with an extra dose of friendly.
It is on the ramp, has an outside patio and the obligatory runway view.
The food is really uninspired and unimpressive. I have been back
because I like the people.

RIVERSIDE/RUBIDOUX/, CA (FLABOB - RIR)
Aprt Mgr: LEO L DOIRON **PH:** 951-683-2309
Field Elevation: 764 **CTAF:** 122.800 **FUEL:** 100LL80
Runway: 06/24 **Length:** 3200 **Width:** 50 **Surface:** ASPH-F

***** Flabob Airport Café - (951) 787-1866**
Open:
Mon - Sun: 6:30am-3:00pm
Restaurant Website: www.flabobairport.org
PIREP:
The airport is a step back in time and that's probably worth the trip.
The restaurant is on the ramp and has a great view of the runways and
the brown desert mountains. The food is very standard airport café
faire. The service is good. What makes this place work for me is the
customers. This is a great place to hangar fly and learn things you never
knew you never knew.

ROSAMOND, CA (ROSAMOND SKYPARK - L00)
Airport Manager: JOHN WILSON **PH:** 888-397-6290
Field Elevation: 2415 **CTAF:** 122.900 **FUEL:** 100LL
Runway: 08/26 **Length:** 3600 **Width:** 50 **Surface:** ASPH-F

*** El Indio Mexican Restaurant – (661) 256-6737**
Rosamond Skypak is a jewel in the desert for aviator's who want to live
with their plane. Fortunately it is a public use airport.
El Indio is right next to the runway. Mexican food in SoCal is always
worth seeking out and at an airport it's priceless. I'm a cheese
enchilada guy and theirs are excellent. This is a somewhat upscale
please you'll be very pleased. I was.

SACRAMENTO, CA (SACRAMENTO EXECUTIVE - SAC)
Aprt Mgr: JOHN DOWNEY **PH:** 916-875-9035
Field Elevation: 24 **CTAF:** 119.500 **FUEL:** 100LLA
Runway: 16/34 **Length:** 3485 **Width:** 150 **Surface:** ASPH-G
Runway: 12/30 **Length:** 3836 **Width:** 100 **Surface:** ASPH-G
Runway: 02/20 **Length:** 5503 **Width:** 150 **Surface:** ASPH-G

Sacremento Jet Center – 916-428-8292
FBO Website: www.sacjet.com

Affiliate: UNK
Self Service: YES
Pilot Supplies: YES
Hours: M-F 6:30 - 9:00 Sat/Sun 8:00 - 4:30

*** Aviator's Restaurant - (916) 424-1728
Open:

Mon – Sun: 7am - 3pm

Fri - Sat: 5pm - 9pm

Restaurant Website:
www.sacramento.aero/sac/facilities_services/businesses/
PIREP:
Aviator's Restaurant is on the second floor of the terminal building and provides the great runway view you would expect from that vantage point. The décor is a nice mix of brick and wood. It has a very folksy feel. I came here for breakfast and was glad I did. Imagine eggs and hash browns set beside a gravy covered chicken fried steak. It cannot get any better than that. Breakfast and lunch on one plate!

SALINAS, CA (SALINAS MUNI - SNS)
Aprt Mgr: GARY PETERSEN **PH:** 831-758-7214

Field Elevation: 85 **CTAF:** 119.400 **FUEL:** 100LLA
Runway: 14/32 **Length:** 1900 **Width:** 50 **Surface:** ASPH-G
Runway: 13/31 **Length:** 4825 **Width:** 150 **Surface:** ASPH-G
Runway: 08/26 **Length:** 6003 **Width:** 150 **Surface:** ASPH-G

Jet West – 831-422-9400
FBO Website: www.jetwestsns.com
Affiliate: UNK
Self Service: YES
Pilot Supplies: YES
Hours: 7:00 - 7:00 7 days

SAN CARLOS, CA (SAN CARLOS - SQL)
Aprt Mgr: MARK LARSON **PH:** 650-573-3700
Field Elevation: 5 **CTAF:** 119.000 **FUEL:** 100LLA
Runway: 12/30 **Length:** 2600 **Width:** 75 **Surface:** ASPH-G

Rabbit AV – 650-591-5857
FBO Website: www.rabbitksql.com
Affiliate: UNK
Self Service: NO
Pilot Supplies: YES

Hours: 7:00 - 8:00 7 days

***** Izzy's Steakhouse - (650) 654-2822

Open:

Mon – Fri: 11:30am – 10pm

Sat – Sun: 5pm – 10pm

Restaurant Website: www.izzyssteaks.com

PIREP:

We don't hand out five stars lightly. This is a great place. Park by the Hiller Museum. It is a very short walk from there to **Izzy's**. The original **Izzy's** is in the San Francisco Marina district. It is a steakhouse. Yes they serve fish but pass on that come here for MEAT! For a steak to be good it has to be aged and that is what Izzy's does. They buy the best Midwestern beef that's available and then they age it for 21 days. Next they cook it to perfection in accordance with your taste. Bring a client here for lunch. Bring your significant other here for dinner. I look forward to my next visit.

***** Sky Kitchen Cafe - 650-595-0464

Proprietor: Ben Abolmoluki

Open:

Mon – Sun: 6am – 3pm

Restaurant Website: www.skykitchencafe.com

PIREP:

This too is one of my favorites. It is a very California kind of place. Clean and modern with a menu filled with fresh, healthy items. They offer 40 different kinds of omelets for breakfast. If none of them float your boat number 41 is titled U-Do-It. I like the Chili and Cheese which exposes my Texas roots.

Hiller Aviation Museum - 650-595-0464

Director: Jeffery Bass

Open:

Mon – Sun: 10am – 5pm

Museum Website: www.hiller.org

Museum Email: jeff@hiller.org

PIREP:

After clearing the runway contact the Ground Frequency and ask for the Northwest Transient parking. There is a walkthrough gate that leads out behind **Izzy's** restaurant. It is a short walk to the museum. (Remember the gate code. You'll need it to re-enter). There are several wonderful exhibits here my two favorites are the **1945 Hiller 360** *(first inherently-stable helicopter to be licensed by the FAA)* and the fully accessible Boeing 747 cockpit.

SAN DIEGO/EL CAJON, CA (GILLESPIE FIELD - SEE)

38

Aprt Mgr: ROGER GRIFFITHS **PH:** 619-956-4805
Field Elevation: 388 **CTAF:** 120.700 **FUEL:** 100LLA
Runway: 09R/27L **Length:** 2738 **Width:** 60 **Surface:** ASPH-G
Runway: 17/35 **Length:** 4145 **Width:** 100 **Surface:** ASPH-G
Runway: 09L/27R **Length:** 5342 **Width:** 100 **Surface:** ASPH-G

Jet Air – 877-253-8247
FBO Website: www.jetairsystems.com
Affiliate: UNK
Self Service: NO
Pilot Supplies: YES
Hours: 7:00 - 8:00 7 days

High Performance Aircraft – 858-576-5000
FBO Website: www.hpair.com
Affiliate: UNK
Self Service: NO
Pilot Supplies: YES
Hours: 24/7

Golden State Aviation – 800-277-4568
Affiliate: UNK
Self Service: NO
Pilot Supplies: YES

*** Gillespie Field Cafe - (619) 448-0415
Proprietor: Roxanne & Peter Oliver
Open:
        Mon – Sun: 7am – 3pm
Restaurant Website: www.gillespiecafe.com
Restaurant Email: cafe@gillespiecafe.com
PIREP:
A nice place to talk airplanes, watch airplane and grab a decent meal.
The food is the basic sandwich-and-fries fare. The service is always
excellent. There is outdoor seating, as well as a few tables inside for
those 2 days a year when the weather isn't perfect.

SAN DIEGO, CA (MONTGOMERY FIELD - MYF)
Aprt Mgr: ERNIE GESELL **PH:** 858-573-1440
Field Elevation: 427 **CTAF:** 119.200 **FUEL:** 100LLA
Runway: 05/23 **Length:** 3400 **Width:** 150 **Surface:** ASPH-G
Runway: 10R/28L **Length:** 3401 **Width:** 60 **Surface:** ASPH-G
Runway: 10L/28R **Length:** 4577 **Width:** 150 **Surface:** ASPH-G

Crown Air Aviation – 858-292-1181
FBO Website: www.crownairaviation.com

Affiliate: UNK
Self Service: NO
Pilot Supplies: YES
Hours: 7 days 5:30 - 9:00

Gibbs Flying Service – 858-277-0310
FBO Website: www.gibbsflyingservice.com
Affiliate: UNK
Self Service: NO
Pilot Supplies: YES
Hours: 7 days 6:30 - 8:30

***** 94ᵗʰ Aero Squadron - (858) 560-6771
Open:
> Mon-Thurs: 11:00 am-9:00 pm
> Fri: 11:00 am-11:00 pm
> Sat: 11:00 am-10:00 pm
> Sun: 9:00 am.-3:00 pm

Restaurant Website: 94thsandiego.com
Restaurant Email: 94thsd@sbcglobal.net
PIREP:
If you've never eaten at a **94ᵗʰ AERO Squadron** you need to. If you've visited another location you'll be shocked at how much better this one is. Zagat rates it, as one of America's Top Restaurants with "very good to Excellent" review for 2013. I agree. It is probably the BEST place in San Diego county for Brunch.

** Casa Machado - (858) 292-4716
Open:
> Mon – Sun: 11:00am - 9:00pm

Restaurant Website: casamachadomex.com
Restaurant Email:
PIREP:
Casa Machado is easy to find right at transient parking next to the terminal. I'm a huge Mexican food fan and this is good Mexican food. For me, breakfast is best. I like the Manchaca.

SAN DIEGO, CA (BROWN FIELD MUNI - SDM)
Aprt Mgr: CHRIS COOPER **PH:** 619-424-0456
Field Elevation: 526 **CTAF:** 126.500 **FUEL:** 100LLA
Runway: 08L/26R **Length:** 7972 **Width:** 150 **Surface:** CONC-G
Runway: 08R/26L **Length:** 3180 **Width:** 75 **Surface:** ASPH-G

San Diego Jet Center – 866-736-5382
FBO Website: www.sandiegojetcenter.com
Affiliate: UNK

Self Service: YES
Pilot Supplies: YES
Hours: 24/7

---

* The Landing Strip Café & Bar - (619) 661-6038
Open:
> Mon – Sat: 8am – 11pm
> Sun: 8am – 2pm

Restaurant Email: bbrown923©yahoo.com
PIREP:
It's on the airport so I am including it but……. This is not a place I would ever go to. It seems to be a down market bar with a small restaurant tacked on. So the ambiance is someplace between really bad to non-existent. The food is reported to be pretty good. The offset is the service, which is often described as rude.

SAN LUIS OBISPO, CA (SAN LUIS COUNTY RGNL - SBP)
Aprt Mgr: RICHARD HOWELL **PH:** 805-781-5205
Field Elevation: 212 **CTAF:** 124.000 **FUEL:** 100LLA
Runway: 07/25 **Length:** 2500 **Width:** 100 **Surface:** ASPH-G
Runway: 11/29 **Length:** 6100 **Width:** 150 **Surface:** ASPH-G

Avis Car Rental – (805) 544-0630
> Sun 9:00 AM - 12:00 AM
> Mon - Thu 8:00 AM - 12:00 AM
> Fri 8:00 AM - 10:00 PM
> Sat 9:00 AM - 5:00 PM

ACI Jet – 805-782-9722
FBO Website: www.acijet.com
Affiliate: UNK
Self Service: YES
Pilot Supplies: YES
Hours: 24/7

*** The Spirit of San Luis - (805) 549-9466
Proprietor: Doug and Julie Wagnon
Open:
> Mon - Sat: 9:00 am - 8:00 pm
> Sun: 9:00 am - 3:00 pm

Restaurant Website: www.sloairport.com/dining-options/
PIREP:
The Spirit of San Luis Restaurant is located to the east of the terminal building. The outdoor patio has a great view of the runways. The food and the service are very good. The menu is a step above the normal airport burger and fries place.

41

John Purner

SANTA MONICA, CA (SANTA MONICA MUNI - SMO)
Aprt Mgr: ROBERT TRIMBORN **PH:** 310-458-8591
Field Elevation: 177 **CTAF:** 120.100 **FUEL:** 100LLA
Runway: 03/21 **Length:** 4973 **Width:** 150 **Surface:** ASPH-G

Atlantic Aviation – 310-396-6770
FBO Website: www.atlanticaviation.com
Affiliate: UNK
Self Service: NO
Pilot Supplies: YES
Hours: 24/7

*** Spitfire Grill - (310) 397-3455
Proprietor: John Clarizio
Open:
> Sunday – Thursday 7:30am ~ 10:00pm
> Friday – Saturday 7:30am ~ 10:00pm

Restaurant Website: www.spitfiregrill.net
Restaurant Email: Team@spitfiregrill.net
PIREP:
The Spitfire offers a broader menu than typical for an airport place but the food is mediocre. It has a cute aviation theme & art but **no view of the airport**. It is actually across the street and behind a building.

SANTA PAULA, CA (SANTA PAULA - SZP)
Aprt Mgr: ROWENA MASON **PH:** 805-933-1155
Field Elevation: 243 **CTAF:** 122.900 **FUEL:** 100LL
Runway: 04/22 **Length:** 2713 **Width:** 60 **Surface:** ASPH-G

*** Flight 126 Café - (805) 525-7200
Open:
> Mon-Fri: 6:30 am – 2:30 pm
> Sat-Sun: 7 am - 2 pm

Restaurant Website: flight126.com
PIREP:
There are two perfect times to come here; breakfast any day and lunch on Friday. For breakfast I go for the Chickenfried steak and eggs. I grew up in Texas, which explains my choice. I've never been disappointed. Lunch on Friday features Clam Chowder. That's the only time they make it. If that doesn't float your boat, you can always order the Chickenfried steak, its available everyday!

*** Costeau on the Go – (707) 43-1972

Open:

42

Monday - Friday 7:30 am - 3:00 pm
Restaurant Website: www.costeaux.com/bakery-cafe/on-the-go/
PIREP:
Small coffee shop with sandwiches and salads. High quality food from the Costeau Bakery.

Located on the north side of Sonoma Jet Center, with the entrance facing the driveway for the airline terminal.

SANTA ROSA, CA (SONOMA COUNTY - STS)
Aprt Mgr: JON G. STOUT **PH:** 707-565-7243
Field Elevation: 128 **CTAF:** 118.500 **FUEL:** 100LLA
Runway: 01/19 **Length:** 5004 **Width:** 100 **Surface:** ASPH-G
Runway: 14/32 **Length:** 5119 **Width:** 150 **Surface:** ASPH-G

Kaiser Air – 707-528-7400
FBO Website: www.kaiserair.com
Affiliate: UNK
Self Service: YES
Pilot Supplies: YES
Hours: 5:00 - 9:00 7 days

Sonoma Jet – 707-523-2800
FBO Website: www.sonomajetcenter.com
Affiliate: UNK
Self Service: YES
Pilot Supplies: YES
Hours: 6:00 - 9:00 summer 6:00 - 8:00 winter 7 days

Avis Car Rental – **(707) 571-0465**
Sun 9:30 AM - 9:30 PM
Mon - Fri 8:30 AM - 9:30 PM
Sat 9:30 AM - 9:30 PM

*** Sky Lounge Steakhouse & Sushi Bar – **(707) 542-9400**
Open:
Mon – Sun: 8am – 9pm
Restaurant Website: www.santarosaskylounge.com
PIREP:
Sky Lounge Steakhouse & Sushi Bar is right at the terminal. It's a short walk from Sonoma Jet Center where you can park for free. You can watch the runways and the commuter airline service from the patio. The food is good but not great. It is served quickly and with a smile. Avoid the sushi.

SOUTH LAKE TAHOE, CA (LAKE TAHOE - TVL)

Aprt Mgr: SHERRY MILLER **PH:** 530-542-6182
Field Elevation: 6269 **CTAF:** 122.950 **FUEL:** 100LLA
Runway: 18/36 **Length:** 8541 **Width:** 100 **Surface:** ASPH-E

*** The Flight Deck Restaurant and Bar - 530-542-3325
Proprietor: Tom & Diane Miller
Open:
Mon-Fri: 11 am - 10 pm
Sat-Sun: 10 am - 10 pm
Restaurant Website: cityofslt.us/Document Center/Home/View/943
PIREP:
The flight in is beautiful though somewhat challenging. It is in the mountains after all. Park the plane at Mountain West Aviation and go out the door to the building next door. You look directly over the airport and the mountains beyond. During the summer they have dining on the deck. The owner is a personable guy who will make you feel welcome. The food is very good and they have a full bar and an OK wine list.

STOCKTON, CA (STOCKTON METROPOLITAN - SCK)
Aprt Mgr: PATRICK CARRENO **PH:** 209-468-4700
Field Elevation: 33 **CTAF:** 120.300 **FUEL:** 100 100LLA
Runway: 11R/29L **Length:** 4448 **Width:** 75 **Surface:** ASPH-G
Runway: 11L/29R **Length:** 10650 **Width:** 150 **Surface:** ASPH-G

Atlantic Aviation – 209-982-1622
FBO Website: www.atlanticaviation.com
Affiliate: UNK
Self Service: NO
Pilot Supplies: YES
Hours: 24/7

*** Top Flight Grill and Catering - (209) 944-7780
Proprietor: Tommy Joyce
Open:
Mon 10:30 am - 8 pm
Tue-Sat 10:30 am - 5 pm
Restaurant Website: www.facebook.com/TopFlightGrillandCatering
PIREP:
It's a burger and fries on the ramp airport restaurant with an unusual interior and an outdoor seating area.

TEHACHAPI, CA (MOUNTAIN VALLEY - L94)
Aprt Mgr: LARRY G BARRETT **PH:** 661-822-5267
Field Elevation: 4220 **CTAF:** 123.000 **FUEL:**
Runway: 09L/27R **Length:** 4890 **Width:** 36 **Surface:** ASPH

Runway: 09R/27L **Length:** 4890 **Width:** 36 **Surface:** ASPH

*** Raven's Nest Sandwich Shop – (661) 822-5267
Open:
Mon – Sun: 8am – 3pm
Restaurant Website: skylarknorth.com/services.html
PIREP:
The fun of this trip is **NOT** the food. This is a glider port that welcomes power pilots and their planes. I always take a blanket and a great pair of sunglasses. I lie on my back on the blanket and watch the sailplanes doing their cloud dance through the sky above me. Eventually I need a break from my labors and body fuel. **The Raven's Nest** provides subsistence food and that's all I'm looking for. It specializes in breakfasts, deli sandwiches, fresh salads, homemade soups, breads and gooey handheld desserts.

TRUCKEE, CA (TRUCKEE-TAHOE - TRK)
Aprt Mgr: KEVIN SMITH **PH:** 530-587-4119
Field Elevation: 5901 **CTAF:** 122.800 **FUEL:** 100LLA A1+
Runway: 01/19 **Length:** 4650 **Width:** 75 **Surface:** ASPH-G
Runway: 10/28 **Length:** 7000 **Width:** 100 **Surface:** ASPH-G

Truckee Tahoe – 530-587-4119
FBO Website: www.atlanticaviation.com
Affiliate: UNK
Self Service: NO
Pilot Supplies: YES
Hours: 7:00 - 7:00 7 days

*** Red Truck on the Runway - (530) 587-1394
Proprietor: Larry Abney
Open:
Mon – Sun: 11am – 2pm
Restaurant Website: www.redtrucktahoe.com/cafe.html
Restaurant Email: yum@redtrucktahoe.com
PIREP:
Chef Larry Abney prepares and serves sustainable organic eats with bold flavors. For four years prior to opening his restaurant at the airport Chef Abney has been serving the same food out of a Big Red Food Truck which wonders the streets of Tahoe and caterings local events. If you are into sustainable organic eats with bold flavors, this is your place. If you're looking for a cheese burger – keep on flying.

UPLAND, CA (CABLE - CCB)
Aprt Mgr: CHARLES R BARNETT **PH:** 909-982-6021

Field Elevation: 1444 **CTAF:** 123.000 **FUEL:** 100LLA
Runway: 06/24 **Length:** 3863 **Width:** 75 **Surface:** ASPH-E

Cable Air – 909-982-6021
FBO Website: www.cableairport.com
Affiliate: UNK
Self Service: YES
Pilot Supplies: YES
Hours: 24/7

*** Maniac Mike's - (909) 982-9886
Open:
      Mon – Sun: 7am - 3pm
Restaurant Website: www.maniac-mikes.com
Restaurant Email: maniac@ maniac-mikes.com
PIREP:
I like the place you will too. It has all of the dishes that you would expect at an airport diner for breakfast and lunch and a few that will surprise you. I think I may have gone a little too Californian because my favorite item is the salmon burger. It is really good.

VAN NUYS, CA (VAN NUYS - VNY)
Aprt Mgr: JESS ROMO **PH:** 424-442-6500
Field Elevation: 802 **CTAF:** 119.300 **FUEL:** 100LLA
Runway: 16L/34R **Length:** 4011 **Width:** 75 **Surface:** ASPH-G
Runway: 16R/34L **Length:** 8001 **Width:** 150 **Surface:** ASPH-G

Signature – 818-464-9500
FBO Website: www.signatureflight.com
Affiliate: UNK
Self Service: NO
Pilot Supplies: YES
Hours: 24/7

Castle & Cook Aviation – 818-988-8385
FBO Website: www.castlecookeaviation.com
Affiliate: UNK
Self Service: NO
Pilot Supplies: YES
Hours: 24/7

Clay Lacy Aviation – 800-423-2904
FBO Website: www.claylacy.com
Affiliate: UNK
Self Service: NO
Pilot Supplies: YES

Hours: 24/7

***** The 94th Aero Squadron - (818) 994-7437

Proprietor: David Mashagh

Open:

Lunch:

Mon - Thur: 11am - 4pm
Fri & Sat: 11am - 4pm

Dinner:

Mon - Thur: 4pm - 9pm
Fri & Sat: 4pm - 10pm
Sun: 4pm - 9pm

Brunch:

Sun: 9:00am - 3pm

Restaurant Website: www.94thvannuys.com

PIREP:

You come here because its fun and you'll enjoy your meal ass you overlook Runway 16R, the most famous runway in general aviation. It was the movie that immortalized it that brought me in for Sunday Brunch. Van Nuys is also the world's busiest GA airport with about 1,000 operations each day. You won't be bored. I like the food. The service is unhurried. Many believe it is over-priced and that's probably true but it is a very nice aviation themed restaurant with an amazing view. I think it's worth every penny they ask. The issue here is getting to it. The restaurant does not have a ramp so you MUST park at one of the FBOs and get a ride to the restaurant.

**** The Landing - 818-997-7412

Proprietor: Executive Chef Desi Szonntagh

Open:

Mon-Sun: 6 am - 9 pm

Restaurant Website: www.airtelplaza.com

Restaurant Email: jdunn@airtelplaza.com

PIREP:

The Landing Restaurant is located in the **Airtel Plaza Hotel** which has its own ramp. Taxi over, tie-down and walk to the lobby. **The 94th Aero Squadron** wins the ambiance battle but The Landing scores on food service and price. I had dinner here and thoroughly enjoyed a New York Strip steak which was cooked by a person that knew what to do.

***** The Airtel Plaza Hotel - 818-997-7412

Open:

Always

Hotel Website: www.airtelplaza.com

John Purner

Hotel Email: jdunn@airtelplaza.com
If you are flying into the LA area on business this is where you stay, no
question about it. I like the hotel and I like the restaurants in it. I am
also a huge fan of this airport. The hotel is right on the runway so there
is noise. I love the sound of airplanes. It puts me to sleep.

WATSONVILLE, CA (WATSONVILLE MUNI - WVI)
Aprt Manager: DON FRENCH **PH:** 831-728-6064
Field Elevation: 163 **CTAF:** 122.800 **FUEL:** 100LLA
Runway: 08/26 **Length:** 3999 **Width:** 100 **Surface:** ASPH-G
Runway: 02/20 **Length:** 4501 **Width:** 150 **Surface:** ASPH-G

*** Ella's at the Airport – (831) 722-0480
Open:
> 11-9 Tues-Thurs, 11-10pm Fri & Sat, 9-9:pm Sundays

Restaurant Website: ellasinwatsonville.com
PIREP:
This is a very nice restaurant. Sunday brunch is my favorite time to go
because I can get one of my favorite dishes – Chicken & Waffles. They
do it really, really well.

WILLOWS, CA (WILLOWS-GLENN COUNTY - WLW)
Aprt Mgr: ANNETTE CHAVEZ **PH:** 530-934-6546
Field Elevation: 141 **CTAF:** 122.800 **FUEL:** 100LL
Runway: 13/31 **Length:** 3788 **Width:** 60 **Surface:** ASPH-F
Runway: 16/34 **Length:** 4125 **Width:** 100 **Surface:** ASPH-G

**** Nancy's Airport Cafe - (530) 934-7211
Open:
> Sun – Thurs: 5am – 10pm
> Fri – Sat: 5am -Midnight

PIREP:
This is a well-established, family run, airport diner. The food is really
very good, and the service is tops. I come here for the airport. Things
happen here. The Forest Service runs their fire control operations out of
Willows during fire season. They have an amazing arsenal of aircraft.
On weekends many private aviators head here for breakfast. I hope to
be among them again very soon. On the flight line you will find, LSAs,
Experimentals, certified machines and warbirds sporting propellers and
jet engines.

WOODLAKE, CA (WOODLAKE - O42)
Aprt Mgr: CRUZ DOMINGUEZ **PH:** 559-564-8055
Field Elevation: 425 **CTAF:** 122.900 **FUEL:** 100LL
Runway: 07/25 **Length:** 2203 **Width:** 50 **Surface:** ASPH-TRTD-G

*** The Runway Café - (559) 697-1213
Proprietor: Thelma Venturella
Open:

Mon – Sun: 7am – 2pm

PIREP:

Woodlake is a small *(3320ft X 50ft)* airport nestled at the foot of the Sierras about 15 min. north of Porterville. They offer Chevron self-serve and plenty of parking right in front of the restaurant. The restaurant is rustic. It resembles an old wooden cabin. The food is good with a wide selection. I have been here for breakfast, which is my favorite meal of the day probably because it is difficult to mess-up. I had biscuits and am pleased to report that they were expertly made onsite.

FlyIn Colorado

COLORADO SPRINGS, CO (COLORADO SPRINGS MUNI - COS)
Aprt Mgr: MARK N. EARLE **PH:** 719-550-1900
Field Elevation: 6187 **CTAF:** 0.000 **FUEL:** 100LLA
Runway: 13/31 **Length:** 8269 **Width:** 150 **Surface:** ASPH-G
Runway: 17R/35L **Length:** 11022 **Width:** 150 **Surface:** ASPH-G
Runway: 17L/35R **Length:** 13501 **Width:** 150 **Surface:** CONC-G

Cutter Aviation – 719-591-2065
FBO Website: www.cutteraviation.com
Affiliate: Phillips 66
Self Service: NO
Pilot Supplies: NO
Hours: 6:00 - 10:00 7 days

Colorado Jet Center – 719-591-2288
FBO Website: www.jetcenters.com
Affiliate: UNK
Self Service: YES
Pilot Supplies: YES
Hours: 24/7

Avis Car Rental – (719) 596-2751
Sun - Sat 6:00 AM - 12:00 AM

*** The Airplane Restaurant - (719) 570-7656
Proprietor: Steve Kanatzar
Open:
Mon - Thurs: 11:00 am - 9:00pm
Fri – Sun: 11:00 am - 10:00pm
Restaurant Website: www.solosrestaurant.com
Restaurant Email: Solosrestaurant@aol.com
PIREP:
The Airplane Restaurant is a short walk from the Colorado Jet Center
and is immediately adjacent to the Radisson. The decor is wonderful. A
mammoth Boeing KC-97 tanker is glued onto the restaurant's main
building. You can actually dine on it if you like. The servers introduce
themselves as "flight attendants". The food very good, I highly
recommend the Rueben paired with the onion rings.

DENVER, CO (ROCKY MOUNTAIN METROPOLITAN - BJC)
Aprt Mgr: KENNETH MAENPA **PH:** 303-271-4850
Field Elevation: 5673 **CTAF:** 118.600 **FUEL:** 100LLA
Runway: 02/20 **Length:** 3600 **Width:** 75 **Surface:** ASPH-F

Runway: 11R/29L **Length:** 7002 **Width:** 75 **Surface:** ASPH-G
Runway: 11L/29R **Length:** 9000 **Width:** 100 **Surface:** ASPH-G

Landmark Aviation – 303-466-2336
FBO Website: www.landmarkaviation.com
Affiliate: Shell
Self Service: YES
Pilot Supplies: NO
Hours: 6:00 - 10:00 7 days

**** The Bluesky Bistro - 720-628-5213
Proprietor: Dan and Sherise
Open:
Mon – Fri: 7:00am-2:00pm
Restaurant Website: www.blueskybistro.com
Restaurant Email: info@blueskybistro.com
PIREPS:
The Bluesky Bistro is located in the Main Terminal. It offers fantastic views of the Flatirons and the runways from the patio or upper level of the Terminal. The food is just south of awesome. Plan to show up Wednesday through Friday so you may have the option of enjoying their BBQ.

DENVER, CO (CENTENNIAL - APA)
Aprt Mgr: ROBERT OLISLAGERS **PH:** 303-790-0598
Field Elevation: 5885 **CTAF:** 0.000 **FUEL:** 100LLA
Runway: 10/28 **Length:** 4800 **Width:** 75 **Surface:** ASPH-G
Runway: 17R/35L **Length:** 7000 **Width:** 77 **Surface:** ASPH-G
Runway: 17L/35R **Length:** 10001 **Width:** 100 **Surface:** ASPH-G

X Jet – 303-649-9538
FBO Website: www.xjet.com
Affiliate: Avfuel
Self Service: NO
Pilot Supplies: YES
Hours: 24/7

TAC Air – 303-790-2575
FBO Website: www.tacair.com
Affiliate: Phillips 66
Self Service: YES
Pilot Supplies: YES
Hours: 24/7

Denver Jet Center – 800-343-3143
FBO Website: www.jetcenters.com

John Purner

Affiliate: UNK
Self Service: NO
Pilot Supplies: YES
Hours: 24/7

Signature Flight Support – 303-799-8388
FBO Website: www.signatureflight.com
Affiliate: UNK
Self Service: NO
Pilot Supplies: YES
Hours: 24/7

***** The Perfect Landing - (303) 649-4478
Proprietor: Jim and Sean Carter
Open:

> Sun – Mon: 7am-9pm
> Tue – Sat: 7am to 10pm

Restaurant Website: www.theperfectlanding.com
PIREP:
Good food, fast attentive service, drinks for your passengers and wonderful airport and mountain views. Park at the Jet Center, fuel is priced well and they will put you right in front of the restaurant's window. This is one of the great on-field restaurants. Go on a Friday night and get a few dances in by the piano. In the evening the ambiance changes considerably. The white table clothes come out; candles are placed on each table and the piano bar fires up. It is a great place to take a date. **The Perfect Landing** is my favorite restaurant in the mountain states.

DENVER, CO (FRONT RANGE - FTG)
Aprt Mgr: ROBERT OLISLAGERS **PH:** 303-790-0598
Field Elevation: 5885 **CTAF:** 0.000 **FUEL:** 100LLA
Runway: 10/28 **Length:** 4800 **Width:** 75 **Surface:** ASPH-G
Runway: 17R/35L **Length:** 7000 **Width:** 77 **Surface:** ASPH-G
Runway: 17L/35R **Length:** 10001 **Width:** 100 **Surface:** ASPH-G

Front Range Airport – 303-261-9100
FBO Website: www.ftg-airport.com
Affiliate: Avfuel
Self Service: YES
Pilot Supplies: YES
Hours: 7 – 9 7 days

** Aviator Bar & Grill – (303) 261-4054
Open:

52

Tues - Sat 8:00AM - 2:30PM
Restaurant Website: www.ftg-airport.com/aviator_cafe.php
Restaurant Email: info@AviatorBarandGrill.com
PIREP:
If you're here and you're hungry you can get a meal. The food has a manufactured quality. There is just nothing special about this café.

GREELEY, CO (GREELEY-WELD COUNTY - GXY)
Aprt Mgr: GARY CYR **PH:** 970-336-3000
Field Elevation: 4697 **CTAF:** 122.800 **FUEL:** 100LLA
Runway: 09/27 **Length:** 5801 **Width:** 100 **Surface:** ASPH-G
Runway: 16/34 **Length:** 10000 **Width:** 100 **Surface:** ASPH-G

Peak Flight Support – 970-336-3010
FBO Website: www.gxy.net
Affiliate: UNK
Self Service: YES
Pilot Supplies: NO
Hours: 6 – 8 7 days

*** Barnstormer Restaurant – (970) 336-3020
Proprietor: Linda Belleau
Open:
Mon – Sat: 7:00am - 2:30pm
Sun: 7:00am- 12:00pm
Restaurant Website: barnstormerrestaurant.com
Restaurant Email: lindabelleau@comcast.net
PIREP:
The Barnstormer Restaurant has been in business since 1990. Clearly, they're doing something right. Initially it goes to location. They are in the airport terminal, right in front of the ramp area. I like seeing my plane while I eat breakfast. I can do that here. Next it's the food and service which are good if not spectacular. Expect airport diner fare and you won't be disappointed. Finally, it's the view which is spectacular. You can see the runway which is pretty standard but you can also see the mountains.

LONGMONT, CO (VANCE BRAND - LMO)
Aprt Mgr: TIM BARTH **PH:** 303-651-8431
Field Elevation: 5055 **CTAF:** 122.975 **FUEL:** 100LLA MOGAS
Runway: 11/29 **Length:** 4800 **Width:** 75 **Surface:** CONC-G

** Flight Deck Grill – (303) 682-8888
Open:
0700-1400 Wednesday thru Sunday
Restaurant Website: www.flightdeckgrill.com/

PIREP:
This is a food truck permanently parked between the FBO and Self
Serve 100LL. This is the cleanest kitchen you will ever see, and the
food and the service is top-notch. Tables with umbrellas to keep you
out of the sun with a great view of the flight line. They open in April
and close when the weather turns in the late fall.

PUEBLO, CO (PUEBLO MEMORIAL - PUB)
Aprt Mgr: MARK LOVIN **PH:** 719-553-2760
Field Elevation: 4729 **CTAF:** 119.100 **FUEL:** 100LLA
Runway: 08R/26L **Length:** 3767 **Width:** 75 **Surface:** ASPH-G
Runway: 17/35 **Length:** 8310 **Width:** 150 **Surface:** ASPH-G
Runway: 08L/26R **Length:** 10498 **Width:** 150 **Surface:** ASPH-G

Rocky Mountain Flower – 719-948-3316
FBO Website: www.rockymoutainflowerfbo.com
Affiliate: Avfuel
Self Service: NO
Pilot Supplies: NO
Hours: 7 – 8 7 days

** Pete's Landing Bar and Grill - (719) 948-9000
Open:
          Tues – Sun: 7:30am - 0:00pm
Restaurant Website: N/A
PIREP:
Pete's Landing is located in the terminal. It's an easy stroll from either
of the FBOs. The food is OK, the service is attentive, you'll be glad
you came not because of the food but the awesome view of the
mountains and airport.

FlyIn Connecticut

WINDSOR LOCKS, CT (BRADLEY INTL - BDL)
  Aprt Mgr: "ERIC WALDRON, A.A.E. ACE" **PH:** 860-292-2001
  Field Elevation: 173 **CTAF:** 0.000 **FUEL:** 100LLA
  Runway: 06/24 **Length:** 9510 **Width:** 200 **Surface:** ASPH-E
  Runway: 01/19 **Length:** 4268 **Width:** 100 **Surface:** ASPH-F
  Runway: 15/33 **Length:** 6847 **Width:** 150 **Surface:** ASPH-F

Signature Flight Support – 860-623-3940
FBO Website: www.signatureflight.com
Self Service: No
Pilot Supplies: Yes
Hours: 24/7

Avis Car Rental – (860) 627-3500
  Sun - Sat 5:00 AM - 1:30 AM

New England Air Museum - (860) 623-3305
Open:
  Mon – Sun: 10:00am - 5:00pm
Museum Website: www.neam.org
Museum Email: staff@neam.org
PIREP:
Park at either **Signature Flight Support** or **Tac Air**, both provide courtesy shuttle service to and from the museum. I used Signature and was pleased that they provided passes to the museum and waived the tiedown fee for a small fuel purchase. They are very nice people. This is a great museum with some wonderful exhibits including a Lockheed 10A Electra. Three times each year this Museum has an Open Cockpit Day. You will be invited to climb into the pilot's seat of 12 aircraft selected from their collection of WWII fighters, jet fighters, airliners, helicopters, and civilian aircraft. This is a great chance to get some photos of these old birds interior. You may never have a chance like this again, don't let it pass you by.

---

* New England Air Museum - (860) 623-3305
Open:
  Mon – Sun: 10:00am - 5:00pm
PIREP:
What about food? They have a small dining area with vending machines offering snacks and beverages. You won't starve, though you may wish you had.

55

FlyIn Delaware

GEORGETOWN, DE (SUSSEX COUNTY - GED)
Aprt Mgr: JIM HICKIN **PH:** 302-855-7774
Field Elevation: 53 **CTAF:** 123.000 **FUEL:** 100LLA
Runway: 10/28 **Length:** 3109 **Width:** 75 **Surface:** ASPH
Runway: 04/22 **Length:** 5000 **Width:** 150 **Surface:** ASPH-G

Georgetown Air Services – 860-623-3940
FBO Website: www.georgetownair.com
Affiliate: Unknown
Self Service: NO
Pilot Supplies: NO
Hours: 7 Days 8am – 6pm

**** Arena's at the Airport - 302-856-3297
Open:
> Mon-Thurs: 11am-9pm
> Friday: 11am-10pm
> Sat: 9am-10pm
> Sun: 9am- 9pm

Restaurant Website: www.arenasdeli.com
PIREP:
Come on the weekend and enjoy breakfast. **Arena's** is a five location deli that has been in the area for over 20 years. Deli's do breakfast right and this one is no exception. For me it's a corn beef and cheese omelet with an onion bagel.

FlyIn Florida

DAYTONA BEACH, FL (SPRUCE CREEK - 7FL6)
    Aprt Mgr: VERN HENDERSHOTT **PH:** 386-872-1430
    Field Elevation: 24 **CTAF:** 0.000 **FUEL:** 100LLA A+
    Runway: 05/23 **Length:** 4000 **Width:** 176 **Surface:** ASPH-G

Spruce Creek – 386-760-5884
FBO Website: www.7fl6.com
Affiliate: UNK
Self Service: YES
Pilot Supplies: NO
Hours: 7 Days: 8am – 5pm

** The Downwind Cafe - (386) 756-8811
Open:
        Tue - Sun: 11am – 9pm
Restaurant Website: www.downwindcafe.com
Restaurant Email: downwindcafe@gmail.com
PIREP:
You **MUST** phone **The Downwind** for permission to land before going, as Spruce Creek is a private airport. Be certain to ask were you can park. They have a large area for transient aircraft near the restaurant. There is an outside seating area, but you can't see the runway from it. That's OK as there are airplanes everywhere. The food used to be good and the service splendid, but it has slipped to awful on both counts following a change of ownership.

Spruce Creek is the largest and nicest flyin community in the world with every amenity you can imagine including an 18-hole golf course, a tennis club and much, much more. You're likely to meet several very nice pilots while you're here. The problem with going to Spruce Creek is that it's hard to leave Spruce Creek, as it is where every pilot wants to live.

DELAND, FL (DELAND MUNI-SIDNEY H TAYLOR FIELD - DED)
    Aprt Mgr: NICKOLIS LANDGRAFF **PH:** 386-740-6955
    Field Elevation: 80 **CTAF:** 123.075 **FUEL:** 100LLA
    Runway: 05/23 **Length:** 4301 **Width:** 75 **Surface:** ASPH-G
    Runway: 12/30 **Length:** 6001 **Width:** 100 **Surface:** ASPH-G

Deland Aviation – 386-740-1955
FBO Website: www.delandaviation.com
Affiliate: UNK

elf Service: YES
Pilot Supplies: YES
Hours: 8:00 - 6:00 M-F/ 9:00 - 5:00 Sat/ 10:00 - 4:00 Sun

*** Airport Restaurant and Gin Mill – (386) 734-9755
Proprietor: John DeWitt & Scott Pollitt
Open:
> Mon - Sat: 11:00 am - 2:00 am
> Sun: 11:00 am - 10:00 pm

Restaurant Website: www.airportginmill.com
Restaurant Email: bestburger@airportginmill.com
PIREP:
Great little airport bar and grill with a rustic pilot atmosphere. Excellent cheeseburgers but also have chicken or fried fish sandwiches - all the same price. It is set back off runway 5 behind some tall bushes, but the glowing neon beer signs in the windows give it away. Watch the skydivers all day long and listen to live music when the sun goes down. Try it out, you will like it.

DESTIN, FL (DESTIN-FORT WALTON BEACH - DTS)
Aprt Mgr: MICHAEL J. STENSON **PH:** 850-651-7160
Field Elevation: 22 CTAF: 123.075 Fuel: 100LLA
Runway: 14/32 **Length:** 5001 **Width:** 100 **Surface:** ASPH-G

Destin Jet – 850-424-6890
FBO Website: www.destinjet.com
Airport Website: www.flydts.com
Affiliate: AVFuel
Pilot Supplies: YES
Hours: 24/7

Hertz – 850-837-2768

FORT LAUDERDALE, FL (FT LAUDERDALE EXEC - FXE)
Aprt Mgr: RUFUS JAMES **PH:** 954-828-4955
Field Elevation: 13 CTAF: 0.000 **FUEL:** 100LLA JETA
Runway: 13/31 **Length:** 4000 **Width:** 100 **Surface:** ASPH-G
Runway: 09/27 **Length:** 6002 **Width:** 100 **Surface:** ASPH-G

Banyan Air Service – 954-491-3170

Banyan Pilot Shop – 888-280-9272
FBO Website: www.banyanair.com
Affiliate: Avfuel
Self Service: NO
Pilot Supplies: YES

Hours: 24/7

***** Jet Runway Cafe - 954 958 9900
Proprietor: Mike Linder & Mitch Amsterdam
Open:
Monday- Friday: 7:30am - 3pm
Saturday: 7:30am - 2pm
Restaurant Website: www.jetrunwaycafe.com
Restaurant Email: info@ jetrunwaycafe.com
PIREP:
This is my second Florida favorite. If I get to choose this is where we go for lunch. The reason is the Honey Lime Salmon. Great ambiance, great food and great service and a BIG plus factor; Banyan Air Service. They are the BEST FBO I've ever found. They have an amazing pilot shop and they have amazing service. When you get ready to fly to the Bahamas, this is where you leave from. They will walk you through the process and fill out all of the forms for you. If you need life vests (which you must have) or a life raft (which you should have) they can sell or rent them to you.

FORT PIERCE, FL (ST LUCIE COUNTY INTL - FPR)
Aprt Mgr: TODD COX **PH:** 772-462-1732
Field Elevation: 23 **CTAF:** 128.200 **FUEL:** 100LLA
Runway: 10L/28R **Length:** 4000 **Width:** 75 **Surface:** ASPH-G
Runway: 14/32 **Length:** 4755 **Width:** 100 **Surface:** ASPH-G
Runway: 10R/28L **Length:** 6492 **Width:** 150 **Surface:** ASPH-G

APP Jet Center – 772-489-2285
Affiliate: UNK
Self Service: YES
Pilot Supplies: NO
Hours: 7 days 7:00 - 9:00 PM

**** The Airport Tiki - (772) 489-2285
Proprietor: Errol Houck
Open:
Mon- Sun: 7am – 5pm
PIREP:
When you land just say, *"Taxi to Tiki"* and the controller will get you to the correct ramp. That's important. There are three great reasons to go to **The Airport Tiki.** First, it's the food and the food here measures up. Next it's the service, and the service here is what you'd want even when it's really busy. Here's the PLUS factor. When you return from the Bahamas *(it's on your bucket list isn't it?)* you will most likely clear customs at Ft. Pierce and custom's at Ft. Pierce is right next door to **The Airport Tiki.**

John Purner

LAKELAND, FL (LAKELAND LINDER RGNL - LAL)
  Aprt Mgr: "EUGENE B. CONRAD, III" **PH:** 863-834-3298
  Field Elevation: 142 **CTAF:** 124.500 **FUEL:** 100LLA
  Runway: 05/23 **Length:** 5005 **Width:** 150 **Surface:** ASPH-G
  Runway: 09/27 **Length:** 8499 **Width:** 150 **Surface:** ASPH-G

Sheltair Aviation – 863-647-3911
FBO Website: www.sheltairaviation.com
Affiliate: UNK
Self Service: YES
Pilot Supplies: YES
Hours: 7 days 6:00AM - 9:00 PM

*** Hilton Garden Inn – (863) 647-0666
Open:
  Daily: Breakfast, lunch, dinner *(no lunch on Sat & Sun)*
PIREP:
Park on the Columbia FBO ramp (no fee) just north of the tower. Walk through the terminal building and across the parking lot to the hotel. Breakfast is a high quality buffet with a broad selection including omelets to order. The above rating is for breakfast only as I have not tried lunch or dinner. Lunch is what you'd expect. The service is good and the surroundings crisp and clean.

**** WACO Kitchen – COMING Summer of 2022
Proprietor: DIETER MORSZECK & SVEN LEPSCHY
Open:
  Summer of 2022
Restaurant Website: www.wacokitchen.com

PIREP:
This is the home airport of the 2nd greatest show in aviation, **Sun 'n Fun**. On the opposite side of the field from the show site, an amazing new restaurant is coming. The **WACO Kitchen** will be on the 2nd floor.

We don't usually add a restaurant that we haven't been too. As a matter of fact, this is a first. The **WACO Kitchen** is a second home for its sister restaurant which is located in Battlecreek, Michigan. They share the same name and of course the same owners and management team.

The Battlecreek location has earned a five start rating from the $100 Hamburger and I am certain the Lakeland venue will not disappoint.

60

Visit as soon as you can and please send a PIREP if you get there before I do.

MIAMI, FL (MIAMI INTL - MIA)
Aprt Mgr: "JOSE ABREU, P.E." **PH:** 305-876-7077
Field Elevation: 9 **CTAF:** 0.000 **FUEL:** 100 A
Runway: 08L/26R **Length:** 8600 **Width:** 150 **Surface:** ASPH-G
Runway: 12/30 **Length:** 9355 **Width:** 150 **Surface:** ASPH-G
Runway: 08R/26L **Length:** 10506 **Width:** 200 **Surface:** ASPH-G
Runway: 09/27 **Length:** 13016 **Width:** 150 **Surface:** ASPH-G

Avis Car Rental – (305) 876-1800
Sun - Sat open 24 hrs

Landmark Aviation – 305-874-1477
FBO Website: www.landmarkaviaiton.com
Affiliate: UNK
Self Service: NO
Pilot Supplies: YES
Hours: 24/7

*** The 94th Aero Squadron - (305) 261-4220
Proprietor: Pamela Ambroci
Open:
Mon - Sat: 11am - 11pm
Restaurant Website: www.94thmiami.com
PIREP:
There are several **94th Aero Squadron's** across the country and I have visited all of them. They are all aviation themed restaurants centered on the WWI period. The restaurants are all fashioned to look like a French farmhouse of that period. All are located to overlook the runway at an airport and all have superior food and service priced to match. None of them have ramp access. This one is no exception. You must pick the FBO that suits you and they will shuttle you to and from the restaurant. Miami International is not my first pick as a piston powered GA friendly place. It is a busy. That is the reason we rate the Miami **94th Aero Squadron** as a three rather than four-star stop.

NEW SMYRNA BEACH, FL (NEW SMYRNA BCH MUNI - EVB)
Aprt Mgr: RHONDA WALKER **PH:** 386-424-2199
Field Elevation: 10 **CTAF:** 119.675 **FUEL:** 100LLA
Runway: 02/20 **Length:** 4000 **Width:** 100 **Surface:** ASPH-F
Runway: 11/29 **Length:** 4319 **Width:** 100 **Surface:** ASPH-G
Runway: 07/25 **Length:** 5000 **Width:** 75 **Surface:** ASPH-G

61

Airgate Aviation – 386-478-0600
FBO Website: www.flyairgate.com
Affiliate: UNK
Self Service: NO
Pilot Supplies: NO
Hours: 7days: 7:00 - 7:00 summer: 7:00 - 6:00 winter

*** Island Hopperz - 386-478-0601
Open:
> 7 Days: 10am - 6pm
Restaurant Website: flyairgate.com/airgate-cafe/

PIREP:
The Airgate Café has been renamed **Island Hopperz. It** is located at the north side of **Airgate Aviation's** (FBO) hangar. It is best to park on the ramp just south of the self-serve fuel facility. The café is small and somewhat plain inside with four outdoor tables also available. The food and service are first rate. It is pricey. The menu and the food have not changed, as a matter of fact, the Airgate Café menu remains on the **Island Hopperz** website.

OCALA, FL (OCALA INTL-JIM TAYLOR FIELD - OCF)
Aprt Mgr: MR. MATTHEW GROW **PH:** 352-629-8377
Field Elevation: 90 **CTAF:** 119.250 **FUEL:** 100LLA1+
Runway: 18/36 **Length:** 7467 **Width:** 150 **Surface:** ASPH-E
Runway: 08/26 **Length:** 3009 **Width:** 50 **Surface:** ASPH-G

***** Elevation89 - (863) 467-6828 (352) 655-2880
Open:
> OPEN DAILY: 11 AM TO 9 PM

PIREP:
This a Fantastic restaurant right on the field... Its gourmet style but casual. The food is some of the best you will have at an airport restaurant. The prices are reasonable.

The Eggs Benedict is unbelievable!! Shrimp with a Cajun Sauce! excellent.
If its lunch your after grab a hold of the Grouper sandwich

The only Bad thing about this place it is there will be a mandatory $15.00 service fee imposed by the FBO unless you purchase fuel (*very high prices*). It may ruin a great airport restaurant. A mandatory fee to eat there will chase many away. Me for instance!

So, **FIVE** stars for the **Elevation 89** and **ONE** star for the FBO.

OKEECHOBEE, FL (OKEECHOBEE COUNTY - OBE)
Aprt Mgr: KATHY SCOTT **PH:** 863-467-5505
Field Elevation: 33 **CTAF:** 123.000 **FUEL:** 100LLA
Runway: 14/32 **Length:** 4001 **Width:** 75 **Surface:** ASPH-G
Runway: 05/23 **Length:** 5000 **Width:** 100 **Surface:** ASPH-G

*** The Landing Strip - (863) 467-6828
Open:
>   Mon-Sun: 6 am - 3 pm

PIREP:
Nice cross runways, easy landing in any wind. Great seats outside where we could watch the traffic. Park on their ramp right. Cheap self-serve fuel. OK cheap is a relative term. They serve breakfast all day which works for me as breakfast is my favorite meal of the day.

ORMOND BEACH, FL (ORMOND BEACH MUNI - OMN)
Aprt Mgr: STEVEN LICHLITER **PH:** 386-615-7019
Field Elevation: 29 **CTAF:** 119.075 **FUEL:** 100LLA
Runway: 17/35 **Length:** 3702 **Width:** 100 **Surface:** ASPH-G
Runway: 08/26 **Length:** 4003 **Width:** 75 **Surface:** ASPH-G

Sunrise Aviation – 386-677-5724
FBO Website: www.flysunrise.com
Affiliate: Shell
Self Service: YES
Pilot Supplies: YES
Hours: 7:00 - 7:00 Mon-Sat 9:00 - 4:00 Sunday

River Bend Golf Club - 386-673-6000 ext. 14
Head Pro: Ken Van Leuven
Open: Tue - Sun:
Restaurant Website: www.riverbendgolf.info
Restaurant Email: proshop@playriverbendgolf.com
PIREP:
From the air, it looks like a very well laid out course. Golf and flying in the same day is hard to beat. There is one little problem and be aware of it. Daytona area flight schools flock to Ormond as a practice destination. It is a good field and it is towered. Keep a smile on your face and your head on a swivel. All things considered; you'd have to work at being unhappy with this destination. Green fees and cart rentals vary by time of day and season. Together they max out at less than 50 bucks.

PALM COAST, FL (FLAGLER COUNTY - FIN)
Aprt Mgr: ROY SIEGER JR **PH:** 386-437-0401

Field Elevation: 33 **CTAF:** 118.950 **FUEL:** 100LLA
Runway: 11/29 **Length:** 4999 **Width:** 100 **Surface:** ASPH-F
Runway: 06/24 **Length:** 5000 **Width:** 100 **Surface:** ASPH-G

*** Highjackers Restaurant - (386) 586-6078
Manager: Lisa Setien
Open:
　　　　Daily: 11AM to 10PM
Restaurant Website: www.highjackers.com
PIREP:
Highjackers is more than a burger run. It's like a mini-vacation to the South Pacific. The food is pretty darn good. I go just for the key lime pie.

PANACEA, FL (WAKULLA COUNTY - 2J0)
Aprt Mgr: RICHARD W. THORNBURG **PH:** 850-926-1201
Field Elevation: 11 **CTAF:** 122.900 **FUEL:**
Runway: 18/36 **Length:** 2590 **Width:** 70 **Surface:** TURF-F

*** Las Palmas Mexican Restaurant - (850) 524-0914
Open:
　　　　Mon - Sat: 9:00am to 11:00pm
PIREP:
"HAMAKNOCKERS" is no more. Looks like COVID did them in. Not to worry a new restaurant has opened in its place. The feature is Mexican food which is one of my favorites. This is Excellent Mexican cuisine.

It's a semi-short grass strip that is semi-lumpy. Take care.

The restaurant is at the north end.

PUNTA GORDA, FL (PUNTA GORDA - PGD)
Aprt Mgr: GARY QUILL **PH:** 941-639-1101
Field Elevation: 26 **CTAF:** 119.550 **FUEL:** 100LLA A+
Runway: 15/33 **Length:** 5688 **Width:** 150 **Surface:** ASPH-G
Runway: 04/22 **Length:** 7193 **Width:** 150 **Surface:** ASPH-G
Runway: 09/27 **Length:** 2636 **Width:** 60 **Surface:** ASPH-P

Avis Car Rental – (941) 575-7567
　　　　Sun 8:00 AM - 10:45 PM
　　　　Mon 8:00 AM - 11:00 PM
　　　　Tue 8:00 AM - 10:30 PM
　　　　Wed 8:00 AM - 11:00 PM
　　　　Thu 8:00 AM - 10:45 PM
　　　　Fri - Sat 8:00 AM - 11:00 PM

Punta Gorda FBO – 941-639-4119
FBO Website: www.flypgd.com
Affiliate: UNK
Self Service: YES
Pilot Supplies: YES
Hours: 24/7

*** Skyview Cafe - 941 637-6004
Proprietor: Edward Gallagher
Open:

Mon – Thu: 7:00am - 2:00pm
Fri: 7:00am - 8:00pm
Sat – Sun: 7:00am - 2:00pm

Restaurant Website: www.flypgd.com/main-terminal/dining/
PIREP:
This is a towered airport and that is served by one airline. The result is a TSA presence which means that you can't park in front of the restaurant and you can't walk across the redlines that are painted on the terminal ramp. So, you park at the FBO and use a little foot power to get to the restaurant. The walk from the FBO is short. The "crunchy" French Toast" is really, really good and you want it. You can sit outside but be warned that it is a smoking zone.

RIVER RANCH, FL (RIVER RANCH RESORT - 2RR)
Aprt Mgr: DEAN MADDUX **PH:** 863-692-0727
Field Elevation: 55 **CTAF:** 122.800 **FUEL:** 100LL
Runway: 16/34 **Length:** 4950 **Width:** 75 **Surface:** ASPH-F

Westgate River Ranch – 863-692-0727
FBO Website: www.westgateresorts.com
Affiliate: UNK
Self Service: YES
Pilot Supplies: YES
Hours: 24/7 credit card self-serve

**** The Westgate Smokehouse Grill - (863) 692-1321
Open:

Serving breakfast, lunch and dinner
(Seasonal hours; please call ahead)

Restaurant Website:
www.westgatedestinations.com/florida/westgate-river-ranch/dining
PIREP:
Pick up a golf cart and a map at the FBO/Golf Course Pro Shop. It'll set you back 5 bucks for two hours but it'll save you a long walk. **The Westgate Smokehouse Grill** overlooks the Kissimmee River. The

John Purner

menu offers steaks, seafood, baby back ribs, burgers, sandwiches and salads. You can eat on the large screened-in porch and watch the birds feeding and spot alligators. Days and hours of operation vary by season, so make sure to call ahead before making the flight.

ST AUGUSTINE, FL (NORTHEAST FLORIDA RGNL - SGJ)
Aprt Mgr: ED WUELLNER **PH:** 904-209-0090
Field Elevation: 10 **CTAF:** 127.625 **FUEL:** 100LLA
Runway: 06/24 **Length:** 2701 **Width:** 60 **Surface:** ASPH-E
Runway: 02/20 **Length:** 2610 **Width:** 75 **Surface:** ASPH-F
Runway: 13/31 **Length:** 8002 **Width:** 150 **Surface:** ASPH-G

Avis Car Rental – (904) 825-1505
Sun 9:00 AM - 12:00 PM
Mon 8:00 AM - 6:30 PM
Tue 8:00 AM - 5:00 PM
Wed 8:00 AM - 6:30 PM
Thu 8:00 AM - 5:00 PM
Fri 8:00 AM - 6:30 PM
Sat 9:00 AM - 2:00 PM

Atlantic Aviation – 904-824-1995
FBO Website: www.atlanticaviation.com
Affiliate: UNK
Self Service: YES
Pilot Supplies: YES
Hours: M-F 6:00 - 12:00 Sat/Sun 6:00 - 10:00

**** The Hangar One Bistro – (904) 602-6003
Open:

DINNER
Mon, Wed-Sun 5:00 pm – 9:00 pm

BRUNCH
Fri 11:30 am – 3:00 pm
Sat, Sun 10:30 am – 3:00 pm

Restaurant Website: www.hangaronebistro.com
PIREP:
First rate. Very good food, most tables have a nice view of the runway. Go for brunch and try the Apple Pancakes. I think they're worth the
flight.

Check it out. This place deserves your attention.

66

ST PETERSBURG, FL (ALBERT WHITTED – SPG)
Aprt Mgr: RICH LESNIAK **PH:** 727-893-7657
Field Elevation: 7 **CTAF:** 127.400 **FUEL:** 100LLA A1
Runway: 18/36 **Length:** 2864 **Width:** 150 **Surface:** ASPH-G
Runway: 07/25 **Length:** 3677 **Width:** 75 **Surface:** ASPH-G

---

* Sheltair Aviation – 727-824-8220
FBO Website: www.sheltairaviation.com
Affiliate: UNK
Self Service: YES
Pilot Supplies: YES
Hours: 7 days 6:00 - 9:00

**** The Hangar Restaurant & Flight Lounge – 727-822-PROP
Open:
            Mon - Sun: 8am – 10pm
Restaurant Website: www.thehangarstpete.com
PIREP:
Albert Whitted is everything a general aviation airport should
be...convenient location, beautiful scenery, multiple runways and an
very good restaurant. The restaurant is modern, clean and attractive
with seating both outdoors and inside. Both the food and service are
outstanding. For me it's the Grilled Ham & Cheese followed by the
seven-layer carrot cake. By the way, the ham is pit grilled and cheese is
Brie. The spoiler is the FBO's insistence on a $15 ramp fee or a fuel
purchase.

SEBASTIAN, FL (SEBASTIAN MUNI - X26)
Aprt Mgr: JOE GRIFFIN **PH:** 772-633-0151
Field Elevation: 21 **CTAF:** 123.050 **FUEL:** 100LL
Runway: 08/26 **Length:** 3200 **Width:** 75 **Surface:** ASPH-G
Runway: 04/22 **Length:** 4024 **Width:** 75 **Surface:** ASPH-G

Sebastian Muni – 772-388-8228
FBO Website: www.sebastianairport.com
Affiliate: UNK
Self Service: YES
Pilot Supplies: YES
Hours: 24/7

---

* ZOO BAR - 772-388-5672
Proprietor: Jim Iannaccone
Open:
            Mon - Sun: 9am - sunset
Restaurant Website: www.skydiveseb.com/skydiving-facilities.htm

Restaurant Email: myzoobar@gmail.com
PIREP:
The Zoo Bar and Restaurant is open for breakfast and lunch. It has
more of a snack bar than restaurant feel. They serve beer and wine
inside and on the observation deck. Sebastian is a skydiving center so
keep your head on a swivel and listen closely for traffic advisories
when arriving and departing. That said I really enjoy watching the
antics of those who choose to jump out of planes as they return to earth.
They all return to earth, that's the one certainty for folks who chose to
jump out of airplanes.

SEBRING, FL (SEBRING RGNL - SEF)
Aprt Mgr: MIKE WILLINGHAM **PH:** 863-655-6444
Field Elevation: 62 **CTAF:** 122.700 **FUEL:** 100LLA MOGAS
Runway: 14/32 **Length:** 4990 **Width:** 100 **Surface:** ASPH-G
Runway: 18/36 **Length:** 5234 **Width:** 100 **Surface:** ASPH-G

Volo Aviation – 863-655-6455
FBO Website: www.sebring-airport.com
Affiliate: UNK
Self Service: YES
Pilot Supplies: NO
Hours: M-F 7:30 - 6:00 Sat - Sun 7:30 - 5:00

*** JR's Runway Cafe - 863-655-0732
Proprietor: Michael Leone
Open:
>   Monday – Friday: 8am - 2:30pm
>   Saturday - Sunday: 7am - 2:30pm

Restaurant Website: sebring-airport.com/flight-center/runway-cafe/
PIREP:
Sebring is a great destination. If you go on a weekend you are almost
guaranteed and see and hear activity on the world famous race track
which abuts the airport and is on the backside of the restaurant. Yes,
you can easily walk over and have a look. The food and service at the
restaurant are adequate – think **Denny's**. If you are interested in LSA's
walk next door to Lockwood aviation they are a local dealer from some
of the finest ones and they are renowned as a repair and service center
for ROTAX engines.

TAMPA, FL (TAMPA NORTH AERO PARK - X39)
Aprt Mgr: CHARLES W. BRAMMER **PH:** 813-973-3703
Field Elevation: 68 **CTAF:** 123.050 **FUEL:** 100LLA
Runway: 14/32 **Length:** 3541 **Width:** 50 **Surface:** ASPH-F

Tampa North Flight Svc – 813-973-3703

FBO Website: www.tampanorth.com
Affiliate: UNK
Self Service: NO
Pilot Supplies: YES
Hours: 8:00 - 4:30 7 days

*** Happy Hangar Café - 813-973-3703
Proprietor: Keith Carver
Open:
Tue-Sun: 7am - 2pm
Restaurant Website: www.tampanorth.com
Restaurant Email: HappyHangar@gmail.com
PIREP:
The airport has new owners who are making serious efforts to improve and expand services. After landing taxi to the ramp area near the self-serve fuel pump and park in any space you like on the paved ramp or in the grass area behind it. Food and service are average airport fare at **The Happy Hangar Café**. Their plus factor is that everything is made from scratch including biscuits and pancakes. I've had the pancakes. They are very, very good. The restaurant's windows overlook the approach end of runway 32 as does the porch, which has picnic tables.

VENICE, FL (VENICE MUNI - VNC)
Aprt Mgr: "CHRIS ROZANSKY, C.M." **PH:** 941-486-2711
Field Elevation: 18 **CTAF:** 122.725 **FUEL:** 100LLA
Runway: 13/31 **Length:** 4999 **Width:** 150 **Surface:** ASPH-F
Runway: 04/22 **Length:** 5000 **Width:** 150 **Surface:** ASPH-P

SunCoast Air Center – 941-485-1799
FBO Website: www.suncoastaircenter.com
Affiliate: UNK
Self Service: YES
Pilot Supplies: YES
Hours: 7:30 - 7:30 7 days

*** SunCoast Cafe - 941-484-0100
Open:
Mon - Sun: 7:30am – 3:30pm
Restaurant Website: www.suncoastcafe.com
Restaurant Email: dduboulay@suncoastcafe.com
PIREP:
This is your basic airport restaurant. The menu and the food it represents are very standard. The wait staff provides yeoman like service. It's worth the stop if you're heading this way.

VERO BEACH, FL (VERO BEACH MUNI - VRB)

69

Aprt Mgr: MR. ERIC MENGER **PH:** 772-978-4930
Field Elevation: 24 **CTAF:** 126.300 **FUEL:** 100 A
Runway: 11L/29R **Length:** 3504 **Width:** 75 **Surface:** ASPH-G
Runway: 04/22 **Length:** 4974 **Width:** 100 **Surface:** ASPH-G
Runway: 11R/29L **Length:** 7314 **Width:** 100 **Surface:** ASPH-G

Sun Aviation – 772-562-2848
FBO Website: www.suncoastaircenter.com
Affiliate: UNK
Self Service: YES
Pilot Supplies: NO
Hours: 6:00 - 9:00 7 days

***** CJ Cannon's - 772-567-7727
Proprietor: Charles J Cannon III
Open:
> Mon – Sat: 7:00am till 9:00pm
> Sun: 7:00am till 2:00pm

Restaurant Website: www.cjcannons.com/
PIREP:
I have been coming here for many years. It is consistently wonderful. Park your airplane and walk right up to the door. Great food and ambiance. Can't be beat for quality and convenience. Call Piper before you go and see if they can arrange a plant tour for you. Their plant is further down the ramp.

WILLISTON, FL (WILLISTON MUNI - X60)
Airport Manager: JOE BALL **PH:** 352-528-4900
Field Elevation: 76 **CTAF:** 122.800 **FUEL:** 100LLA
Runway: 14/32 **Length:** 4399 **Width:** 100 **Surface:** ASPH-G
Runway: 05/23 **Length:** 6668 **Width:** 100 **Surface:** CONC-G

*** Pyper Kub Cafe and Restaurant – 352-528-0376
Open:
> Sun – Thur: 7:00am – 3:00pm
> Fri: 7:00am – 8:00pm
> Sat: 7:00am – 9:00pm

PIREP:
It's right next to the FBO. Fun diner-type food, excellent breakfasts and fun aviation theme décor. Plus, great in-wing fuel service and nice, friendly staff.

WINTER HAVEN, FL (WINTER HAVEN'S GILBERT - GIF)
Airport Manager: DEBBIE MURPHY **PH:** 863-291-5678

Field Elevation: 145 **CTAF:** 123.050 **FUEL:** 100LLA MOGAS
Runway: 05/23 **Length:** 5005 **Width:** 100 **Surface:** ASPH-F
Runway: 11/29 **Length:** 4001 **Width:** 100 **Surface:** ASPH-G

*** Flightline Cafe & Catering – 863-875-5869
Open:
        Tue – Thur: 9:00am till 2:00pm
        Fri – Sun: 8:00am – 8:00pm
Restaurant Website: flightlinecafe.com
Restaurant Email: FlightlineCafe@gmail.com
PIREP:
The restaurant is in the terminal and offers a fairly good view of the flightline. It has suffered a few management changes which has made it spotty, sometimes good sometimes not so much. Recently, I've been happy and hope you be as well. Let's give it a thumbs up for now and hope for more consistency in the future.

FlyIn Georgia

ATLANTA, GA (COBB COUNTY-MC COLLUM FIELD - RYY)
Aprt Mgr: KARL A VON HAGEL **PH:** 770-528-1615
Field Elevation: 1041 **CTAF:** 125.900 **FUEL:** 100LLA1+
Runway: 09/27 **Length:** 6311 **Width:** 100 **Surface:** CONC-G

Hawthorne Global Aviation Services – 770-422-4300
FBO Website: www.hawthorne.aero
Affiliate: UNK
Self Service: NO
Pilot Supplies: NO
Hours: 6:00 10:00 Mon-Friday 7:00 - 9:00 Sat/Sun

***** Elevation Chophouse - (770) 485-7469**
Proprietor: Michael Bowman
Open:
>Tue–Fri 5pm–10pm
>Sat 11am–10pm
>Sun 11am–9pm

Restaurant Website: www.elevationatlanta.com
Restaurant Email: info@elevationgeorgia.com
PIREP:
Elevation is certainly a cut above most airport cafes. The food choices vary between ordinary and unusual. My test is always a simple medium rare, New York Strip steak which is easy to screw up. The one I was presented was excellent. Test passed – grade A. The service is attentive. They also make their own ice cream using liquid nitrogen. Is it good? I really don't know – I passed.

ATLANTA, GA (DEKALB-PEACHTREE - PDK)
Aprt Mgr: Mario Evans **PH:** 770-936-5440
Field Elevation: 1003 **CTAF:** 120.900 **FUEL:** 100 A A1
Runway: 09/27 **Length:** 3383 **Width:** 150 **Surface:** ASPH-G
Runway: 02L/20R **Length:** 3746 **Width:** 150 **Surface:** ASPH-G
Runway: 16/34 **Length:** 3967 **Width:** 150 **Surface:** ASPH-G
Runway: 02R/20L **Length:** 6001 **Width:** 100 **Surface:** CONC-G

Epps Aviation – 770-458-9851
FBO Website: www.eppsaviation.com
Affiliate: Shell
Self Service: NO
Pilot Supplies: NO
Hours: 24/7

Atlantice Aviation – 770-454-5000
FBO Website: www.atlanticaviation.com
Affiliate: UNK
Self Service: NO
Pilot Supplies: NO
Hours: 24/7

Signature Flight Support – 770-452-0010
FBO Website: www.signatureflight.com
Affiliate: UNK
Self Service: NO
Pilot Supplies: NO
Hours: 24/7

Epps Aviation – 770-458-9851
FBO Website: www.eppsaviation.com
Affiliate: UNK
Self Service: NO
Pilot Supplies: NO
Hours: 24/7

***** The Downwind - 770/452-0973**
Proprietor: Andreas Mammas and Jenifer Hardee
Open:
        Monday - Friday: 11am - 10pm
        Saturday - noon - 10pm

Restaurant Email: www.downwindrestaurant.com
Restaurant Email: downwindrest@aol.com
PIREP:
The Downwind was established in 1989 and its been going strong ever since. It's a family owned business started by Jenifer Hardee and her stepfather, Andreas Mammas. They offer great burgers, sandwiches, Greek specialties, and seafood. Its runway location offers terrific views. The Downwind really does have the *"Best Hamburger in Town"*. Get one!

Park at Atlantic, they don't charge a ramp fee or require a fuel purchase if you're there less than two hours. That's plenty of time to wolf down a burger. PDK is BUSY! Pay attention to the controller's instructions and make certain he knows what your intentions are.

I love using this airport as there is a MARTA stop just outside its gate, that's the quickest way to get into town, do your business and get back to the 'port. Atlanta has killer auto traffic. The MARTA saves you the

John Purner

trouble.

***** 57th Fighter Group Restaurant - 770-234-0057
Manager: Gregg Herndon
Open:
> Sunday Brunch: 10:00am–2:30pm
> Sunday Dinner 5:00pm–9:00pm
> Tues–Sat: Lunch 11:00am–2:30pm
> Tues–Sat: Dinner; 5:00pm–9:00pm

Restaurant Website: www.the57threstaurant.com
Restaurant Email: Itamar57th@gmail.com
PIREP:
The only bad part about 57th is that you can't taxi to the restaurant's ramp. It doesn't have one. Pilots, passengers and friends are welcomed at Epps Aviation where they will be given a complimentary shuttle to the restaurant. Problem solved!

I'm a meat and potatoes kinda' guy. The 57th is right in my wheelhouse. If its dinner, I go for the Prime Rib; lunch is all about the Pot Roast "Samwich". The food is great and the service respectful but the reason for this stop is the homage it pays to aircraft. The setting is pilot perfect.

PDK is Atlanta's second busiest airport; which guarantees an airplane active view on the other side of the huge windows. This is the only restaurant I've ever been to that makes headsets available to those who want to listen while they watch.

Put this one on your list. You'll thank me.

FT VALLEY, GA (CAMERON FIELD - GA81)
> **Airport Manager:** DAVID MURPHY **PH:** 478-954-0225
> **Field Elevation:** 380 **CTAF:** 0.000 **FUEL:**
> **Runway:** 18/36 **Length:** 3000 **Width:** 100 **Surface:** TURF

*** Peachtree Cafe and Bakery
Open:
> Open 7am to 6pm daily

Restaurant Website: www.lanesouthernorchards.com
PIREP:
Unique is the best word to describe this stop. You set down on a soft grass strip that sits in the middle of a 6,000-acre peach and pecan orchard. I love peaches and things folks make with them. Peach pie is at the top of my list, well right underneath Pecan.

Located at the north end of the field, is the **Peachtree Café and Bakery**. Tie down and walk across the road. They feature a homemade southern style menu. You'll find something to love on the menu. I come for breakfast and always leave with two pies – peach and pecan.

JEKYLL ISLAND, GA (JEKYLL ISLAND - 09J)
Aprt Mgr: RONNIE SMITH **PH:** 912-635-4091
Field Elevation: 11 **CTAF:** 123.000 **FUEL:**
Runway: 18/36 **Length:** 3715 **Width:** 75 **Surface:** ASPH-G

***** Jekyll Island Club Grand Dining Room - (912) 635-5155
Proprietor: Executive Chef Abigail Hutchinson
Open:
> Monday – Saturday: 7:00am – 10:00pm
> Sunday Brunch: 10:45am – 2:00pm

Restaurant Website: www.jekyllclub.com/dining/
Restaurant Email: concierge@jekyllclub.com
PIREP:
The Jekyll Island Club was once a Rockefeller resort. It shows. The landing strip is in great shape and is a short stroll along a picturesque lane lined with moss draped oaks to the hotel. Come for Sunday Brunch. Everything you might care to eat is elegantly presented and perfectly prepared. The ambiance is white table clothes with service to match and the food matches up nicely. Don't miss this one.

LAWRENCEVILLE, GA (GWINNETT COUNTY - LZU)
Aprt Mgr: MATT SMITH **PH:** 770-822-5196
Field Elevation: 1062 **CTAF:** 124.100 **FUEL:** 100LLA1+
Runway: 07/25 **Length:** 6000 **Width:** 100 **Surface:** ASPH-G

Aircraft Specialists Jet Center – 770-277-9000
FBO Website: www.asjet.com
Affiliate: UNK
Self Service: NO
Pilot Supplies: NO
Hours: 24/7

*** The Flying Machine - (770) 962-2262
Proprietor: Hokey Sloan
Manager: Joy Hoge
Open:
> Mon – Thurs: 11 am - 9 pm
> Fri & Sat: 11 am - 10 pm
> Sun: 11 am - 3 pm

Restaurant Website: www.theflyingmachine.com
Restaurant Email: mail@ theflyingmachine.com

PIREP:

If you're close, you should put this on your list. It is really, really a great restaurant. Downhome comfort food served by people that seem genuinely glad that you dropped by. Come on Wednesday, Friday or Saturday nigh and you'll hear some wonderful music. The last time I was here I went with the $100 Hamburger *(what else)* and finished up with the Cobbler of the day *(lucky me it was apple)*. I'll be back.

WILLIAMSON, GA (PEACH STATE - GA2)

Aprt Mgr: RON ALEXANDER **PH:** 770-467-9490
Field Elevation: 926 **CTAF:** 122.800 **FUEL:** 100LL
Runway: 13/31 **Length:** 2400 **Width:** 100 **Surface:** TURF-F

*** Barnstormer's Grill - (770) 227-9989
Proprietor: Trudy Gill
Open:

> Tues – Thurs: – 11:30am – 9:00pm
> Fri: 11:30am – 9:30pm
> Sat: 9:00am – 9:30pm
> Sun: 11:00am – 3:00pm

Restaurant Website: www.barnstormersgrill.com
Restaurant Email: barnstormersgril@bellsouth.net
PIREP:

This is a great airport restaurant with wonderful service and one **BIG** problem. The runway is a bit hilly and rough. It's fine for tail draggers or high wing planes with plenty of prop clearance but "puckering" for a low wing with limited prop clearance like a Mooney or an Aztec. Wonderful improvements are being made at this airport surrounding the development of the **Candler Field Museum**. They're rebuilding Atlanta's principal airport as it was in the days of the Barnstormer. They have and will add more exhibits.

FlyIn Idaho

BIG CREEK, ID (BIG CREEK - U60)
Airport Manager: DIV ADMIN **PH:** 208-334-8775
Field Elevation: 5743 **CTAF:** 122.900 **FUEL:** N/A
Runway: 01/19 **Length:** 3550 **Width:** 110 **Surface:** TURF-G

*** Big Creek Lodge - (208) 375-4921
Manager: Mike & Theresa Giery
Open:
mid-May through mid-October
BREAKFAST: OPEN 7:30 AM TO 10:00 AM – **$20**/MEAL
LUNCH: OPEN NOON TO 1 PM – **$15**/MEAL
DINNER: OPEN 5:30 PM TO 7 PM – **$30**/MEAL
Restaurant Website: www.bigcreeklodgeidaho.com
Restaurant Email: managers@bigcreeklodgeidaho.com
PIREP:
Big Creek badly needed a refresh and got it in spades. It's no longer a shack in the outback.

A 15-minute flight from McCall and a 50-minute flight from Boise, Big Creek has been a beloved destination for backcountry pilots for nearly a century. The landing strip is 3,500 feet long and 5,743 feet in elevation, so it can be challenging. The Idaho Division of Aeronautics offers a detailed pilot's guide on flying into Big Creek.

https://itd.idaho.gov/wp-content/uploads/2020/06/BigCreek_SOP_Aero.pdf

The food is rustic and wonderful. Get here if you can. Dream about it if you can't.

CALDWELL, ID (CALDWELL INDUSTRIAL - EUL)
Aprt Mgr: ROB OATES **PH:** 208-459-9779
Field Elevation: 2432 **CTAF:** 122.700 **FUEL:** 100LLA
Runway: 12/30 **Length:** 5500 **Width:** 100 **Surface:** ASPH-G

Silver Hawk Aviation – 208-453-8577
FBO Website: www.silverhawkaviation.net
Affiliate: UNK
Self Service: YES
Pilot Supplies: NO
Hours: 24/7

*** Caldwell Airport Café - (208) 546-2233
Proprietor: Carol Cameron
Open:
> Mon – Sat: 7:00am - 2:30pm
> Sun: 7:00am - 1:30pm

PIREP:
A reasonably long, wide turf strip brings you to the rustic back country building that houses **The Caldwell Airport Café**. Mountain men fly in here for a breakfast of homemade biscuits and gravy. Expect to do some hanger flying.

COOLIN, ID (CAVANAUGH BAY - 66S)
Aprt Mgr: DIVISION ADMIN **PH:** 208-334-8775
Field Elevation: 2484 **CTAF:** 122.900 **FUEL:**
Runway: 15/33 **Length:** 3100 **Width:** 120 **Surface:** TURF-G

*** Cavanaugh Bay Resort & Marina - (208) 443-2095
Proprietor: Mike Belles
Open:
> **Fall Hours**
> Sun: 11am - 8pm
> Monday – Wednesday: CLOSED
> Thursday & Friday: 4pm - 9pm
> Saturday: 11am - 9:30pm

Restaurant Website: https://www.cavsresort.com/
PIREPS:
The restaurant is just across the road from the airstrip, which is the usual turf that you expect in the backcountry. The deck is right on Priest Lake. The Prime Rib sandwich is very good, and the onion rings are about the best I ever had.

DRIGGS, ID (DRIGGS-REED MEMORIAL - DIJ)
Aprt Mgr: TOM HUNTER **PH:** 208-313-5077
Field Elevation: 6231 **CTAF:** 122.700 **FUEL:** 100LLA
Runway: 03/21 **Length:** 7300 **Width:** 100 **Surface:** ASPH-E

Teton Aviation – 800-472-6382
FBO Website: www.tetonaviation.com
Affiliate: UNK
Self Service: NO
Pilot Supplies: YES
Hours: 8:00 - 5:00 winter 7:00 - 7:00 summer 7 days

**** Warbirds Cafe - (208) 354-2550
Proprietor: Michael Bowman
Open:

Tue – Sun: 11am – 9pm
Winter Hours
Tue – Sun: 4pm – 9pm
Restaurant Website: http://tetonaviation.com/warbirds-cafe/
Restaurant Email: info@tetonaviation.com
PIREP:
This is the place we've all been looking for. The restaurant is clean, well-staffed, large, bright, new and sparkling. In the summer, sit outside along the taxiway with your handheld radio on CTAF and eat gourmet food in full view of the Tetons in all of their majesty. The Warbirds Museum is under the same roof and is free. What a treat!!!

One Burger PIREPer put it this way:

Our first visit to Warbirds was for the Sunday brunch. The quality and selection of food was outstanding and reasonably priced. I can't say enough about the friendly and professional staff, who actually thanked us for choosing to join them the minute we walked in the door, and sincerely invited us back to visit again once we had eaten more than we will openly admit.

We really enjoyed the aircraft/hangar decor, which fostered all the adventures of aviation, yet with a pleasingly simplistic and upscale feel. My husband especially enjoyed the aircraft photos and historical information under the glass tabletops at the booth seating, and of course, the fact that we were practically seated on the taxi way, with a beautiful mountain view just beyond. The clever menu, printed on sectionals and including aviation term specials, such as Lower Your Flaps Jack pancakes, the Bi Plane Bagel featuring Norwegian smoked salmon, 3G Granola from the locals, and the B-1 Buffalo Burger, was a favorite of mine. We ran a quick reconnaissance on the dinner menu, and plan on returning soon for the Lobster Brie Quesadilla appetizers, Pepper Seared Duck Breast, Prime Rib, or a Rocky Mountain Elk Burger. By the way, there are plenty of tempting choices on the menus for those who prefer a more vegetarian type meal.

If you find yourself anywhere near the western base of the Teton Mountain range in Idaho, navigate to the airport north of Driggs, follow the signs to the Warbirds Cafe, and do exactly what the emblem inscribed in the stained concrete floor as you enter indicates. Check your attitude... and get ready for a dining experience you won't soon forget.

WARREN, ID (WARREN /USFS/ - 3U1)
Aprt Mgr: PAYETTE FOREST **PH:** 208-634-0746

John Purner

Field Elevation: 5902 **CTAF:** 122.900
Runway: 11/29 **Length:** 2765 **Width:** 50 **Surface:** DIRT-G

*** The Baum Shelter - (208) 382-4336
Open:

Mon – Thurs.: 11am – 8pm
Fri - Sun: 11am - 9pm

Restaurant Website: www.baumsheltertoo.com
Restaurant Email: info@baumsheltertoo.com
PIREPS:
The Baum Shelter has a restaurant, full bar and lodging in the beautiful
Idaho backcountry. Warren, Idaho is a rustic, historical mining
community that hasn't changed much in the last 100 years. The runway
parallels Main Street and ends in "downtown". The Baum Shelter is
about 100 yards away. I have only been there for lunch and had a really
good B.L.T.

FlyIn Illinois

ALTON/ST LOUIS, IL (ST LOUIS RGNL - ALN)
    Aprt Mgr: DAVID MILLER **PH:** 618-259-2531
    Field Elevation: 545 **CTAF:** 126.000 **FUEL:** 100LL/JetA
    Runway: 17/35 **Length:** 6500 **Width:** 100 **Surface:** ASPH-G
    Runway: 11/29 **Length:** 8098 **Width:** 150 **Surface:** ASPH-G

*** High Flyers Grille - (618) 251 8500
Proprietor: Chris King
Open:
        Tue-Thu: 11:00 am – 10:00 pm
        Fri-Sat: 11:00 am – 10:30 pm
        Sun: 11:00 am – 9:00 pm
Restaurant Website: highflyersgrille.wordpress.com
Restaurant Email: highflyersgrille@gmail.com
PIREP:
Right on the runway – check!
Outside patio – check!
Amazing food – check!
Best Illinois Airport Restaurant – 2014 – double check!

I go here for the hand-crafted soda. We're talking REAL homemade root beer. It just doesn't get better than that unless it is served up with a build it yourself pizza which is exactly what I order.

I'd like it here a whole lot better if they did breakfast.

BLOOMINGTON/NORMAL, IL (BLOOMINGTON - BMI)
    Aprt Mgr: CARL G. OLSON **PH:** 309-663-7383
    Field Elevation: 871 **CTAF:** 124.600 **FUEL:** 100LLA
    Runway: 11/29 **Length:** 6525 **Width:** 150 **Surface:** ASPH-CONC-G
    Runway: 02/20 **Length:** 8000 **Width:** 150 **Surface:** CONC-G

Avis Car Rental – (309) 664-0781
    Sun 8:00 AM - 10:30 PM
    Mon - Fri 7:00 AM - 10:30 PM
    Sat 8:00 AM - 10:30 PM

Image Air – 309-663-2303
FBO Website: www.imageair.com
Affiliate: Phillips 66
Self Service: NO
Pilot Supplies: NO

Hours: 7:00 - 10:30 7 days

Synergy Flight Center – 309-828-4448
FBO Website: www.synergyfbo.com
Affiliate: UNK
Self Service: NO
Pilot Supplies: YES
Hours: 7:00 - 10:00 7 days

BOLINGBROOK, IL (BOLINGBROOK'S CLOW INTL - 1C5)
Aprt Mgr: JOSEPH DE PAULO **PH:** 630-378-0479
Field Elevation: 670 **CTAF:** 122.900 **FUEL:** 100LLA
Runway: 18/36 **Length:** 3362 **Width:** 50 **Surface:** ASPH-G

*** Charlie's - (630) 771-0501
Proprietor: Chris King
Open:
Mon – Sun: 7:00 am – 3:00 pm
Restaurant Website: http://ordercharliesrestaurant.com
Restaurant Email: donnayoung129@gmail.com
PIREP:
Clow International is a Class E asphalt strip southwest of Chicago and just outside O'Hare's class B. **Charlie's** has picture windows overlooking the ramp area. The menu is extensive. You'll have **NO** trouble finding a dish that interests you. The crowd is eclectic from mothers with kids to businessmen to senior aviators swapping stories.

CHICAGO/WEST CHICAGO, IL (DUPAGE - DPA)
Aprt Mgr: DAVID BIRD **PH:** 630-584-2211
Field Elevation: 758 **CTAF:** 0.000 **FUEL:** 100LLA
Runway: 15/33 **Length:** 3399 **Width:** 100 **Surface:** ASPH-G
Runway: 10/28 **Length:** 4750 **Width:** 75 **Surface:** ASPH-G
Runway: 02R/20L **Length:** 5101 **Width:** 100 **Surface:** CONC-G
Runway: 02L/20R **Length:** 7571 **Width:** 100 **Surface:** CONC-G

Dupage Flight Center – 630-208-5600
FBO Website: www.dupageflightcenter.com
Affiliate: UNK
Self Service: YES
Pilot Supplies: YES
Hours: 24/7

** Kitty Hawk Cafe - (630) 208-6189
Proprietor: Erin
Open:
Mon - Fri: 9:00 am - 2:00 pm

Restaurant Website: dupageflightcenter.com/gallery/kitty-hawk-cafe/
PIREP:
The Kitty Hawk is located in the terminal building. It is nice and clean with a great view. The food service is very, very basic.

CHICAGO/SCHAUMBURG, IL (SCHAUMBURG RGNL - 06C)
Aprt Mgr: KARYN ROBLES **PH:** 847-923-3859
Field Elevation: 801 **CTAF:** 123.000 **FUEL:** 100LLA
Runway: 11/29 **Length:** 3800 **Width:** 100 **Surface:** CONC-G

***** Pilot Pete's - (847) 891-5100)
Proprietor: John Minginas
Open:
　　　　Mon – Sun: 11am – 9pm
Restaurant Website: www.pilot-petes.com
PIREP:
One of our $100 Hamburger website subscribers said it better than I ever could. So, here's his review not mine:

Pilot Pete's deserves 6 stars if you ask me! I flew myself and a date there for dinner once. Dinner was as exciting as the flight! The atmosphere is a Jimmy Buffet meets the 'classic international' Juan Trippe/PanAm era with a mix of every aviation generation to follow! A funky mix of mood lighting creatively illuminates all of the wall murals and both large and small model airplanes hanging from the ceiling! The food was excellent – Pete's has a traditional American menu with its own unique twist. The prices are very reasonable, and the proportions are not disappointing. I had no problem getting into the airport – I flew in from Michigan VFR – followed the lake shore from Gary north, right past the Chicago skyline – passengers are plastered to the window! I went direct DEERE-OBK-06C – north of PWK, no problems, Chicago ATC was friendly getting in and out. I highly recommend **Pilot Pete's** for a date with your lady or a trip with the guys – either way it's a great time!

DECATUR, IL (DECATUR - DEC)
Aprt Mgr: JOSEPH ATTWOOD **PH:** 217-428-2423
Field Elevation: 682 **CTAF:** 118.900 **FUEL:** 100LLA
Runway: 12/30 **Length:** 6799 **Width:** 150 **Surface:** ASPH-CONC-G
Runway: 06/24 **Length:** 8496 **Width:** 150 **Surface:** ASPH-CONC-G
Runway: 18/36 **Length:** 5298 **Width:** 150 **Surface:** ASPH-G

Avis Car Rental – (217) 422-4337
　　　　Sun 2:00 PM - 6:00 PM
　　　　Mon - Fri 8:00 AM - 5:00 PM
　　　　Sat 10:00 AM - 2:00 PM

John Purner

Gaitros Aviation – 217-423-9903
FBO Website: www.gaitrosaviation.com
Affiliate: Phillips 66
Self Service: NO
Pilot Supplies: NO
Hours: M-F 5:00 - 9:00 Sat 5:00-7:00 Sunday 7:00 - 7:00

MATTOON/CHARLESTON, IL (COLES COUNTY - MTO)
Aprt Mgr: ANDREW FEARN **PH:** 217-234-7120
Field Elevation: 722 **CTAF:** 122.700 **FUEL:** 100LLA
Runway: 06/24 **Length:** 5799 **Width:** 100 **Surface:** ASPH-G
Runway: 11/29 **Length:** 6501 **Width:** 150 **Surface:** CONC-G
Runway: 18/36 **Length:** 1080 **Width:** 250 **Surface:** TURF

***** The Airport Steakhouse - (217) 234-9433
Proprietor: Ron Bean
Open:
>Mon - Sat: 7am – 8pm
>Sun: 7am – 7pm
>Closed Major Holidays

Restaurant Website: airportsteakhouse.net
PIREP:
You can't park closer to a restaurant anywhere else. This is a solid 5 burger destination. Best GIANT pork tenderloins anywhere; HUGE and hand breaded. They call it the Elephant Ear. Don't leave without one. This is the **BEST** airport restaurant in Illinois – really is.

MOLINE, IL (QUAD CITY INTL - MLI)
Aprt Mgr: BRUCE CARTER **PH:** 309-764-9621
Field Elevation: 590 **CTAF:** 119.400 **FUEL:** 100LLA
Runway: 13/31 **Length:** 7301 **Width:** 150 **Surface:** ASPH-CONC-F
Runway: 09/27 **Length:** 10002 **Width:** 150 **Surface:** CONC-E
Runway: 05/23 **Length:** 5015 **Width:** 150 **Surface:** CONC-G

Avis Car Rental – (309) 762-3606
>Sun 8:00 AM - 11:00 PM
>Mon - Fri 7:00 AM - 11:00 PM
>Sat 8:00 AM - 10:00 PM

Elliott Aviation – 309-799-3183
FBO Website: www.elliottaviation.com
Affiliate: Phillips 66
Self Service: NO
Pilot Supplies: NO
Hours: M-F 6:00 - 10:00 Sat/Sun 8:00-5:00

84

MOUNT VERNON, IL (MOUNT VERNON - MVN)
Aprt Mgr: CHRIS COLLINS **PH:** 618-242-7016
Field Elevation: 480 **CTAF:** 123.000 **FUEL:** 100LLA
Runway: 05/23 **Length:** 6496 **Width:** 150 **Surface:** ASPH-E
Runway: 15/33 **Length:** 3146 **Width:** 100 **Surface:** ASPH-G

SRT Aviation – 618-244-7746
FBO Website: www.mtvernonairport.com
Affiliate: Shell
Self Service: YES
Pilot Supplies: YES

*** Bonnie Café - (618) 242-1110
Open:
    Mon-Sat 6:00 AM - 8:00 PM
    Sun 6:00 AM - 3:00 PM
Restaurant Website: thebonniecafe.com
PIREP:
This family owned and operated restaurant serves breakfast, lunch, and dinner all day long. Enjoy a daily buffet with changing entrees and sides. Friday night buffet includes catfish, clam strips, crab cakes, and more. On Saturday evenings order all you can eat crab legs. Great Buffet!

PEORIA, IL (GENERAL DOWNING - PEORIA INTL - PIA)
Airport Manager: GENE OLSON **PH:** 309-697-8272
Field Elevation: 661 **CTAF:** 0.000 **FUEL:** 100LLA
Runway: 04/22 **Length:** 8004 **Width:**150 **Surface:** ASPH-F
Runway:13/31 **Length:** 10104 **Width:**150 **Surface:** CONC-G

*** Hangar Too – 309-633-0811
Open:
    M-F 6:30am – 6:30pm
    Sat Sun 6:30am – 5:00pm
PIREP:
PIA hosts several commercial flights, it's not that busy but it's definitely not a sleepy country airport. Park at Byerly's FBO ramp. It's about a three-minute walk outside the fence to the main terminal. Byerly will give you a ride if prefer. Good menu had a burger naturally. Reasonable prices, quick service.

QUINCY, IL (QUINCY RGNL-BALDWIN FIELD - UIN)
Airport Manager: MARTY STEGEMAN **PH:** 217-885-3285
Field Elevation: 769 **CTAF:** 123.000 **FUEL:** 100LLA
Runway: 18/36 **Length:** 5877 **Width:** 150 **Surface:** ASPH-CONC-G

Runway: 04/22 **Length:** 7098 **Width:** 150 **Surface:** ASPH-CONC-G
Runway: 13/31 **Length:** 5397 **Width:** 150 **Surface:** ASPH-G

*** Blue Haven Café – 217-885-3010
Open:

Mon-Sat 6 am - 8 pm
Sun 6 am - 2 pm

PIREP:

Not fancy, just a simple menu at reasonable prices. The food is great and the service attentive. This is a pretty standard airport restaurant. It makes you happy you're a pilot and get to enjoy breakfast, spell avgas and hangar fly while mere mortals are home cutting the grass.

ROCHELLE, IL (ROCHELLE MUNI AIRPORT - RPJ)

Aprt Mgr: DON ELLIOT **PH:** 815-562-2494
Field Elevation: 781 **CTAF:** 122.800 **FUEL:** 100LLA
Runway: 07/25 **Length:** 4225 **Width:** 75 **Surface:** ASPH-G

Rochelle Avionics – 815-562-8619
FBO Website: www.rochelleavionics.com
Affiliate: UNK
Self Service: YES
Pilot Supplies: YES

*** Flight Deck Bar and Grill - (815) 561-3664
Proprietor: C J & Doug Stolfa
Open:

Mon: 11:00am - 9:00pm
Tue – Fri: 11:00am - 10:00pm
Sat: 11:00am - 10:00pm
Sun: 11:00am - 9:00pm
Last Sunday of the month - Breakfast: 8:00am - 10:30am

Restaurant Website: www.flightdeckbar.com
Restaurant Email: info@ flightdeckbar.com
PIREP:

Arriving aircraft should check to see if the jump planes are up on CTAF 122.97. If they're not on that frequency, check 121.0 to see if their talking to Rockford Approach. **The Flight Deck Bar and Grill is** located in **Chicagoland Skydiving Center's** facilities just east of the T-hangars towards the approach end of runway 25. Park on the main ramp and use the sidewalk located on the south side of the airport that runs along the T-hangars. **The Flight Deck Bar and Grill** is not the normal snack shack that you find at skydiving centers. It is a large, clean, nicely decorated restaurant that provides very good food and friendly, efficient service. Your receipt from dining at the restaurant gets you a 10-cent per gallon discount on your fuel.

FlyIn Indiana

COLUMBUS, IN (COLUMBUS MUNI - BAK)
Aprt Mgr: ROD BLASDEL **PH:** 812-376-2519
Field Elevation: 656 **CTAF:** 118.600 **FUEL:** 100LLA
Runway: 14/32 **Length:** 5000 **Width:** 100 **Surface:** ASPH-F
Runway: 05/23 **Length:** 6400 **Width:** 150 **Surface:** ASPH-G

Jeff Air Pilot Services – 812-372-1819
FBO Website: www.jeffairfbo.com
Affiliate: UNK
Self Service: YES
Pilot Supplies: YES
Hours: M-F 6:00 - 8:00 Sat 7:00 - 8:00 Sunday 8:00 - 7:00

*** Blackerby's Hangar 5 Restaurant - 812-378-4010
Proprietor: Wayne Blacherby
Open:
> Monday – Sunday: 6:30am-2:00pm

Restaurant Website: www.blackerbyshangar5.com
Restaurant Email: info@ blackerbyshangar5.com
PIREP:
The restaurant is right beside the tower. The FBO and the restaurant are in a fairly new building with refreshed decor. It's a good size place, with booths along the plate glass windows overlooking the runway. The menu is standard airport café breakfast and lunch selections. You won't be disappointed or impressed.

GRIFFITH, IN (GRIFFITH-MERRILLVILLE - 05C)
Aprt Mgr: CRAIG ANDERSON **PH:** 219-924-0207
Field Elevation: 634 **CTAF:** 123.000 **FUEL:** 100LLA
Runway: 08/26 **Length:** 4899 **Width:** 75 **Surface:** ASPH-G

Griffith Aviation – 219-924-0207
FBO Website: www.griffithairport.com
Affiliate: UNK
Self Service: YES
Pilot Supplies: YES
Hours: M-F 7:30 - 8:00 Sat/Sun 8:00 - 6:00

*** Mi Tierra - (219) 922-3633
Proprietor: Jesse & Anna Toledo
Open:
> Tue – Sat: 10:30am - 9:30pm

Restaurant Website: https://www.restaurantji.com/in/griffith/mi-tierra-/

PIREP:
This is one of the spots that I have never been to, which is sad as I LOVE Mexican food. I am including a **PIREP** from one of the $100 Hamburger website subscribers.

"Great destination for those in the Chicago area. I flew on a Wednesday night, from the Wisconsin/Illinois border, skirting the Chicago class B airspace. The views of Chicago and Midway traffic were great. This is a good time to use VFR flight following. You will mix with heavy traffic and get good experience listening. I was handed off 4 times in 1.3 hours. The airport is well lit at night. No taxiway. Easy to find the huge general aviation parking area. Enter the FBO (fuel truck is available) and go down the hall to the restaurant. But get into your airplane by 8pm closing time. Looking for another excuse to have my dinner there, a $100 quesadilla!"

INDIANAPOLIS, IN (EAGLE CREEK AIRPARK - EYE)
Aprt Mgr: MICHAEL T. MEDVESCEK **PH:** 317-487-5024
Field Elevation: 823 **CTAF:** 122.800 **FUEL:** 100LLA
Runway: 03/21 **Length:** 4200 **Width:** 75 **Surface:** ASPH-G

Eagle Creek Aviation Services – 317-293-6935
FBO Website: www.eagle-creek.com/fbo
Affiliate: UNK
Self Service: YES
Pilot Supplies: YES
Hours: M-F 7:00 - 8:00 Sat/Sun 8:00 - 7:00

***** Rick's Cafe Boatyard - (317) 290-9300)
Proprietor: Rick Albrecht
Open:
> Mon - Thurs: 11am to 10pm
> Fri - Sat: 11am to 11pm
> Sun: 10am to 10pm

Restaurant Website: ricksboatyard.com
PIREP:
Rick's is across the street from the FBO. It is a short 50-yard walk. If the weather is good go for a spot on the large deck. They run heaters if it's a little cool. You'll have a great view of boating activity on the lake as well as arriving and departing aircraft from the airport. The food is really near the top of anyone's expectations and the service is equal. I am a carnivore, so I go for flame kissed cow.

TERRE HAUTE, IN (SKY KING - 3I3)

Aprt Mgr: STEVE BROWN **PH:** 812-466-2229
Field Elevation: 496 **CTAF:** 122.800 **FUEL:** 100LL
Runway: 18/36 **Length:** 1978 **Width:** 50 **Surface:** ASPH-F
Runway: 08/26 **Length:** 3557 **Width:** 50 **Surface:** ASPH-F

*** Fox's Meat Market & Grocery - (812) 466-5825
Proprietor: Richard Fox
Open:
>   Daily: Lunch

Restaurant Email: foxsmeatmarket@aol.com
PIREP:
This is a grocery store/meat market that abuts the airport. They serve dynamite sandwiches at lunch and you want one. Eating on the curb outside of a small-town grocery store brings me back to my youth in Texas. Once you have landed at this airport back taxi to the office and park on the ramp. The market is just a short walk across a two-lane road that is literally off the end of runway 26. Walk into **Fox's** for a sandwich, a side and a drink. Be warned that this is a flight school. During the school year it might be busier than many controlled airports.

FlyIn Iowa

BELMOND, IA (BELMOND MUNI - Y48)
 Aprt Mgr: LEE ANN WALTZING **PH:** 641-444-4183
 Field Elevation: 1201 **CTAF:** 122.900 **FUEL:**
 Runway: 17/35 **Length:** 3245 **Width:** 95 **Surface:** TURF-G

**** Cattleman's at the Club – (641) 583-5221
Proprietor: DuWayne and Deb Abel
Open:
 Seasonal:
Restaurant Website: www.cattlemansattheclub.com
PIREP:
"Solid, simple and honest food". Their motto is also a very good description. In warm weather I enjoy eating on the outside deck. It overlooks the golf course and gives a "leaners" view of the landing strip. I've never had a bad steak here and neither will you.

Stay a while and play a round. Why not!

CEDAR RAPIDS, IA (THE EASTERN IOWA - CID)
 Aprt Mgr: MR. TIM BRADSHAW, A.A.E. **PH:** 319-362-3131
 Field Elevation: 869 **CTAF:** 118.700 **FUEL:** 100LLA
 Runway: 13/31 **Length:** 6199 **Width:** 150 **Surface:** ASPH-CONC-E
 Runway: 09/27 **Length:** 8600 **Width:** 150 **Surface:** CONC-E

Avis Car Rental – (319) 366-6418
 Sun 8:00 AM - 12:00 AM
 Mon - Fri 7:00 AM - 12:00 AM
 Sat 9:00 AM - 8:30 PM

Landmark Aviation – 319-366-1925
FBO Website: www.landmarkaviation.com
Affiliate: UNK
Self Service: YES
Pilot Supplies: YES
Hours: 7 days 4:00 - 10:00

CLINTON, IA (CLINTON MUNI - CWI)
 Aprt Mgr: MICHAEL NASS **PH:** 563-242-3292
 Field Elevation: 708 **CTAF:** 122.800 **FUEL:** 100LLA
 Runway: 03/21 **Length:** 5204 **Width:** 100 **Surface:** ASPH-F
 Runway: 14/32 **Length:** 4201 **Width:** 75 **Surface:** CONC-G

* Airport Snack Machines - (563) 242-3292
PIREP:
We're talking about a microwave, a sandwich machine, a pop machine, and candy machine. Obviously, this isn't a dining destination. If you are here for fuel or for some other reason and you are starving, food is available. It is very low-quality food, but it is food. 'Nuff said

MASON CITY, IA (MASON CITY MUNI - MCW)
Aprt Mgr: MS PAMELA OSGOOD **PH:** 641-421-3397
Field Elevation: 1214 **CTAF:** 123.000 **FUEL:** 100LLA
Runway: 12/30 **Length:** 5502 **Width:** 150 **Surface:** ASPH-E
Runway: 18/36 **Length:** 6501 **Width:** 150 **Surface:** ASPH-G

North Iowa Air Service – 641-424-9366
FBO Website: www.northiowaair.com
Affiliate: UNK
Self Service: NO
Pilot Supplies: NO
Hours: 7:00 - 7:00 7 days

John Purner

FlyIn Kansas

BEAUMONT, KS (BEAUMONT HOTEL - 07S)
Airport Manager: Jeanne Squier **Phone Number:** 785-841-3100
Field Elevation: 1617 **CTAF:** 0.000 **FUEL:**
Runway: 18/36 **Length:** 2400 **Width:** 80 **Surface:** TURF-G

***** The Beaumont Hotel – (620) 843-2422
Open:
> Wed - Fr: 11AM - 8PM
> Sat: 7AM - 8PM
> Sun: 7AM - 3PM

Restaurant Website: beaumonthotelks.com/dining/
PIREP:
I get a kick out of landing on the grass airstrip and taxiing down Main Street for a block or so to reach the front door of the Beaumont Hotel. So do many others. Often there are more planes tied down across the street than there are cars in the parking lot.

Charles Kuralt did a piece on them a few years ago; there's a video on YouTube here: ***www.youtube.com/watch?v=TadNEte0rdA*** . Its old but you'll enjoy watching it. I know I do.

Breakfast is about what you'd expect at any Midwest Mom and Pop kinda' place. Good, honest and hearty. Lunch? Well its even better.

I'll be back again– many times I hope.

BENTON, KS (LLOYD STEARMAN FIELD - 1K1)
Aprt Mgr: DWAYNE CLEMENS **PH:** 316-648-0132
Field Elevation: 1364 **CTAF:** 123.075 **FUEL:** 100LLA
Runway: 17/35 **Length:** 5106 **Width:** 60 **Surface:** ASPH-G

Benton Airpark – 316-778-1035
Affiliate: UNK
Self Service: NO
Pilot Supplies: NO
Hours: 24/7

*** Stearman Field Bar & Grill – (316) 778-1612
Proprietor: Dwayne Clemens
Open:
> Mon - Thur: 11am - 10pm
> Fri: 11am – 12am

Sat: 8am – 12am
Sun: 8am – 10pm
Restaurant Website: www.stearmanbarandgrill.com
Restaurant Email: stearmanfield@gmail.com
PIREP:
The restaurant is at the very north end of the runway, right by the self-service fuel pumps. The service is good, and the food is interesting. Many places can whip up a batch of fried pickles. The Stearman also has fried green beans. They're mighty good. They have a great wedge salad – extra bacon is the key. I come here for the Country Fried Steak. It's hard to beat.

GARDEN CITY, KS (GARDEN CITY RGNL - GCK)
Aprt Mgr: MS. RACHELLE POWELL **PH:** 620-276-1190
Field Elevation: 2891 **CTAF:** 118.150 **FUEL:** 100LLA
Runway: 17/35 **Length:** 7300 **Width:** 100 **Surface:** CONC-E
Runway: 12/30 **Length:** 5700 **Width:** 100 **Surface:** CONC-G

Saker Aviation – 620-275-5055
FBO Website: www.sakeraviation.com
Affiliate: UNK
Self Service: YES
Pilot Supplies: YES
Hours: 6:00 - 10:00 7 days

***** Napoli's - (620) 271-1490**
Open:
Tue - Thur: 11:00am – 9:00pm
Fri - Sat: 11:00am – 10:00pm
Sun: 11:00am – 9:00pm
PIREP:
Really good Italian food. Garden City Regional is several miles outside of town, but there is always a crowd of local customers; a very good indication of the quality of the food.

HUTCHINSON, KS (HUTCHINSON MUNI - HUT)
Manager: MR. PIETER MILLER **PH:** 620-694-2692
Field Elevation: 1543 **CTAF:** 118.500 **FUEL:** 100LLA
Runway: 13/31 **Length:** 7004 **Width:** 100 **Surface:** ASPH-E
Runway: 17/35 **Length:** 4252 **Width:** 75 **Surface:** ASPH-F
Runway: 04/22 **Length:** 6000 **Width:** 100 **Surface:** ASPH-F

Wells Aircraft – 888-496-5545
FBO Website: www.wellsaircraft.com
Affiliate: UNK
Self Service: NO

Pilot Supplies: YES
Hours: 8:00 - 6:00 M-F Sat Sun 8:00 - 5:00

**** The Airport Steak House - (620) 662-4281
Proprietor: Kevin & Ralph Bowen
Manager: Eddie Wells
Open:
> Mon – Thurs: 8:00am to 8:00pm
> Fri: 8:00am to 9:00pm
> Sat: 11:00am to 9:00pm
> Sun: 11:00am to 8:00pm

Restaurant Website: www.hutchinsonairportsteakhouse.com
PIREP:
The steaks are better than other menu offerings. They cook them in front of you over an open charcoal pit using the same Kingsford® Charcoal you probably use at home. The restaurant is in the terminal building about fifty steps from the ramp. The entrance above the doorway leading into the eating area is the tail section of a 1/2 scale biplane positioned as though it has just flown through the wall.

LUCAS, KS (LUCAS - 38K)

Airport Manager: GARY BRETZ **Phone Number:** 785-525-6425
Field Elevation: 1485 **CTAF:** 122.900 **FUEL:**
Runway: 17/35 **Length:** 2904 **Width:** 50 **Surface:** ASPH-G

*** K-18 – (785) 525-6262
Open:
> Every day: 6AM – 10PM

Restaurant Website: www.k18cafe.com
PIREP:
Chicken Fried Steak and eggs perfectly prepared using perfect ingredients is a good enough reason to come. That's what I ordered, and I finished breakfast off with a perfect cinnamon roll. Lunch is an even better deal. The **K-18 Special** is a perfectly prepared 1/2 lb. Hamburger, Choice of Potatoes, and Pop, Coffee or Tea for a very reasonable price. Friends you can't beat that deal with a stick!

PAOLA, KS (MIAMI COUNTY - K81)

Aprt Mgr: WAYNE HARCLERODE **PH:** 913-755-2345
Field Elevation: 943 **CTAF:** 122.800 **FUEL:** 100LL
Runway: 03/21 **Length:** 3398 **Width:** 60 **Surface:** ASPH-E
Runway: 15/33 **Length:** 2572 **Width:** 60 **Surface:** TURF-F

**** We-B-Smokin' - (913) 256-6802
Proprietor: Terry Bright
Open:

Tues- Fri: 11am – 8pm
Sat Breakfast: 7:30 am – 8pm
Sunday Breakfast: 7am – 1pm

Restaurant Website: www.websmokin.com/bbq_menu.html
Restaurant Email: info@websmokin.com/
PIREP:
Be very careful at this airport. It attracts many pilots flying antique aircraft without radios. Keep your head on a swivel and strictly follow normal traffic procedures. What about the food? They have very good BBQ. It is certainly worth the trip. They even made our **$100 Hamburger Best of the Best** list more than once. It is not quite as good now as it was then but it is still worth a stop.

TOPEKA, KS (PHILIP BILLARD MUNI - TOP)
Aprt Mgr: ERIC M. JOHNSON **PH:** 785-862-2362
Field Elevation: 881 **CTAF:** 118.700 **FUEL:** 100LLA
Runway: 04/22 **Length:** 3002 **Width:** 100 **Surface:** ASPH-F
Runway: 18/36 **Length:** 4331 **Width:** 75 **Surface:** ASPH-G
Runway: 13/31 **Length:** 5099 **Width:** 100 **Surface:** ASPH-G

Kansas Air Center – 785-234-2602
FBO Website: www.kansasair.com
Affiliate: UNK
Self Service: NO
Pilot Supplies: YES
Hours: 7:00 - 9:00 M-F Sat Sun 7:00 -8:00

*** Tammy's Billard Airport Restaurant - (785) 232-3669
Proprietor: Tammy Bailey
Open:
Wed – Mon: 7:00 am - 2:00 pm
Restaurant Website:
www.mtaa-topeka.org/billard-airport/billard-amenities
PIREP:
The place is right next to the ramp, and as you walk inside, it looks a bit run down, but don't be discouraged! This restaurant has been serving good ole' hot American food for more than half a century. Don't expect fancy but do expect wonderful down-home food. I love this place.

FlyIn Kentucky

FALLS-OF-ROUGH, KY (ROUGH RIVER STATE PARK - 2I3)
Aprt Mgr: CHUCK TEMPFER **PH:** 270-257-2311
Field Elevation: 577 **CTAF:** 122.800 **FUEL:**
Runway: 02/20 **Length:** 3200 **Width:** 75 **Surface:** ASPH-G

***** Grayson's Landing Restaurant - (270) 257-2311
Proprietor: Chef Connell
Open:

> Thurs: 4:30pm to 8:00pm
> Fri & Sat: 7:00am - 8:00pm
> Sun: 7:00am - 3:00pm

Restaurant Website: www.parks.ky.gov/parks/resortparks/rough-river
Restaurant Email: michael.ricks@ky.gov
PIREP:
There are no instrument approaches so save this for a nice day. The landing strip is in very good shape and there is a pilot lounge. Be sure to bring your own chocks and tiedowns and remember the airport is unattended. The walk to the lodge is very short. You will eat overlooking a lake. A very pleasant experience all-and-all. The food is very good and the service is admirable.

*** Rough River General Store – (270) 257-2245
Open:

> Breakfast, Lunch and Dinner: 7 Days

Restaurant Website: www.parks.ky.gov/parks/resortparks/rough-river
Restaurant Email: michael.ricks@ky.gov
PIREP:
The other end of the runway from the Lodge you'll find the Rough River General Store. There's a parking area at the end of Runway 20 with room enough for five airplanes. I had my regular breakfast of eggs, sausage with biscuit and gravy fare. It was excellent. I liked it because it was cooked to order and not part of an unattended food buffet. They also serve lunch and dinner with specials each day. The food is cheap and tasty, a great combination. It's about a quarter mile walk from the airplane parking area.

LONDON, KY (LONDON-CORBIN ARPT-MAGEE FLD - LOZ)
Aprt Mgr: LARRY CORUM **PH:** 606-232-1452
Field Elevation: 1212 **CTAF:** 123.000 **FUEL:** 100LLA+
Runway: 06/24 **Length:** 5751 **Width:** 150 **Surface:** ASPH-G

London Corbin Airport – 606-878-9100

FBO Website: www.london-corbinairport.com
Affiliate: UNK
Self Service: YES
Pilot Supplies: YES
Hours: 7:00 - 8:00 M-F 8:00 - 8:00 Sat/Sun

LOUISVILLE, KY (BOWMAN FIELD - LOU)
Aprt Mgr: PH: 502-458-1475
Field Elevation: 546 **CTAF:** 119.500 **FUEL:** 100LLA
Runway: 06/24 **Length:** 4326 **Width:** 75 **Surface:** ASPH-F
Runway: 15/33 **Length:** 3579 **Width:** 75 **Surface:** ASPH-G

Atlantic Aviation – 502-368-1515
FBO Website: www.atlanticaviation.com
Affiliate: UNK
Self Service: NO
Pilot Supplies: NO
Hours: 24/7

***** Bistro Le Relais - **502-451-9020**
Proprietor: Anthony Dike
Chef: Alexander Dulaney
Open:
>Fri: 11:30am – 2pm
>Tues – Sun: 5:30pm – 10pm

Restaurant Website: www.lerelaisrestaurant.com
Restaurant Email: lerelaisrst@bellsouth.net
PIREP:
Without doubt this is the best airport restaurant in Kentucky. It may be **the best restaurant** in Kentucky period. Come for dinner and plan on spending the night so you can enjoy a nice wine with your meal. The price is formidable but commensurate with the quality of the meal you will enjoy. It is located in the old terminal building. It's like going back in time to the 1930s. The food is French. The décor reminds you of Rick's Café in the movie Casablanca. Don't miss this one.

PRESTONSBURG, KY (BIG SANDY RGNL - K22)
Aprt Mgr: GARY COX **PH:** 606-298-5930
Field Elevation: 1221 **CTAF:** 123.050 **FUEL:** 100LLA+
Runway: 03/21 **Length:** 5000 **Width:** 100 **Surface:** ASPH-G

Cox Aviation – 606-298-5930
FBO Website: www.bigsandyregional.com
Affiliate: UNK
Self Service: NO
Pilot Supplies: NO

John Purner

Hours: 8:00 - dusk 7 days

*** Cloud 9 Café - (606) 298-2799
Proprietor: Gary Cox
Open:
        Mon - Sun: 11am – 8pm
PIREP:
This friendly café is located right next to the terminal. On the front
porch you'll find several rocking chairs. Pick one out and sit a spell.
It's kinda' like a mini Cracker Barrel! In the evening you may see some
elk. There is a herd nearby and sometimes they show up.

FlyIn Louisiana

JENNINGS, LA (JENNINGS - 3R7)
    Aprt Mgr: DWAYNE BEBEE **PH:** 337-616-2370
    Field Elevation: 23 **CTAF:** 122.800 **FUEL:** 100LLA
    Runway: 13/31 **Length:** 3601 **Width:** 75 **Surface:** ASPH-E
    Runway: 08/26 **Length:** 5002 **Width:** 75 **Surface:** ASPH-E
    Runway: 17/35 **Length:** 1977 **Width:** 150 **Surface:** TURF-G

    ★ **King Buffett - (337) 824-8848**
Proprietor: Chef Connell
Open:
        Mon - Sun: 11am – 8pm
PIREP:
Don't expect much and you won't be disappointed.

The King Buffet is an all you can eat Chinese buffet kinda' place. Park your plane on the east side of airport. Walk past the Quality Inn and the King Buffet is located inside the Days Inn. The reviews of this Days Inn range someplace between wretched and barely adequate. I have never stayed here and probably never will. The hosting facility gives you a view of what to expect at **The King Buffet**.

If you're really hungry it will work.

MONROE, LA (MONROE RGNL - MLU)
    Aprt Mgr: CLEVE NORRELL **PH:** 318-329-2461
    Field Elevation: 79 **CTAF:** 118.900 **FUEL:** 100LLA
    Runway: 18/36 **Length:** 5001 **Width:** 150 **Surface:** ASPH-G
    Runway: 04/22 **Length:** 7505 **Width:** 150 **Surface:** ASPH-G
    Runway: 14/32 **Length:** 4999 **Width:** 150 **Surface:** ASPH-P

    JPS Aviation – 318-387-0222
FBO Website: www.jpsaviation.com
Affiliate: Ascent
Self Service: YES
Pilot Supplies: YES
Hours: Mon – Fri 24 hrs. Weekends – 4am – 11pm

NEW IBERIA, LA (ACADIANA RGNL - ARA)
    Aprt Mgr: F. JASON DEVILLIER **PH:** 337-365-7202
    Field Elevation: 24 **CTAF:** 125.000 **FUEL:** 100LLA
    Runway: 16/34 **Length:** 8002 **Width:** 200 **Surface:** CONC-G

John Purner

**** Freeman Jet Center Acadiana - (337) 367-1401

Proprietor: Edward Lasalle
Open:
Mon - Sun: 7am - Sunset
PIREP:
Pricey but it will be one of the best airport meals you've ever had.

The FBO, **Freeman Jet Center Acadiana** now caters through Landry's Seafood between 11am - 1:30pm & 5pm-7:30pm. This works very well as Landry's is one of the best restaurants on the Gulf Coast. Seriously good food.
Call ahead to order and we can have it waiting for you when you get here!

They also now offer crew cars to take into town to explore in town restaurants. People in Louisiana live in order to eat and they eat very well. Call ahead to reserve one of their cars.

NEW ORLEANS, LA (LAKEFRONT - NEW)
Aprt Mgr: FRED PRUITT **PH:** 504-243-4010
Field Elevation: 7 **CTAF:** 119.900 **FUEL:** 100LLA
Runway: 09/27 **Length:** 3114 **Width:** 75 **Surface:** ASPH-G
Runway: 18L/36R **Length:** 3697 **Width:** 75 **Surface:** ASPH-G
Runway: 18R/36L **Length:** 6879 **Width:** 150 **Surface:** ASPH-G

**** Messina's Runway Café - (504) 241 -5300
Executive Chef: Leon West
Open:
Tue – Sun 8 a.m. to 3 p.m.
Restaurant Website: https://messinasrunwaycafe.com
PIREP:
This place has great food and service. I always go on Tuesday for lunch. The $11.95 Blue Plate Special that day is: southern style fried chicken with macaroni and cheese, collard greens and corn bread. That's as good as it needs to be!

FlyIn Maine

AUGUSTA, ME (AUGUSTA STATE - AUG)
   Aprt Mgr: JOHN GUIMOND **PH:** 207-626-2306
   Field Elevation: 352 **CTAF:** 123.000 **FUEL:** 100LLA
   Runway: 17/35 **Length:** 5001 **Width:** 150 **Surface:** ASPH-F
   Runway: 08/26 **Length:** 2703 **Width:** 75 **Surface:** ASPH-G

   ✈ **Maine Instrument Flight** – 888-643-3597
   FBO Website: www.maineinstrumentflight.com
   Affiliate: UNK
   Self Service: NO
   Pilot Supplies: NO
   Hours: 7:00-7:00 7 days weeks

BANGOR, ME (BANGOR INTL - BGR)
   Aprt Mgr: REBECCA HUPP **PH:** 207-992-4600
   Field Elevation: 192 **CTAF:** 0.000 **FUEL:** 100LLA
   Runway: 15/33 **Length:** 11440 **Width:** 200 **Surface:** ASPH-G

   ★★ **Refueler Pub - (207) 947-4375**
   Open:
      Mon – Sun: 10am – 5pm
   PIREP:
   Bangor International is a somewhat active commercial airport that also
   handles many transatlantic GA flights. When you land you'll be
   directed to the GA ramp. The FBO will be happy to give you a lift to
   the domestic terminal, where you can take refuge in the **Refueler Pub**.
   The food is pretty standard commercial airport fare as is the service.
   While this is not a destination Burger run, it is a great place to eat if
   you have another reason to be at Bangor International.

LIMINGTON, ME (LIMINGTON-HARMON - 63B)
   Airport Manager: ANDREW POMEROY **PH:** 207-637-2121
   Field Elevation: 292 **CTAF:** 122.700 **FUEL:** 100LL
   Runway: 11/29 **Length:** 2973 **Width:** 50 **Surface:** ASPH-F

   *** **Runway Restaurant - 207-637-2210**
   Proprietor: Lindsay Bradeen & Jennifer Gamble
   Open:
      Breakfast and Lunch Daily
   Restaurant Website: www.runwayrestaurant.com
   PIREP:

Prompt service, from a farm to table experience serving breakfast ALL day long, I like that. Sometime I want breakfast at noon. I can get that need fulfilled here. It's located just 50 yards from the base of runway 29. I've heard that they serve a wild jerked chicken wrap. I'm not a jerk chicken fan but you may be.

ROCKLAND, ME (KNOX COUNTY RGNL - RKD)
Aprt Mgr: JEFF NORTHGRAVES **PH:** 207-594-4131
Field Elevation: 56 **CTAF:** 123.050 **FUEL:** 100LLA
Runway: 03/21 **Length:** 4000 **Width:** 100 **Surface:** ASPH-G
Runway: 13/31 **Length:** 5007 **Width:** 100 **Surface:** ASPH-G

Downeast Air – 207-594-2171
FBO Website: www.downeastair.com
Affiliate: UNK
Self Service: NO
Pilot Supplies: NO
Hours: 24/7

Owl's Head Transportation Museum - (207) 594-4418
Proprietor: Kevin Bedford
Open:
Mon - Sun: 10am – 5pm
Restaurant Website: www.ohtm.org
Restaurant Email: info@ohtm.org
PIREP:
Let's be clear, you do not come here for the food. It is merely a concession stand. You show-up to visit the Museum which is really pretty cool. Check out their website and plan accordingly. The aviation portion of the Museum is light but interesting.

SANFORD, ME (SANFORD RGNL - SFM)
Aprt Mgr: DANA H. PARRY **PH:** 207-432-0596
Field Elevation: 244 **CTAF:** 123.075 **FUEL:** 100LLA
Runway: 14/32 **Length:** 4999 **Width:** 100 **Surface:** ASPH-G
Runway: 07/25 **Length:** 6389 **Width:** 100 **Surface:** ASPH-G

✦ Southern Maine Aviation – 207-324-8919
FBO Website: www.flyingsma.com
Affiliate: UNK
Self Service: YES
Pilot Supplies: YES
Hours: 7:00 - 5:00 and 7:00 to 7:00 summer hours 7 days

*** The Cockpit Cafe - (207) 324-7332
Proprietor: Daniel Bowden and Ronald Farrington.

Executive Chef: Richard Martin
Open:
> Thur – Sun: 9am - 9pm

Restaurant Website: www.pilotscovecafe.com
PIREP:
The **Pilots Cove Cafe** is in the main terminal building, next to Southern Maine Aviation. There is plenty of no charge ramp parking. This is a good place to come for breakfast. Expect a crowd on the weekends as many locals show up. I always go with the lobster omelet, as it is not something, I can get anywhere else and it is very tasty.

John Purner

FlyIn Maryland

CAMBRIDGE, MD (CAMBRIDGE-DORCHESTER - CGE)
Aprt Mgr: ROBERT TENANTY **PH:** 410-228-4571
Field Elevation: 20 **CTAF:** 122.700 **FUEL:** 100LLA
Runway: 16/34 **Length:** 4477 **Width:** 75 **Surface:** ASPH-G

**** Katie's at The Airport - (410) 901-8844
Open:

Mon - Sat: 8:00 AM - 8:00 PM
Sunday – 8:00 AM - 3:00 PM
CLOSED WEDNESDAYS

Restaurant Email: homecook99@gmail.com
PIREP:
Home cooked food, family atmosphere, and great service can all be found at this locally owned and operated restaurant located in the Dorchester County Airport Terminal. I have had the crab cakes here and they are pretty darn good. Well worth a stop.

EASTON, MD (EASTON/NEWNAM FIELD - ESN)
Aprt Mgr: MIKE HENRY **PH:** 410-770-8055
Field Elevation: 72 **CTAF:** 118.525 **FUEL:** 100LLA
Runway: 04/22 **Length:** 5500 **Width:** 100 **Surface:** ASPH-E
Runway: 15/33 **Length:** 4003 **Width:** 100 **Surface:** ASPH-G

*** Sugar Buns Airport Cafe and Bakery - 410-820-4220
Open:

Daily: 7:00 AM - 3:00 PM

Restaurant Website: www.sugarbuns.com
PIREP:
I like coming here because it has a different focus. Sugarbuns is a bakery and yes, they are known for their praiseworthy Cinnamon Rolls.

For lunch I also go with the CrabZilla which is their signature dish: 6 legs of bacon, one-inch heirloom tomato, Super Lump Crabcake, homemade onion rings, lettuce on Texas Toast with two olive eyes, served on an island of fries.

Worth the trip!

FREDERICK, MD (FREDERICK MUNI - FDK)
Aprt Mgr: KEVIN DAUGHERTY **PH:** 301-600-2201
Field Elevation: 306 **CTAF:** 122.725 **FUEL:** 100LLA
Runway: 12/30 **Length:** 3600 **Width:** 75 **Surface:** ASPH-G
Runway: 05/23 **Length:** 5219 **Width:** 100 **Surface:** ASPH-G

Landmark Aviation – 301-662-8156
FBO Website: www.landmarkaviation.com
Affiliate: UNK
Self Service: YES
Pilot Supplies: YES
Hours: 7:00 - 8:00 7 days

*** Airways Inn of Frederick - (301) 228-2100
Proprietor: Jang Sewell
Open:

> Mon: 7:30am – 3pm
> Tues - Thurs: 7:30am – 8pm
> Fri: 7:30am - 9pm
> Sat: 7am – 9pm
> Sun: 7am – 7pm

Restaurant Website: www.airwaysinnoffrederick.com
Restaurant Email: airwaysinn@frederick.com
PIREP:
Many pilots like to come to Frederick because it is home to AOPA. I come here to visit **Airways Inn of Frederick**. It's that good. My choice is the steamed shrimp. I became aware of them when I lived in Newport News. I love them.

GAITHERSBURG, MD (MONTGOMERY COUNTY - GAI)
Aprt Mgr: JOHN LUKE III **PH:** 301-963-7100
Field Elevation: 539 **CTAF:** 123.075 **FUEL:** 100LLA
Runway: 14/32 **Length:** 4202 **Width:** 75 **Surface:** ASPH-G

DC Metro Aviation – 301-963-8043
FBO Website: www.dcmetroaviation.com
Affiliate: UNK
Self Service: YES
Pilot Supplies: YES

*** Café Sophie – (240) 261-4189
Proprietor: Sandy Poe
Open:

> Daily: 8am – 3pm
> CLOSED TUESDAY

Restaurant Website: www.cafesophie.net

PIREP:

Sophie is a Golden Doodle with a big smile. Tom and Sandy run the place. I have stopped in twice for breakfast and to pet Sophie, I'm a sucker for dogs. This is the only place I have ever been too in America where you can get a decent authentic pub style English breakfast compete with two sunny side up eggs, one banger sausage, tomato beans, fired tomatoes, mushrooms. and toast. They have several European dishes on the menu as well as many American favorites. I like this place. The service the friendly, the ambiance pleasing, the food delicious and prices fair.

HAGERSTOWN, MD (HAGERSTOWN RGNL - HGR)
Aprt Mgr: PHIL RIDENOUR **PH:** 240-313-2777
Field Elevation: 703 **CTAF:** 120.300 **FUEL:** 100LLA A1
Runway: 02/20 **Length:** 3165 **Width:** 100 **Surface:** ASPH-G
Runway: 09/27 **Length:** 7000 **Width:** 150 **Surface:** ASPH-G

Rider Jet Center – 301-791-9119
FBO Website: www.riderjetcenter.com
Affiliate: UNK
Self Service: YES
Pilot Supplies: YES
Hours: 5:00 - 10:00 7 days

**** Nick's Airport Inn - (301) 733 8560
Proprietor: Nick, Paul & Tina Giannaris
Open:

> Tue- Fri: 12:00am - 8:00pm
> Saturday: 4:00pm - 8:30pm

Restaurant Website: www.nicksairportinn.com
Restaurant Email: info@ nicksairportinn.com
PIREP:

Nick's is not your typical airport café. It is more like a fine downtown restaurant. Nick's is famous for crab cakes. I ordered them once and quickly understood why. Now I'm in a rut. When I go to Nick's that's what I eat. They have many other great choices that I never tried. I really enjoy the great, friendly service, the excellent atmosphere, and the amazing food.

*** The Grille at Runways – (240) 707-6466
Open:

> Mon - Sat: 8am – 9pm
> Sun: 8am – 3pm

Restaurant Website: www.thegrillehgratrunways.com
PIREP:

The Grille at the Runways is on the ramp -- in fact, it is in the Rider Jet Center.
 terminal. Rider gave me a $0.75 per gallon discount on full-service 100LL for patronizing the restaurant, which brought the cost down to the self-serve price.
Hopefully they're still doing that. If not go for Self- Serve.

I came here for Sunday brunch and jumped all over the Meat Lovers Omelet.
Perfect!

FlyIn Massachusetts

CHATHAM, MA (CHATHAM MUNI - CQX)
>**Aprt Mgr:** TIMOTHY HOWARD **PH:** 508-945-9000
>**Elevation:** 64 **CTAF:** 122.800 **FUEL:** 100LL
>**Runway: 06/24 Length: 3001 Width: 100 Surface: ASPH-G**

**** Hangar B Eatery - (508) 593-3655
Proprietor: Tracy Shields
Open:
>WED - MON 7am – 2pm
>CLOSED TUESDAY

Restaurant Website: hangarbchatham.com
Restaurant Email: tracy.erskine@gmail.com
PIREP:
Hangar B has turned into one of my favorites. Chef Brian Erskine brings his skills honed in San Francisco, Los Angeles and Chicago to bear on locally sourced food products. The results are amazing!

EDGARTOWN, MA (KATAMA AIRPARK - 1B2)
>**Aprt Mgr:** MICHAEL CREATO **PH:** 508-627-9018
>**Field Elevation:** 18 **CTAF:** 122.800 **FUEL:** 100LL
>**Runway: 17/35 Length: 2600 Width: 50 Surface: TURF-G**
>**Runway: 06/24 Length: 2700 Width: 50 Surface: TURF-G**
>**Runway: 03/21 Length: 3700 Width: 50 Surface: TURF-G**

Katama Airpark – 508-627-9018
Affiliate: UNK
Self Service: YES
Pilot Supplies: YES
Hours: 7:30 - 8:00 7 days

*** Katama Kitchen - (774) 549-5345
Open:
>Open every day in the season for breakfast and lunch.
>Serving dinner every evening except Wednesdays.

Restaurant Website: www.katamakitchen.com
PIREP:

This is an airport that we ALL want to visit. It is a beautiful well-maintained turf airport with three runways and two parking areas. I have come here twice to spend the day at the beach. Park at the opposite end of the airport from the restaurant and walk a path to the Atlantic. You'll have to cross the street. You should come early and stay a few hours at the sandy beach. There is a small fee that you pay at the restaurant, that is used to maintain the field. What about the food? Well, it's pretty darn good. Sit on their large deck and enjoy breakfast lunch or dinner.

I'm a beach guy so I get a burger and a drink to go and sit on the beach for most of the afternoon.

It's nice!!

FITCHBURG, MA (FITCHBURG MUNI - FIT)
Aprt Mgr: ALFRED P. GUERTIN PH: 978-345-9580
Field Elevation: 348 CTAF: 122.700 FUEL: 100LLA
Runway: 02/20 Length: 3504 Width: 75 Surface: ASPH-G
Runway: 14/32 Length: 4510 Width: 100 Surface: ASPH-G

Fitchburg Muni – 978-345-9580
Affiliate: UNK
Self Service: NO
Pilot Supplies: YES
Hours: 8:00 - 7:00 7 days

LAWRENCE, MA (LAWRENCE MUNI - LWM)
Aprt Mgr: MICHAEL MILLER PH: 978-794-5880
Field Elevation: 148 CTAF: 119.250 FUEL: 100LLA
Runway: 14/32 Length: 3900 Width: 100 Surface: ASPH-F
Runway: 05/23 Length: 5001 Width: 150 Surface: ASPH-G

Lawrence Jet Center – 978-685-7500
Affiliate: UNK
Self Service: NO
Pilot Supplies: YES
Hours: 7:00 - 900 M-F; 7:00 - 3:00 Sat; 7:00 - 5:00 Sunday

Eagle East Aviation – 978-683-3314
FBO Website: www.eagleeastaviation.com
Affiliate: Shell
Self Service: NO
Pilot Supplies: YES
Hours: 8:00 - 6:00 7 days

Falcon Air – 978-689-4492
Affiliate: UNK
Self Service: NO
Pilot Supplies: YES
Hours: 8:00 - 5:00 M-F   8:30 - 2:00 Sat

*** **Dominic's Diner - (978) 682-8822**
Open:
> Mon – Sun: 7:00am – 2:00pm
> Lunch starts at 11am
> Sundays Breakfast ONLY

Restaurant Website: www.dominicsdiner.com
PIREP:
The menu is filed with the ordinary American dishes that you expect plus a list of Mediterranean foods that will surprise and delight you. I am glad to come here when I need a break from hamburgers and pancakes. Plus they have homemade beer battered onion rings.

MANSFIELD, MA (MANSFIELD MUNI - 1B9)
Aprt Mgr: DAVID DINNEEN **PH:** 508-339-3624
Field Elevation: 122 **CTAF:** 123.000 **FUEL:** 100LL
Runway: 14/32 **Length:** 3500 **Width:** 75 **Surface:** ASPH-G
Runway: 04/22 **Length:** 2200 **Width:** 100 **Surface:** TURF-G

*** **Hangar12 -** (774) 284-4782
Open:
> Mon – Sun: 7am-2pm

Restaurant Website: www.katamakitchen.com
PIREP:
For starters I like this airport. Heck I like any airport that has a turf strip to compliment the paved runway. I almost always land on pavement but I love looking over the airplanes that normally land on grass. They're fun to get close to and they're fun to watch as they are typically taildraggers. The pilots that fly them are loaded with great hangar flying yarns.

The restaurant has a patio that holds about 35 people and give a great view of the ramp. Inside there is room for another 25 to 30 folks. The menu is best described as interesting. I had the Double Cheeseburger which is best described as "Pretty Darn Good." You could have a Kale Salad. They have one on the menu. I don't eat Kale life is too long to suffer. If you're there for breakfast, try the Chicken and Waffles. One of the taildragger pilots told me it was better than "Pretty Darn Good." Any young lady who pilots a CUB is to be believed.

NANTUCKET, MA (NANTUCKET MEMORIAL - ACK)

Aprt Mgr: ALFRED G. PETERSON **PH:** 508-325-5300
Field Elevation: 47 **CTAF:** 118.300 **FUEL:** 100LLA
Runway: 12/30 **Length:** 2696 **Width:** 50 **Surface:** ASPH-F
Runway: 15/33 **Length:** 4000 **Width:** 100 **Surface:** ASPH-G
Runway: 06/24 **Length:** 6303 **Width:** 150 **Surface:** ASPH-G

Nantucket Memorial Airport – 508-325-5307
Affiliate: Phillips 66
Self Service: YES
Pilot Supplies: YES
Hours: 24/7

*** Crosswinds Restaurant & Bar - 508-228-6005
Open:
   Mon - Sun: 5:30am - 9:00pm
Restaurant Website: www.crosswindsnantucket.com
Restaurant Email: eat@crosswindsnantucket.com
PIREP:
The Nantucket Memorial Airport was home to the *"Wings"* television series. Some of which was shot in the restaurant. They claim to have a menu that will fill you up without emptying your wallet. I think that's true as the portions are HUGE and the prices are low. My lunch favorite is the chicken pot pie because you can't get it everywhere and the BLT because they use wonderful tomatoes that I suspect are grown locally. I love tomatoes and everybody loves bacon.

NEW BEDFORD, MA (NEW BEDFORD RGNL - EWB)
  Aprt Mgr: THOMAS M. VICK **PH:** 508-991-6160
  Field Elevation: 79 **CTAF:** 118.100 **FUEL:** 100LLA
  Runway: 05/23 **Length:** 4997 **Width:** 150 **Surface:** ASPH-F
  Runway: 14/32 **Length:** 5000 **Width:** 150 **Surface:** ASPH-F

**** The Airport Grille - 508-992-7504
Proprietor: Robert Cassi
Open:
   Mon – Thurs: 11:30 am - 9:00 pm
   Fri – Sat: 11:30 am - 10:00 pm
   Sun: 11:30 am - 9:00 pm
Restaurant Website: www.airportgrille.com
Restaurant Email: info@airportgrille.com
PIREP:
Taxi to the terminal and park on its ramp, the controller tower sits right on top of it. Walk inside and work your way up to the second floor. **The Airport Grille's** elevated position and huge plate glass windows offer an expanse view of the airport. **The Grille** is an upscale modern American bistro providing a warm and relaxing environment. They use

local produce and seafood and also have steaks and chops plus a pretty good wine. For lunch I recommend the wedge salad and the baked codfish.

NORWOOD, MA (NORWOOD MEMORIAL - OWD)
Aprt Mgr: RUSS MAGUIRE **PH:** 781-255-5616
Field Elevation: 49 **CTAF:** 126.000 **FUEL:** 100LLA
Runway: 10/28 **Length:** 3995 **Width:** 75 **Surface:** ASPH-G
Runway: 17/35 **Length:** 4008 **Width:** 100 **Surface:** ASPH-G

Flight Level Aviation – 781-769-8680
FBO Website: www.flightlevelnorwood.com
Affiliate: Shell
Self Service: NO
Pilot Supplies: YES
Hours: 7:00 - 7:00 7 Days

***** Taso's Euro-Cafe – **(781) 278-0001**
Proprietor: Christiana Kapsaskis
Open:

Mon – Thurs: 11:00 am - 9:00 pm
Fri – Sat: 11:00 am - 10:00 pm
CLOSED ON SUNDAYS

Restaurant Email: tasoseurocafe1.com/
PIREP:
This is a family owned and operated Greek restaurant. The food and service are amazing. It is well worth the trip. Go with the baked lamb. It is really, really good. Start with an order of calamari for the table. Be warned they are not opened on Sunday. Be double warned the food is so good its addictive.

ORANGE, MA (ORANGE MUNI - ORE)
Aprt Mgr: LEONARD BEDAW **PH:** 978-544-8189
Field Elevation: 555 **CTAF:** 122.800 **FUEL:** 100LLA
Runway: 14/32 **Length:** 4801 **Width:** 75 **Surface:** ASPH-G
Runway: 01/19 **Length:** 5000 **Width:** 75 **Surface:** ASPH-G

** White Cloud Diner - (978) 544-6821
Proprietor: Sharon Prue
Open:

Mon – Sun: 7am – 2pm
CLOSED TUESDAY

PIREP:
The airport is a very active skydiving center so monitor CTAF and time your arrival to miss theirs. It takes about 5 minutes to walk from the tie-down through the airport office, down the drive and across the street to

the restaurant. It's a big airport so be sure to tie down near the office off the taxiway parallel to 14/32. They make honest food. The service is fast and genuinely friendly.

PLYMOUTH, MA (PLYMOUTH MUNI - PYM)
Aprt Mgr: TOM MAHER **PH:** 508-746-2020
Field Elevation: 148 **CTAF:** 123.000 **FUEL:** 100LLA
Runway: 15/33 **Length:** 3351 **Width:** 75 **Surface:** ASPH-G
Runway: 06/24 **Length:** 4350 **Width:** 75 **Surface:** ASPH-G

Alpha One Flight Services – 508-747-1494
FBO Website: www.alpha-1.com
Affiliate: UNK
Self Service: NO
Pilot Supplies: YES
Hours: 7:00 - 8:00 7 Days

Plymouth Airport – 508-746-2020
Affiliate: UNK
Self Service: NO
Pilot Supplies: YES
Hours: 6:00- 10:00 7 Days

**** Plane Jane's Cafe - (508) 747-9396
Proprietor: Jane Grennell
Open:
> Mon – Wed: 6am to 3pm
> Thurs & Fri: 6am to 9pm
> Sat & Sun: 6am to 5pm

Restaurant Website: www.planejanesplace.com
Restaurant Email: info@planejanesplace.com
PIREP:
For 20 years this Mom and son owned, and operated restaurant has been serving up the **BEST** breakfast in New England. Do no miss any opportunity to land here. Consider how good any airport restaurant has to be to survive for 20 years let alone thrive. These folks continue to expand and improve the place. I enjoy sitting on their deck and eating their Blueberry pancakes with a side of crisp bacon.

STOW, MA (MINUTE MAN AIR FIELD - 6B6)
Aprt Mgr: DONALD MC PHERSON **PH:** 978-897-3933
Field Elevation: 268 **CTAF:** 122.800 **FUEL:** 100LL
Runway: 03/21 **Length:** 2770 **Width:** 48 **Surface:** ASPH-F
Runway: 12/30 **Length:** 1600 **Width:** 70 **Surface:** TURF-GRVL-F

***** Nancy's Air Field Cafe - (978) 897-3934

Proprietor: Nancy McPherson
Open:
> Wed, Thur, Sun: 8am – 3pm
> Fri – Sat: 8am – 9pm

Restaurant Website: www.nancysairfieldcafe.com
Restaurant Email: info@nancysairfieldcafe.com
PIREP:
You can't buy a BETTER meal at any airport anywhere on earth.

This is a great place to come to fuel your body and your plane. The food at **Nancy's** is really good and deserving of the awards and accolades it has received.

The fuel price is one of the lowest in the country and certainly the lowest in New England.

VINEYARD HAVEN, MA (MARTHAS VINEYARD - MVY)
Aprt Mgr: SEAN FLYNN **PH:** 508-693-7022
Field Elevation: 67 **CTAF:** 121.400 **FUEL:** 100LLA
Runway: 15/33 **Length:** 3328 **Width:** 75 **Surface:** ASPH-G
Runway: 06/24 **Length:** 5504 **Width:** 100 **Surface:** ASPH-G

Martha's Vineyard – 508-693-7022
Affiliate: UNK
Self Service: NO
Pilot Supplies: YES
Hours: 24/7

***

* Plane Plane View Restaurant - (508) 693-1886
Proprietor: Robert Jackson
Open:
> Mon – Sun: 7:00 am - 3:00 pm
> Mon – Sun: 7:00 am - 7:00 pm (June 23 through September 5)

PIREP:
I like Martha's Vineyard. It is a good place to visit during the shoulder seasons. The food is good, the service is crisp and the prices are astoundingly low. Can you imagine getting a three-egg cheese omelet for less than five bucks anywhere let alone on MV? This is one of my favorite New England flyin's. I come here eat breakfast, grab a bus and wander the island. The Martha's Vineyard Regional Transit Authority operates public buses from the airport to all of the island villages and many popular island locations. Bus routes also serve several **island beaches** including **State Beach, Oak Bluffs**, and **South Beach** in Edgartown. **The island's bus system is uncommonly clean and efficient and is a model of public transportation systems.**

Sometimes I hang out at the beach all day but that's just me.

FlyIn Michigan

BATTLE CREEK, MI (W K KELLOGG - BTL)
Aprt Mgr: LAWRENCE BOWRON **PH:** 269-966-3470

Field Elevation: 952 **CTAF:** 126.825 **FUEL:** 100LLA
Runway: 05R/23L **Length:** 4100 **Width:** 75 **Surface:** ASPH
Runway: 13/31 **Length:** 4835 **Width:** 100 **Surface:** ASPH-G
Runway: 05L/23R **Length:** 10004 **Width:** 150 **Surface:** ASPH-G

***** WACO Kitchen – (269) 520-1200**
Open:
> Mon-Fri 11am-4pm

Restaurant Website: wacokitchen.com
PIREP:
Outstanding food, great service, located right on the ramp, inexpensive fuel, with windows to the Waco factory next door and a covered outdoor deck with a view of the runway.

Hard to beat!

We stopped on the way to Oshkosh as our usual restaurant was closed Mondays, stopped again on the way home, and hope to visit in the future.

Here's some good news. The next time you go to Sun n' Fun you find a WACO Kitchen in the terminal building. It is opening this summer. The Battle Creek location has earned its five stars. I'm certain the Lakeland location will not disappoint.

BEAVER ISLAND, MI (WELKE - 6Y8)
Aprt Mgr: PAUL WELKE **PH:** 231-448-2071
Field Elevation: 664 **CTAF:** 122.800 **FUEL:** 100LL
Runway: 09/27 **Length:** 2512 **Width:** 30 **Surface:** ASPH-G
Runway: 17/35 **Length:** 3500 **Width:** 140 **Surface:** TURF-F

***** Circle M – (231) 448-2513**
Proprietor: Shawn Avra
Manager: Zach Van Stelle
Open:
> Open for Dinner Daily.
> **SEASONAL**

Restaurant Website: www.beaverisland.org/circle-m/

Restaurant Email: zach@propblastcafe.com
PIREP:

The Circle M is located right on the field, taxi up the grass strip to the north end and park right on their lawn. If that isn't reason enough to go, the food is out of this world, crazy good and reasonably priced. The owner of the restaurant flies out in his C-172 to pick-up the catch of the day, every day. Great atmosphere inside or on the deck right next to your plane. Only downside is being on an island in Michigan it is only open seasonally so call ahead.

COLDWATER, MI (BRANCH COUNTY MEMORIAL - OEB)
Aprt Mgr: RON DOOLEY **PH:** 517-279-7050
Field Elevation: 959 **CTAF:** 122.700 **FUEL:** 100LLA
Runway: 07/25 **Length:** 5350 **Width:** 75 **Surface:** ASPH-F
Runway: 04/22 **Length:** 3500 **Width:** 75 **Surface:** ASPH-G
Runway: 16/34 **Length:** 2400 **Width:** 190 **Surface:** TURF-G

✈ **Elite Air Service** – 517-278-6516
Affiliate: UNK
Self Service: YES
Pilot Supplies: YES
Hours: M-F 8:00 - 4:30 Weekends call out only

*** **Prop Blast Café - 517-781-6000**
Open:
Mon - Sun: 7am to 3pm
Restaurant Website: www.propblastcafe.com
Restaurant Email: zach@propblastcafe.com
PIREP:

The Prop Blast Café like many restaurants we cover closed for COVID. Happily, it reopened June 6, 2022.

The café is located in the FBO building, which is right on the taxiway with plenty of ramp space. This is one of those places that pays careful attention to the ingredients that they place before you. For instance, they serve only romaine lettuce in their salads and on their sandwiches; no iceberg is served here. It is a small homey place with good service.

For lunch I suggest the Mushroom and Swiss Burger Basket or the Chicken Bacon Ranch wrap.

FLUSHING, MI (DALTON - 3DA)
Aprt Mgr: ANTHONY SABOURIN **PH:** 810-624-4001

Field Elevation: 733 **CTAF:** 122.800 **FUEL:** 100LL
Runway: 18/36 **Length:** 2510 **Width:** 50 **Surface:** ASPH-F
Runway: 09/27 **Length:** 1633 **Width:** 130 **Surface:** TURF-G

*** Liberty Family Restaurant - (810) 867-4768
Proprietor: Art & John Panos
Open:

Mon - Sat: 8am - 8pm
Sun: 7am - 4pm

Restaurant Email: www.libertyeats810.com
PIREP:

Dalton is an interesting little airport populated by airplane folks. There are a slew of hangars and a good number of homes with hangars—some very nice and at least one single wide mobile home—with hangar. This is truly an *"everyman's airpark."* Park in the grass at the north end of 18/36 and walk over to the diner. The food is about what you'd expect for a family owned restaurant. Everything is made from scratch. The service is very good. The place fills up with locals on the weekends.

GAYLORD, MI (LAKES OF THE NORTH - 4Y4)
Aprt Mgr: SCOTT BROWN **PH:** 231-585-6000
Field Elevation: 1286 **CTAF:** 122.900 **FUEL:**
Runway: 05/23 **Length:** 4285 **Width:** 40 **Surface:** ASPH-P

** Settings Restaurant - (231) 585-6000
Proprietor: Joe and Jan Lauka
Open:

Mon - Sun: 7:00am - 10:00pm

Restaurant Website: www.settingsrestaurant.com
Restaurant Email: info@settingsrestaurant.com
PIREP:

LAKES OF THE NORTH is the getaway resort area for Michigan. It is scenic and fun with lakes, forest and recreational opportunities everywhere. 'Settings' serves the golfers in the summer and the snowmobilers in the winter. Pilots are welcome year-round. The food is what you'd expect for a muni. golf course clubhouse. I came here to play a round and munch a burger. Both were good but you don't really come here for the food.

*** Deer Run Golf Course – (800) 851-4653
Golf Pro: Mike Alpers
Open:

Seasonal

Restaurant Website: settingsrestaurant.com
Restaurant Email: tcalpers@yahoo.com

PIREP:
You can cart your clubs over from the tie-down. A round with a cart will set you make about $35.00, which is a really good deal.

GLADWIN, MI (SUGAR SPRINGS - 5M6)
Aprt Mgr: RICHARD SAGER **PH:** 989-426-9153
Field Elevation: 940 **CTAF:** 122.900 **FUEL:**
Runway: E/W **Length:** 3800 **Width:** 50 **Surface:** TURF

***** The Hearth Restaurant & Pub - (989) 426-9203
Open:
Daily: 11am – 8pm
Restaurant Website: www.sugarsprings.net/dining/
PIREP:
This is a terrific place to slip away to for a round of golf or a good meal. Remember, this is a PRIVATE airstrip and permission **MUST** be granted before you land. It's easy to obtain. Simply call the Property Owners Association Office at 989-426-4111, the Golf Pro Shop at 989-426-4391, or the Hearth Restaurant at 989-426-9203. Park at the west or east end *(the west end is easier and has an access road)*. Bring your own tie-downs and have a member or guest pass with you. The food, service, ambiance and setting are all excellent. I recommend fish not seafood but local lake fish; either the whitefish or yellow belly perch. They are really worth the trip.

***** Sugar Springs Golf Club - (989) 426-9203
Proprietor: Nancy McPherson
Open:
Seasonal
Restaurant Website:
www.sugarsprings.net/Golf/golfcoursehome.html
PIREP:
Sugar Springs Golf Club is 6,737 yards, par 72, 18-hole championship course, designed by Jerry Matthews. It weaves through a wooded front nine and a more open back nine with subtle elevation changes, water in play on five holes, & greens guarded with bunkers that creates an enjoyable challenge for golfers of all skill levels. The 18th hole green fee is about $30.00! The resort also offers many lakes, an Olympic size pool, archery and tennis.

JACKSON, MI (JACKSON COUNTY-REYNOLDS FIELD - JXN)
Aprt Mgr: KENT L MAURER **PH:** 517-788-4225
Field Elevation: 1001 **CTAF:** 128.475 **FUEL:** 100LLA
Runway: 06/24 **Length:** 5349 **Width:** 150 **Surface:** ASPH-F
Runway: 14/32 **Length:** 4000 **Width:** 100 **Surface:** ASPH-G

John Purner

Skyway Aviation – 517-787-2460
FBO Website: www.skywayjxn.com
Affiliate: Texaco
Self Service: NO
Pilot Supplies: YES
Hours: Mon – Saturday 8:00 - 5:00   Sunday 8:00 - 3:00

*** The Apron Restaurant & Spirits - (517) 783-3616
Proprietor: Dianne Weems
Open:

>   Monday- 7am - 2pm
>   Tuesday - Saturday 7am - 10pm
>   Sunday- 7am - 2pm
>   Kitchen Closes at 9pm Tuesday- Saturday
>   Breakfast ends at noon daily
>   Lunch and Dinner begins at noon daily

Restaurant Website: www.theapron517.com
Restaurant Email: theapron517@gmail.com
PIREP:
Consider this, the Apron has a 3,800 sq. ft. patio directly overlooking the apron and the runaway. It is made better by its proximity to Michigan International Speedway and all of the auto company proving grounds which are scattered nearby. Jackson is a fun stop.

The food? Oh, its terrific and the service is attentive.

KALAMAZOO, MI (KALAMAZOO INTL - AZO)
Aprt Mgr: CLIFTON MOSHOGINIS **PH:** 269-388-3668
Field Elevation: 874 **CTAF:** 118.300 **FUEL:** 100LLA
Runway: 09/27 **Length:** 2800 **Width:** 60 **Surface:** ASPH-G
Runway: 05/23 **Length:** 3438 **Width:** 100 **Surface:** ASPH-G
Runway: 17/35 **Length:** 6502 **Width:** 150 **Surface:** ASPH-G

Duncan Aviation – 269-343-2548
Affiliate: UNK
Self Service: NO
Pilot Supplies: YES
Hours: 24/7

The Air Zoo "Kitty Hawk Cafe" - (866) 524-7966
Proprietor: EMA Enterprises
Open:
>   Mon - Sun: Lunch

Restaurant Website: www.airzoo.org/page.php?page_id=80
Restaurant Email: airzoo@airzoo.org
PIREP:

There is a snack bar on the second floor of the museum. You don't come here for the food but you shouldn't starve if you're that hungry. 'Nuff said!

The KALAMAZOO Air Zoo – (269) 382-6555
Open:
> Mon - Sat: 9:00am - 5:00pm
> Sun: 12:0 pm - 5:00pm

Restaurant Website: www.airzoo.org
Restaurant Email: airzoo@airzoo.org
PIREP:
The Air Zoo features more than 50 rare and historic aircraft, amusement park-style rides, full-motion flight simulators, RealD 3D/4D Missions Theater, as well as historical exhibits and educational activities. The **NEW** Air Zoo is a $19.50 multimedia and aviation experience. The **OLD** Air Zoo with its numerous WWII warbirds is still open and is right on the airport, the **NEW** Air Zoo is a short walk away. Park at Duncan Aviation, they'll show you what to do next.

LUZERNE, MI (LOST CREEK - 5Y4)
> **Aprt Mgr:** CLIFF OLSON **PH:** 734-775-1953
> **Field Elevation:** 1051 **CTAF:** 122.900 **FUEL:**
> **Runway:** 05/23 **Length:** 2200 **Width:** 100 **Surface:** TURF-F
> **Runway:** 18/36 **Length:** 2600 **Width:** 100 **Surface:** TURF-F

*** Lost Creek Sky Ranch - (989) 826-9901
Proprietor: Dennis Kann and Debbie Coulon
Open:
> Monday to Thursday 11Am-11pm
> Friday and Saturday 11Am-2Am
> Sunday 12PM-11PM

Restaurant Website: www.lcskyranch.com/
Restaurant Email: Lostcreekskyranch768@yahoo.com
PIREP:
I have never been here but one of my good friends and $100 Hamburger subscribers has. Here's what Victor Adamko says about this place:
"The 'Lost Creek Sky Ranch' (5Y4) located in Luzerne, Michigan is an excellent choice for just a meal or a weekend destination. The airport is public use with two grass strips 2200' and 2600' in good shape. The flying "R" ranch offers two restaurants, one upstairs serving anything from burgers to steaks, prime rib, BBQ ribs and seafood. The lower restaurant is a pizza joint. I have eaten there on several occasions; the prices are reasonable ($8.00 - $20.00) the food and service has always been very good! They also serve drinks and have a band on the weekends.

Overnight accommodations are available at a very reasonable price! Although I have not seen the rooms the rest of the place is kept up very well! I believe tent camping is still available. The ranch also caters to the horse crowd and horse rental is available for any one crazy enough to ride one of those things! From a quick burger to a weekend getaway, it is certainly a great destination and one of my personal favorites (five burgers). No services are offered so plan your fuel and bring your own tie downs with stakes."

PLAINWELL, MI (PLAINWELL MUNI - 61D)
Aprt Mgr: VIRGIL WILLIAMS **PH:** 269-685-6268
Field Elevation: 722 **CTAF:** 122.800 **FUEL:** 100LL
Runway: 09/27 **Length:** 2650 **Width:** 50 **Surface:** ASPH-F
Runway: 01/19 **Length:** 2550 **Width:** 150 **Surface:** TURF-G

*** Fly Inn Again - (269) 685-1554
Proprietor: Richard and Cathy Dunn
Open:
> Mon - Sat: 7am – 2pm
> Sun: 7am – 12pm

PIREP:
This is a small but wonderful café right on the ramp. These folks care so much about the burgers they serve that they grow their own lettuce and tomatoes, bake their own bread and grind their own meat. Now that's dedication that deserves our support.

FlyIn Minnesota

BRAINERD, MN (BRAINERD LAKES RGNL - BRD)
    Aprt Mgr: RICK ADAIR **PH:** 218-825-2166
    Field Elevation: 1232 **CTAF:** 122.700 **FUEL:** 100LLA
    Runway: 12/30 **Length:** 4080 **Width:** 75 **Surface:** CLOSED
    Runway: 16/34 **Length:** 7100 **Width:** 150 **Surface:** CONC-E
    Runway: 05/23 **Length:** 6514 **Width:** 150 **Surface:** CONC-G

Northpoint Aviation – 218-829-3398
FBO Website: www.northpointaviation.net
Affiliate: Avfuel
Self Service: NO
Pilot Supplies: YES
Hours: 7 days 7:00 - 9:00 summer; 7:00 - 8:00 winter

**** Wings Cafe - (218) 828-0206
Proprietor: Mark Nesheim
Open:
        Daily: 5:30 am to 4:00 pm
Restaurant Website: www.wingsairportcafe.com
PIREP:
Multiple long runways and plentiful ramp space make this a great stop.
The restaurant and FBO are in the same building. The vie of the
runaways from the restaurant is good not the best but certainly
adequate.

Breakfast is served all day. That's a great place to start. This place has
some breakfast treats that get my heart started. It begins with amazing
caramel or cinnamon rolls and rolls right along to my favorite corned
beef hash.

If it's a burger you're after this is the place. They have a full assortment
cooked to your order. The menu is designed to please any appetite,
mine included.

Here's a twist this restaurant is a full bakery. Desserts of course but
also delicious homemade breads which are sold sliced on unsliced. It's
a twist. I grabbed a loaf and a pie and yes a dozen chocolate cookies
just in case.

DULUTH, MN (DULUTH INTL - DLH)
    Aprt Mgr: BRIAN D RYKS **PH:** 218-727-2968

Field Elevation: 1428 **CTAF:** 0.000 **FUEL:** 100LLA
Runway: 03/21 **Length:** 5718 **Width:** 150 **Surface:** ASPH-G
Runway: 09/27 **Length:** 10162 **Width:** 150 **Surface:** CONC-F

Monaco Air – 218-727-2911
Affiliate: UNK
Self Service: YES
Pilot Supplies: YES
Hours: 24/7

** The Aerohead Tap House - (218) 481-7335
Proprietor: Clint Deraas
Open:
> Mon - Sun: 11 am - 9 pm

Restaurant Website: www.duluthairport.com/airport-food.php
PIREP:
Park at North Country Aviation, they'll give you a lift to the passenger terminal where the restaurant is located. Lunch and dinner are standard passenger terminal food. Not good enough to be good or bad enough to be bad. This certainly isn't a flyin destination.

ST CLOUD, MN (ST CLOUD RGNL - STC)
Aprt Mgr: BILL P. TOWLE **PH:** 320-255-7292
Field Elevation: 1031 **CTAF:** 118.250 **FUEL:** 100LLA
Runway: 05/23 **Length:** 3000 **Width:** 75 **Surface:** ASPH-F
Runway: 13/31 **Length:** 7000 **Width:** 150 **Surface:** CONC-G

---

* Rollie's Sub Shop – 320-255-7292, Ext. 4
Proprietor: Hannah and Amanda
Open:
> Spotty at best

Restaurant Website: stcloudairport.com/index.aspx?nid=129
PIREP:
Rollie's offers sub sandwiches made to order with various chips and Coke products. They are available approximately three hours before every major commercial flight (exception of early mornings). This is best described as desperation rather than destination dining.

ST PAUL, MN (ST PAUL DOWNTOWN HOLMAN FLD - STP)
Airport Manager: GREG FRIES **PH:** 651-224-4306
Field Elevation: 705 **CTAF:** 119.100 **FUEL:** 100LLA
Runway: 09/27 **Length:** 3642 **Width:** 100 **Surface:** ASPH-G
Runway: 13/31 **Length:** 4004 **Width:** 150 **Surface:** ASPH-G
Runway: 14/32 **Length:** 6491 **Width:** 150 **Surface:** ASPH-G

**** Holman's Table – 612-800-5298

Proprietor: Troy Reding & Brad Sorenson,
Open:
>Tues–Fri 11AM–10PM
>Sat & Sun 9AM–10PM

Restaurant Website: www.holmanstable.com
Restaurant Email: contact@HolmansTable.com
PIREP:
Enter the old terminal building, which has a beautiful terrazzo floor with a map of the USA. Just imagine, passengers from the 1930s walked through those same doors.

The view? Wonderful!

The food? Amazing!
Holman's Table is an upscale dining spot featuring locally sourced ingredients prepared in a world class manner. Expect a fresh, modern, sophisticated meal. A really imaginative wine list is provided. Ask for a recommendation for a chef inspired pairing.

If you ever wanted a Lamb Burger for lunch this would be the place to have it.

Breakfast? Biscuits and gravy? Certainly, but you could also choose grilled organic salmon.

If it's dinner, go for the bone in Ribeye and bring your wallet – the fat one.

John Purner

FlyIn Mississippi

BAY ST LOUIS, MS (STENNIS INTL - HSA)
Airport Manager: BILL COTTER **PH:** 228-467-7070
Field Elevation: 23 **CTAF:** 127.150 **FUEL:** 100LLA
Runway: 18/36 **Length:** 8497 **Width:** 150 **Surface:** ASPH-G

*** Jet-A-Way Café – (228) 463-2389
Open:
Mon – Fri – 8AM - 6PM
Sat and Sun – Closed
Restaurant Email: info.hsa@millionair.com
PIREP:
The Jet-A-Way Café is located on the second floor of the MillionAir
facility. The view is pretty terrific. It is a MillionAir operation. Here's
an interesting feature crews pay only $1.00 for their meal and that
includes food and drink. Good Deal? You bet! If you're arriving
afterhours just call ahead for a pizza. It'll be waiting for you.

GRENADA, MS (GRENADA MUNI - GNF)
Aprt Mgr: CHARLES WEATHERS **PH:** 662-227-3440
Field Elevation: 208 **CTAF:** 122.800 **FUEL:** 100LLA
Runway: 13/31 **Length:** 7000 **Width:** 150 **Surface:** ASPH-E
Runway: 04/22 **Length:** 4998 **Width:** 99 **Surface:** ASPH-F

Grenada Muni – 662-227-8402
Affiliate: UNK
Self Service: NO
Pilot Supplies: YES
Hours: 24/7

**** Williams Aviation, Inc. - (662) 227-8402
Proprietor: Guy and Tammy Anderson
Open:
Mon - Sun: Lunch
Restaurant Email: foxtrot@willerwireless.com
PIREP:
The operator at Grenada Muni is a supper nice guy. He serves Hot
Dogs and all the fixings every day for **FREE**. He enjoys your
company.

126

FlyIn Missouri

DEXTER, MO (DEXTER MUNI - DXE)
Aprt Mgr: MIKE WILLIAMS **PH:** 573-624-5959
Field Elevation: 304 **CTAF:** 122.800 **FUEL:** 100LLA
Runway: 18/36 **Length:** 5000 **Width:** 100 **Surface:** ASPH-G

FBO: Dexter Airport
Phone: 573-421-6385
Affiliate: UNK
Self Service: YES **Pilot Supplies:** NO

**** Airways Cafe - (573) 624-4377
Proprietor: Teresa and Ashley Cobb
Open:
>Mon - Fri: 6:00 am - 2:00 pm
>Sat: 6:00 am - 1:30 pm

PIREP:
A real pleasure! It is as one reviewer put it, "a slice of hometown America", I totally agree. The day I went, meatloaf was on the menu. I had that with a large piece of apple pie for dessert. It's a good stop.

JEFFERSON CITY, MO (JEFFERSON CITY MEMORIAL - JEF)
Aprt Mgr: RON CRAFT **PH:** 573-634-6469
Field Elevation: 549 **CTAF:** 125.600 **FUEL:** 100LLA
Runway: 12/30 **Length:** 6001 **Width:** 100 **Surface:** ASPH-G
Runway: 09/27 **Length:** 3401 **Width:** 75 **Surface:** CONC-G

Central Missouri Aviation – 573-443-1576
FBO Website:
Affiliate: Phillips 66
Self Service: YES
Pilot Supplies: NO
Hours: M-F 6:30-8:30PM Sat/Sun 8-6PM available for call outs

*** The Landing Zone - (573) 230-4818
Proprietor: Bob Drainer
Open:
>Monday 6am-2pm
>Tues 6am-2pm
>Wed Closed
>Thurs 6am-2pm
>Friday 6am-2pm

Saturday 7am – 2pm
Sunday 7am-2pm

Restaurant Website: landingzonemo.com/
PIREP:
Bob Drainer has been a regular at this airport since he was a teenager.
He is also a great restaurateur. You'll have beautiful views of the
capital, the Missouri River, and the airport. That isn't bad. What's
better? The Por Tenderloin sandwich. It's a killer. Know this. It is rated
as the Best Breakfast in Jefferson City. I can believe that.

MILLER, MO (KINGSLEY AIRFIELD - MO9)
Aprt Mgr: KIMAN KINGSLEY **PH:** 417-452-3831
Field Elevation: 1262 **CTAF:** 122.800 **FUEL:** 100LLA

***** **Hangar Kafe - (417) 452-2277**
Proprietor: Kiman and Darlene Kingsley
Open:

Mon - Thu: 7:00 am - 3:00 pm
Fri - Sat: 7:00 am - 7:00 pm
Sun: 7:00 am - 4:00 pm

Restaurant Website: hangarkafe.com
Restaurant Email: hangarkafe@yahoo.com
PIREP:
Kiman and Darlene Kingsley opened this emporium of home cooking
in April of 2013. It is flourishing and for good reason, the food is great
and priced fairly. They attract the local crowd with inexpensive
airplane rides and parachute jumps. Kiman runs his crop dusting
business out of this 2,700 foot turf strip which sits in the middle of their
family farm.

It's worth the trip!

FlyIn Montana

BOZEMAN, MT (BOZEMAN YELLOWSTONE INTL - BZN)
    Aprt Mgr: BRIAN SPRENGER **PH:** 406-388-6632
    Field Elevation: 4473 **CTAF:** 118.200 **FUEL:** 100 100LLA
    Runway: 03/21 **Length:** 2650 **Width:** 75 **Surface:** ASPH-G
    Runway: 12/30 **Length:** 8994 **Width:** 150 **Surface:** ASPH-G
    Runway: 11/29 **Length:** 3197 **Width:** 80 **Surface:** TURF-G

Arlins's Aircrat Service,Inc.– 406-388-1351
FBO Website: www.arlins.com
Affiliate: AVFuel
Self Service: Yes
Pilot Supplies: Yes
Hours: 7 days 7AM - 7PM

Yellowstone Jetcenter – 800-700-5381
FBO Website: www.ysjet.com

*** The Copper Horse Restaurant - (406) 388-6168
Open:
        Mon - Sun: 5am – 11pm
Restaurant Website: www.thecopperhorserestaurant.com
PIREP:
The restaurant is located in the terminal. This is a really good restaurant with really good food and service. I have been here for lunch and had the chicken fried steak sandwich which was better than I hoped. Views? Well this is Montana so great views.

HAMILTON, MT (RAVALLI COUNTY - 6S5)
    Aprt Mgr: PAGE GOUGH **PH:** 406-375-9149
    Field Elevation: 3642 **CTAF:** 122.800 **FUEL:** 100LLA
    Runway: 16/34 **Length:** 4200 **Width:** 75 **Surface:** ASPH-F

Choice Aviation – 406-363-6471
FBO Website: www.choiceaviation.com
Affiliate: Phillips
Self Service: YES
Pilot Supplies: YES
Hours: 7days 7AM – 7PM

** Hangar Cafe - (406) 363-4478
Proprietor: Max Martz
Open:

Closed Monday
Tues: 9am – 2:30pm
Sat – Sun: 8am – 2pm

PIREP:

The Hanger Cafe is located on the west side of runway 16/34, at the mid-field intersection taxiway. You can park in front or to the south side in a large parking area. They even offer free chocks to use. The food is the standard airport café variety. Service is best described as slow as in molasses.

WEST YELLOWSTONE, MT (YELLOWSTONE - WYS)
Aprt Mgr: DON DEGRAW **PH:** 406-646-7631
Field Elevation: 6649 **CTAF:** 123.000 **FUEL:** 100LLA1+
Runway: 01/19 **Length:** 8400 **Width:** 150 **Surface:** ASPH-G

***** Yellowstone Pilot Campground – (406) 646-7631**
PIREP:

Yellowstone Pilot Campground now open for the season. Enjoy rustic camping right off the apron! It is a first-class free pilots' campground directly north of the general aviation ramp. The campground is heavily forested and has four developed campsites and room for additional rustic-style camping. Campground amenities include running water, restroom facilities, and stocked firewood. For additional information, please contact Airport Operations at 406-646-7631. Complimentary bicycles are provided by the airport and may be accessed by knowing your emergency frequency.

**** The Smokejumper Café – (406) 646-9060**
Proprietor: James Killinger
Open:

Mon: 11:00 am - 4:00 pm
Tue: Closed
Wed – Friday: 11:00 am - 4:00 pm
Sat – Sun: 9:00 am - 4:00 pm

Restaurant Website: www.smokejumpercafe.com
PIREP:

Don't go if you're in a hurry or if you don't like refilling your own coffee, it's a one-man operation but the food you eventually get is good. They have wonderful mountain view seating, inside and outside. Breakfast is the best time to come. This airport is the gateway to Yellowstone National Park. It is also one of the principle bases from which battles against forest fires that ravage the west in the summer are waged. You'll see some interesting aircraft here during those times.

FlyIn Nebraska

NORFOLK, NE (NORFOLK RGNL - OFK)
Aprt Mgr: MS TERRI WACHTER **PH:** 402-371-7210
Field Elevation: 1573 **CTAF:** 122.700 **FUEL:** 100LLA
Runway: 01/19 **Length:** 5800 **Width:** 100 **Surface:** ASPH-G
Runway: 14/32 **Length:** 5800 **Width:** 100 **Surface:** ASPH-G

Norfolk Airport Services – 402-379-7810
FBO Website: www.norfolkairportservices.com
Affiliate: UNK
Self Service: YES
Pilot Supplies: NO
Hours:
> M-F 7:00-7:00
> Sat. 7:00 - 5:00
> Sun 10:00 - 5:00

NORTH PLATTE, NE (NORTH PLATTE RGNL - LBF)
Aprt Mgr: MR. MIKE SHARKEY **PH:** 308-532-1900
Field Elevation: 2777 **CTAF:** 123.000 **FUEL:** 100LLA
Runway: 17/35 **Length:** 4436 **Width:** 100 **Surface:** ASPH-G
Runway: 12/30 **Length:** 8001 **Width:** 150 **Surface:** CONC-E

Trego/Dugan Aviation, Inc. – 308-532-5864
FBO Website: www.trego-dugan.com
Affiliate: Phillips
Self Service: NO
Pilot Supplies: YES
Hours: 7 days 6:00 – 9:00

*** Lincoln Highway Diner - 308-534-4340
Open:
> Mon - Sun: 7:00 am - 8:00 pm
Restaurant Email: neffcafe@gmail.com
PIREP:
If you like people come here on Sunday there'll be a crowd. This is a great Midwestern restaurant with good honest food and courteous service. I have eaten here only twice and have been pleased both times. It doesn't matter much what you eat it's all good but remember don't miss the Blueberry pie. As a matter of fact buy a whole one to take home with you.

SCOTTSBLUFF, NE (WESTERN NEB. RGNL - BFF)

John Purner

Aprt Mgr: DARWIN SKELTON **PH:** 308-635-4941
Field Elevation: 3967 **CTAF:** 123.000 **FUEL:** 100LLA
Runway: 05/23 **Length:** 8002 **Width:** 150 **Surface:** ASPH-G
Runway: 12/30 **Length:** 8279 **Width:** 150 **Surface:** ASPH-G

Valley Airways – 308-635-1331

FlyIn Nevada

DENIO, NV (DENIO JUNCTION - E85)
Aprt Mgr: JOHN RUSSUM **PH:** 775-623-6416
Field Elevation: 4202 **CTAF:** 122.900 **FUEL:** MOGAS
Runway: 07/25 **Length:** 3100 **Width:** 100 **Surface:** DIRT-F
Runway: 02/20 **Length:** 3320 **Width:** 42 **Surface:** DIRT-F
Runway: 13/31 **Length:** 3430 **Width:** 90 **Surface:** DIRT-F

*** Denio Junction Cafe - (775) 941-0171
Proprietor: Bobby Putney
Open:
> Mon - Sun: Breakfast, Lunch and Dinner

PIREP:
This stop is a long way from anywhere but very friendly. It is a dirt strip in really good shape. There is no avgas but you can taxi up to the gas station pumps and fuel up there. The premium blend didn't have any ethanol in it when I was there. The restaurant is friendly and has decent food. This isn't so much a destination as it is a stop along the way.

LAS VEGAS, NV (HENDERSON EXECUTIVE - HND)
Aprt Mgr: DENNIS ANDERSON **PH:** 702-261-4802
Field Elevation: 2492 **CTAF:** 125.100 **FUEL:** 100LLA
Runway: 17L/35R **Length:** 5001 **Width:** 75 **Surface:** ASPH-E
Runway: 17R/35L **Length:** 6501 **Width:** 100 **Surface:** ASPH-E

HND Aero – 702-261-4800
FBO Website: www.hnd.aero
Affiliate: UNK
Self Service: YES
Pilot Supplies: YES
Hours: 7 days 5:30 – 9:30

*** The Landings HND – (702) 616-3337
Proprietor: Marie
Open:
> Mon – Sun : 7:00 am – 4:00 pm

Restaurant Website: www.thelandingslv.com
PIREP:
I have never been here so I am including a **PIREP** from one of the subscribers to the $100 Hamburger website. Here it is:

John Purner

"The restaurant has a more upscale look than your typical airport restaurant. You enter the restaurant through a small and intimate bar. The bar has a casino Sports Book look to it with signed Muhammad Ali boxing gloves and three TV's tuned to different sports channels behind the bar that seats eight people. The restaurant seating area is open and inviting. The second story location of the restaurant allows for a great view of the runways and ramp area with window seat tables running along the entire length of the restaurant. Tie-down areas are generally pretty boring with your weathered 172's but this tarmac is a who's who of shiny corporate jets. At the back end of the restaurant there is a small outdoor seating area with both views of the runways and the lights of the Las Vegas Strip in the distance. I was there for breakfast and my omelet was adequate. But it did have the unusual ingredient of cactus which I have never seen offered before."

MINDEN, NV (MINDEN-TAHOE - MEV)
   Aprt Mgr: BOBBI THOMPSON **PH:** 775-782-9871
   Field Elevation: 4722 **CTAF:** 123.050 **FUEL:** 100LLA
   Runway: 16/34 **Length:** 7400 **Width:** 100 **Surface:** ASPH-E
   Runway: 12/30 **Length:** 5300 **Width:** 75 **Surface:** ASPH-G
   Runway: 12G/30G **Length:** 2200 **Width:** 60 **Surface:** DIRT-G

Sierra Skyport – 775-309-4423
FBO Website: www.sierraskyport.com
Affiliate: UNK
Self Service: YES
Pilot Supplies: NO
Hours: 24/7

Hutt Aviation – 775-782-8277
FBO Website: www.huttaviation.com
Affiliate: UNK
Self Service: NO
Pilot Supplies: YES
Hours: 7 days 8 – 5

*** The Taildragger Café - (775) 782-9500
Proprietor: Mary Getty
Open:
   Mon – Sun: 6:00 am – 8:00 pm
Restaurant Email: taildraggercafe@gmail.com
PIREP:
The scenery alone is worth the flight. There are two soaring outfits on the field. People that know about such things support one and throw stones at the other though honest soaring pilots disagree about which is which. They all seem to agree as do I that the food and service at **The**

Taildragger Café is awesome. I cannot comment on their breakfast as I've only been here for lunch.

YERINGTON, NV (YERINGTON MUNI - O43)
Airport Manager: DAN NEWELL **PH:** 775-463-3511
Field Elevation: 4382 **CTAF:** 122.800 **FUEL:** 100LL
Runway: 01/19 **Length:** 5814 **Width:** 75 **Surface:** ASPH-F

** McDonald's
Open:
> Mon – Sun: Breakfast, Lunch & Dinner

PIREP:
There is a **McDonald's** adjacent to the tie-down area, although perhaps a quarter-mile walk once exiting the perimeter fence gate. Yerington Municipal Airport has a pilot's lounge with restroom. Caution: No-radio aircraft operate out of Yerington as well as turbine aircraft. There have been two mid-air collisions in the past on approach to Runway 1, right over Main Street.

FlyIn New Hampshire

FRANCONIA, NH (FRANCONIA - 1B5)
    Aprt Mgr: JOSEPH M. KWASNIK **PH:** 603-730-7148
    Field Elevation: 978 **CTAF:** 122.800 **FUEL:**
    Runway: 18/36 **Length:** 2305 **Width:** 150 **Surface:** TURF-G

**** The Franconia Inn - 1-800-473-5299
Proprietor: Richard and Alec Morris
Open:
        Breakfast: 7:30am -9:30am
        Dinner: 6:00am -8:30pm
Restaurant Website: www.franconiainn.com
Restaurant Email: reservations@franconiainn.com
PIREP:
The Franconia Inn is an upscale and historic resort with its own turf
strip. They actually have one package which includes a stay at the
resort and a glider ride for each guest. Come up for breakfast once and
you'll be hooked. That's what happened to me. Be sure to make
reservation for breakfast or dinner. The food and service are amazing
and you don't want to be disappointed.

HAMPTON, NH (HAMPTON AIRFIELD - 7B3)
    Aprt Mgr: GEORGE FORREST **PH:** 603-964-6749
    Field Elevation: 93 **CTAF:** 122.800 **FUEL:** 100LLMOGAS
    Runway: 02/20 **Length:** 2100 **Width:** 170 **Surface:** TURF-G

**** Airfield Cafe - (603) 964-1654
Proprietor: The Aversano Family
Open:
        Mon - Sun: 7am – 2pm
Restaurant Website: www.theairfieldcafe.com
Restaurant Email: theairfieldcafe@comcast.net
PIREP:
Plan on a wait but plan to come. This is a wonderful New England
flyin. Breakfast is really good and is served all day. I love their
pancakes and always spring for the Maple Syrup. It cost extra and is
well worth it.

JAFFREY, NH (JAFFREY AIRPORT-SILVER RANCH - AFN)
    GEORGE FORREST 603-964-6749
    Aprt Mgr: HARVEY N SAWYER **PH:** 603-532-8870
    Field Elevation: 1040 **CTAF:** 122.800 **FUEL:** 100LL

Runway: 16/34 **Length:** 2982 **Width:** 134 **Surface: ASPH-TURF-F**

**** Kimball Farm - (603) 532-5765
Proprietor: Mike and Peter Kimball
Open:
SEASONAL
Restaurant Website: kimballfarm.com/jaffrey/
Restaurant Email: theairfieldcafe@comcast.net
PIREP:
OK, I'm bending our rule on this one just a bit. Truth be told it is not on the airport, it's on the airport perimeter. I like this place and I think you'll like it as well. Where else can you get a lobster roll *(hamburger burnout)* and terrific ice cream. This is a really, really great stop. They've been at it for eighty years so they must be doing something right.

NASHUA, NH (BOIRE FIELD - ASH)
Aprt Mgr: ROY RANKIN **PH:** 603-882-0661
Field Elevation: 199 **CTAF:** 133.200 **FUEL:** 100LLA1+
Runway: 14/32 **Length:** 5501 **Width:** 100 **Surface: ASPH**-F

Infinity Aviation – 603-598-4526
FBO Website: www.infinityfbo.com
Affiliate: Shell
Self Service: NO
Pilot Supplies: YES
Hours: 6:00 - 9:00 pm 7 days

*** The Midfield Cafe - (603) 594-0930
Proprietor: Fred Manhack
Open:
Mon - Sun: 7am – 2pm
Restaurant Website: sites.google.com/view/midfieldcafe/home
Restaurant Email: midfieldcafe@yahoo.com
PIREP:
Breakfast. I have been here for breakfast and it was good. It has all of the standard things you expect from an airport café:

You can taxi up and park on their ramp. Check!
They have a good view of the runway. Check!
They have an outdoor deck. Check!
They have a normal American breakfast and lunch menu. Check!

NEWPORT, NH (PARLIN FIELD - 2B3)
Aprt Mgr: RUSSELL KELSEA **PH:** 603-863-1220

John Purner

Field Elevation: 784 **CTAF:** 122.800 **FUEL:** 100LL
Runway: 18/36 **Length:** 3450 **Width:** 50 **Surface: ASPH**-E
Runway: 12/30 **Length:** 1950 **Width:** 80 **Surface:** TURF-G

Parlin Field – 603-863-1220
FBO Website: www.newportnh.net
Affiliate: Phillips
Self Service: YES
Pilot Supplies: YES
Hours: 24/7

FlyIn New Jersey

BLAIRSTOWN, NJ (BLAIRSTOWN - 1N7)
  Aprt Mgr: DENNIS KIERNAN **PH:** 908-362-8965
  Field Elevation: 372 **CTAF:** 123.000 **FUEL:** 100LL
  Runway: 07/25 **Length:** 3088 **Width:** 70 **Surface:** ASPH-G

 ✈ **Blairstown Airport** – 908-362-8956
Affiliate: Phillips 66
Self Service: YES
Pilot Supplies: YES
Hours: 24/7

*** Donna's Runway Cafe - (908) 362-1600
Proprietor: Jeanne Anderson
Open:
   Mon - Sun: Breakfast and Lunch
Restaurant Website: donnasrunwaycafe.net
PIREP:
Excellent parking spaces by the office and café. We're talking the
"pull-through" variety with chocks just sitting there waiting for you.
Very nice! The airport has a lot of gliding activity, but it is manageable.
This is a good place to interact with other pilots and see the gliders land
and takeoff. The food is worth the trip and made better by the attentive
service.

LINCOLN PARK, NJ (LINCOLN PARK - N07)
  Aprt Mgr: PETER DEROSA **PH:** 973-628-7166
  Field Elevation: 182 **CTAF:** 122.800 **FUEL:** 100LL
  Runway: 01/19 **Length:** 2942 **Width:** 40 **Surface:** ASPH-G

Lincoln Park Airport – 973-633-0450
Affiliate: Phillips 66
Self Service: YES
Pilot Supplies: YES
Hours: 24/7

**** Sunset Pub and Grill - 973 694 8700
Proprietor: Frank Skrek
Open:
   Mon –Wed: 11:30 am - 12:00pm
   Thurs: 11:30 am - 1:00 pm
   Fri: 11:30 am - 2:00 am
   Sat: 11:00 am -2:00 am

Sun: 11:00 am -12:00 am
Restaurant Website: www.sunsetpubandgrill.com
PIREP:
N07 is under the NYC class B, Teterboro and Morristown airports. Lots of traffic so be careful. The approach to runway 1 is sloping ground with high trees at the end of runway. If you are looking for a $100 Hamburger but want more of a regular, nice sit-down restaurant feel I recommend **Sunset Pub and Grill**. This is a full bar and restaurant with a large patio on the apron, so you watch airplanes. Think **Friday's** or **Hoolihan's**

LUMBERTON, NJ (FLYING W - N14)
Aprt Mgr: MINDY REDNER **PH:** 609-267-7673
Field Elevation: 49 **CTAF:** 122.800 **FUEL:** 100LLA
Runway: 01/19 **Length:** 3496 **Width:** 75 **Surface:** ASPH-G

**** Flying W - (609) 267-7673**
Proprietor: Heather Cave
Open:
Mon – Sun: 8 am - 2pm
Restaurant Website: www.flyingwairport.com
Restaurant Email: info@flyingwairport.com
PIREP:
This is the cafe in the operations building, not the old **Avion** restaurant. You can taxi right up to the restaurant. It is a burger and breakfast kinda' place in a unique location with amazing entertainment in the evening. Plus they've got a swimming pool.

MILLVILLE, NJ (MILLVILLE MUNI - MIV)
Aprt Mgr: MINDY REDNER **PH:** 609-267-7673
Field Elevation: 49 **CTAF:** 122.800 **FUEL:** 100LLA
Runway: 01/19 **Length:** 3496 **Width:** 75 **Surface:** ASPH-G

***** Verna's Flight Line Restaurant – (856) 825-3200**
Proprietor: Verna Herman
Open:
Mon - Sun: 6:00 am - 2:00 pm
Restaurant Email: vernasflightline@aol.com
PIREP:
In a word – tablecloths. That lets you know that this is a restaurant that sets high standards. The food is wonderful and the service impeccable. They have chalkboard breakfast and lunch specials every day. I once lucked into a COLD meatloaf sandwich – fabulous!

MOUNT HOLLY, NJ (SOUTH JERSEY RGNL - VAY)
Aprt Mgr: MINDY REDNER **PH:** 609-267-3131

Field Elevation: 53 **CTAF:** 122.800 **FUEL:** 100LLA
Runway: 08/26 **Length:** 3881 **Width:** 50 **Surface:** ASPH-G

South Jersey Airport – 609-267-3131
Affiliate: UNK
Self Service: YES
Pilot Supplies: YES
Hours: 8:00 - 6:00 7 days - JetA Self Serve 24/7 no LL Self Serve

---

*** Runway Cafe - (609) 518-0400
Proprietor: Vinci Lunt
Open:
> Tue - Sun: 8:00 am - 3:00 pm

PIREP:
This is a step up from your average $100 Hamburger stop. It's on the ramp and the food good and service is above adequate.

OCEAN CITY, NJ (OCEAN CITY MUNI - 26N)
Aprt Mgr: WILLIAM R COLANGELO **PH:** 609-525-9223
Field Elevation: 5 **CTAF:** 122.700 **FUEL:** 100LL
Runway: 06/24 **Length:** 2973 **Width:** 60 **Surface:** ASPH-G

The Beach

PIREP:

Yes, there was once an on-airport restaurant here. That was pre-COVID. It closed and has not yet been replaced.

This is a review of the entire area, with a huge sandy beach about an 8-minute walk to the East. The south end of the beach - near the airport - is undeveloped, while a further 10-minute walk north on the beach will lead to a well-developed boardwalk area, with the usual stores and restaurants.

This is a family friendly spot. No tattoo parlors, casinos, or even alcohol - I believe this is a 'dry' town - hardly an issue for pilots, of course! So very family oriented.

Be aware that beachgoers might be required to buy a beach pass for the day or season - it's about $10

PITTSTOWN, NJ (SKY MANOR - N40)
>**Aprt Mgr:** SKY MANOR AIRPORT PARTNERS **PH:** 908-996-4200
>**Field Elevation:** 560 **CTAF:** 122.975 **FUEL:** 100LL
>**Runway:** 07/25 **Length:** 2900 **Width:** 50 **Surface:** ASPH-G

>**Sky Manor** – 908-996-4200
>**Affiliate:** UNK
>**Self Service:** YES
>**Pilot Supplies:** YES
>**Hours:** 24/7

>***** Sky Café - (908) 996-3442**
>**Proprietor:** Rosella Caloiero
>**Open:**
>> Tue - Sun – 7:30am to 3:00pm
>
>**Restaurant Website**: skymanorairport.com/sky-cafe.htm
>**PIREP:**
>Rosella Caloiero has taken over this iconic stop from long-time operator Marty Lane. The weekend breakfast buffet is gone, and I miss it. The food and service are consistently good.

ROBBINSVILLE, NJ (TRENTON-ROBBINSVILLE - N87)
>**Aprt Mgr:** WILLIAM DEY **PH:** 609-259-1059
>**Field Elevation:** 118 **CTAF:** 123.000 **FUEL:** 100LL
>**Runway:** 11/29 **Length:** 4275 **Width:** 75 **Surface:** ASPH-F

>**Trenton - Robbins** – 609-259-1059
>**Affiliate:** UNK
>**Self Service:** YES
>**Pilot Supplies:** YES
>**Hours:** 24/7

>**Cutting Edge** – 609-259-0700
>**Affiliate:** UNK
>**Self Service:** YES
>**Pilot Supplies:** YES
>**Hours:** 24/7

SUSSEX, NJ (SUSSEX - FWN)
>**Aprt Mgr:** PAUL STYGER **PH:** 973-875-7337
>**Field Elevation:** 421 **CTAF:** 122.700 **FUEL:** A
>**Runway:** 03/21 **Length:** 3499 **Width:** 75 **Surface:** ASPH-F

>***** Airport Diner - (973) 702-7324**
>**Proprietor:** Laura Marran
>**Open:**

Mon - Sun: Breakfast and Lunch

PIREP:
A standard place with no surprises and one really good thing. The Chicken Caesar is really worth the stop. They have a self-serve pump so you can save a couple of bucks on fuel.

WEST MILFORD, NJ (GREENWOOD LAKE - 4N1)
Aprt Mgr: TIM WAGNER **PH:** 973-728-7721
Field Elevation: 790 **CTAF:** 122.900 **FUEL:** 100LLA
Runway: 06/24 **Length:** 3471 **Width:** 60 **Surface:** ASPH-G

Greenwood Lake Airport – 973-728-7721
Affiliate: Phillips 66
Self Service: YES
Pilot Supplies: YES
Hours: FS 9:00 - 5:00 7 days   Self Serve 24/7

WILDWOOD, NJ (CAPE MAY COUNTY - WWD)
Aprt Mgr: THOMAS BERRY **PH:** 609-886-8652
Field Elevation: 23 **CTAF:** 122.700 **FUEL:** 100LLA
Runway: 01/19 **Length:** 4998 **Width:** 150 **Surface:** ASPH-G
Runway: 10/28 **Length:** 4998 **Width:** 150 **Surface:** ASPH-G

*** The Flight Deck Dinner - 609-886-1105
Proprietor: Sean P. McMullan
Chef: DeJohin Nelson
Open:
Mon - Sun: 7:00 am - 2:00 pm
Restaurant Website: flightdeckdiner.com
Restaurant Email: flightdeckdiner@comcast.net
PIREP:
It is located in the terminal and seats about 40 folks total with 10 at a counter and 30 or so at various tables. They serve breakfast all day. The staff is friendly and the food is great and inexpensive. They are doing a great job. You will need to ask for the code to the gate to get back on the airfield.

John Purner

FlyIn New Mexico

ALAMOGORDO, NM (WHITE SANDS RGNL - ALM)
   Aprt Mgr: MATT MCNEILE **PH:** 575-439-4110
   Field Elevation: 4200 **CTAF:** 122.800 **FUEL:** 100LLA A1+
   Runway: 03/21 **Length:** 7006 **Width:** 150 **Surface:** ASPH-G
   Runway: 16/34 **Length:** 3512 **Width:** 200 **Surface:** DIRT-F

Exile Aviation – 575-437-2474
Affiliate: UNK
Self Service: NO
Pilot Supplies: YES
Hours: 7:00 - 6:00 7 days

**** Airport Grille - (575) 439-1093
Proprietor: Linda Madron
Open:
            Mon - Sat: 8:00am - 2:00pm
PIREP:
Homemade pies, I picked up a Lemon Meringue to take along with me.
This is a small well cared for diner with good food and happy servers.
This is a one woman show. Linda does it all!

RATON, NM (RATON MUNI/CREWS FIELD - RTN)
   Aprt Mgr: KEITH MANGELSDORF **PH:** 575-445-3076
   Field Elevation: 6352 **CTAF:** 122.800 **FUEL:** 100LLA1+
   Runway: 07/25 **Length:** 4404 **Width:** 75 **Surface:** ASPH-F
   Runway: 02/20 **Length:** 6328 **Width:** 75 **Surface:** ASPH-G

Express Aviation Services – 575-445-3076
Affiliate: Phillips 66
Self Service: NO
Pilot Supplies: YES
Hours: 24/7

*** Express Aviation Services - (575) 445-3076
Proprietor: Keith and Fern Manglesdorf
Open:
            Daily: Lunch
Restaurant Website: exaviationservices.com
Restaurant Email: info@exaviationservices.com
PIREP:

Express Aviation Services continues to provide their famous green chili and cheese hamburgers 7 days a week. Just call in your order when you are inbound, and they will have it waiting upon your arrival. I love this place.

SANTA FE, NM (SANTA FE MUNI - SAF)
Aprt Mgr: JAMES H. MONTMAN **PH:** 505-955-2900
Field Elevation: 6348 **CTAF:** 119.500 **FUEL:** 100LLA1 A1+
Runway: 15/33 **Length:** 6307 **Width:** 100 **Surface:** ASPH-E
Runway: 10/28 **Length:** 6300 **Width:** 75 **Surface:** ASPH-G
Runway: 02/20 **Length:** 8342 **Width:** 150 **Surface:** ASPH-G

Jet Center at Santa Fe – 505-780-4455
FBO Website: www.jetcentersf.com
Affiliate: Avfuel
Self Service: NO
Pilot Supplies: YES
Hours: 7:00 9:00 7days

Landmark Aviation – 505-471-2525
FBO Website: www.landmarkaviation.com
Affiliate: Phillips 66
Self Service: YES
Pilot Supplies: YES
Hours: 6:00 - 9:00 7 days

FlyIn New York

GANSEVOORT, NY (HEBER AIRPARK - K30)
Aprt Mgr: JAMES HEBER **PH:** 518-793-8983
Field Elevation: 230 **CTAF:** 122.900 **FUEL:**
Runway: 06/24 **Length:** 2200 **Width:** 24 **Surface:** ASPH-G

*** The Clubhouse Tavern – (518)792-4144
Proprietor: James and Joan Heber
Open:
>   Seasonal
>   Mon - Sun: 11am – 2pm

Restaurant Website: www.airwaymeadowsgolf.com
Restaurant Email: golfing@airwaymeadowsgolf.com
PIREP:
The runway is between the 2nd and 8th fairways, which makes a tricky landing over trees onto runway 6. If you're playing the course, they'll leave a golf-cart at the tie-down for you. The 18-hole course is challenging and worth the flight. The green fee with a cart is less than $50. It's a short walk across 9th fairway to the clubhouse and restaurant. They offer good food in a nice atmosphere.

GLENS FALLS, NY (FLOYD BENNETT MEMORIAL - GFL)
Aprt Mgr: DONALD DEGRAW **PH:** 518-792-5995
Field Elevation: 328 **CTAF:** 123.000 **FUEL:** 100LLA
Runway: 12/30 **Length:** 3999 **Width:** 100 **Surface:** ASPH-E
Runway: 01/19 **Length:** 5000 **Width:** 150 **Surface:** ASPH-G

Rich Air – 518-798-3091
FBO Website: www.flyrichair.com
Affiliate: Phillips 66
Self Service: YES
Pilot Supplies: YES
Hours: 8:00 - 6:00 7 days

ITHACA, NY (ITHACA TOMPKINS RGNL - ITH)
Aprt Mgr: ROBERT A NICHOLAS **Ph:** 607-257-0456
Field Elevation: 1099 CTAF: 119.600 FUEL: 100LLA
Runway: 14/32 **Length:** 6977 **Width:** 150 **Surface:** ASPH-G
Runway: 15/33 **Length:** 2018 **Width:** 50 **Surface:** TURF-E

*** The Second Landing – (607) 229-2880
Open:

Mon - Sun: 6:00am - 6:00pm
Restaurant Website: flyithaca.com/information/cafe/
Pirep:
It is a cafeteria-style food establishment with a limited menu in the main terminal building, a 5-minute walk from the FBO. Seating overlooks the runway. Great burger and fries served by a friendly staff.

It's not a destination unless you're coming in to tour the Glenn Curtis Museum which is nearby.

MILLBROOK, NY (SKY ACRES - 44N)
Aprt Mgr: GINNIE STYLES **PH:** 845-677-5010
Field Elevation: 698 **CTAF:** 122.800 **FUEL:** 100LL
Runway: 17/35 **Length:** 3830 **Width:** 60 **Surface:** ASPH-G

Sky Acres Airport – 845-677-5010
Affiliate: UNK
Self Service: YES
Pilot Supplies: YES
Hours: 24/7

*** Hangars Cafe - (845) 605-1991
Open:
Fri – Sun: 7:00am - 3:00pm
Restaurant Website: www.hangarscafe.com/
PIREP:
Its right next door to *HerGin Aviation's* pilot shop. I like to hang around the place and visit with the local pilot crowd. The Café is a diner at a fun airport with standard food.

MONTAUK, NY (MONTAUK - MTP)
Aprt Mgr: HELEN GILL **PH:** 631-668-3738
Field Elevation: 7 **CTAF:** 122.700 **FUEL:**
Runway: 06/24 **Length:** 3246 **Width:** 75 **Surface:** ASPH-G

***** Inlet Seafood Restaurant - (631) 668-4272
Open:
Seasonal: Mon - Sun: Lunch and Dinner
Restaurant Website: www.inletseafood.com
Restaurant Email: info@inletseafood.com
PIREP:
Walk north 10 minutes or less on the main road, toward the beach, to The Inlet, a great seafood restaurant and bar, complete with a deck overlooking the water and Montauk Harbor. This is another rule breaker as it's not on the airport, but this is such a great spot I decided to include it anyway. They have wonderful sushi, which can't be found

any fresher as The Inlet is owned and operated by six fishermen. While the sushi is good, I ALWAYS go with one of their scallop offerings.

They are all amazing!

After the meal, swim at the public beach (there is a large bathroom for changing); a bathroom and showers are available at KMTP before the flight home. This is one of my all-time favorite stops. It is also the ONLY walk to restaurant in this book. It is worth breaking the rule.

SARANAC LAKE, NY (ADIRONDACK RGNL - SLK)
Aprt Mgr: ROSS DUBARRY **PH:** 518-891-4600
Field Elevation: 1663 **CTAF:** 123.000 **FUEL:** 100LLA
Runway: 09/27 **Length:** 3998 **Width:** 100 **Surface:** ASPH-G
Runway: 05/23 **Length:** 6573 **Width:** 150 **Surface:** ASPH-G

Adirondack Regional – (518) 891-0164
Affiliate: Phillips 66
Self Service: NO
Pilot Supplies: YES
Hours: Winter/Spring 7:00 - 8:00   Summer/Fall 6:00 - 9:00

*** ADK CAVU Cafe – (518) 354-8063
Open:

Tues - Sun 7:00AM - 2:00PM.
Restaurant Website: adirondackairport.com/adirondack-cavu-cafe/
PIREP:
This is a glorious part of the world to fly over. I enjoy sitting down here to have a bite before heading out with my load of fall leaf watchers. The food is better than ordinary and the service acceptable.

WALLKILL, NY (KOBELT - N45)
Aprt Mgr: WILLIAM RICHARDS & KAY HOIBY-GRIEP
PH: 845-255-1087
Field Elevation: 420 **CTAF:** 122.800 **FUEL:** 100LL
Runway: 03/21 **Length:** 2864 **Width:** 50 **Surface:** ASPH-G

*** NU-CAVU – (845) 895-9000
Open:

Wed - Fri 4:00PM - 9:00PM
Sat – Sun 12:00PM – 9:00PM
Restaurant Website: **Restaurant Website:** www.nucavu.com
PIREP:
One of the better high-end restaurants at an airport. Great food and ambiance. Music some nights. Tricky airport to get into when there are cross winds, but worth the effort.

Reservations are required to secure a table on the weekends! Call a week, if not two weeks in advance!

WESTHAMPTON BEACH, NY (FRANCIS S GABRESKI - FOK)
Aprt Mgr: ANTHONY CEGLIO **PH:** 631-852-8095
Field Elevation: 66 **CTAF:** 125.300 **FUEL:** 100LLA
Runway: 01/19 **Length:** 5001 **Width:** 150 **Surface:** ASPH-CONC-G
Runway: 06/24 **Length:** 9001 **Width:** 150 **Surface:** ASPH-CONC-G
Runway: 15/33 **Length:** 5003 **Width:** 150 **Surface:** ASPH-F

Adirondack Regional – 518-891-4600
Affiliate: Phillips 66
Self Service: NO
Pilot Supplies: YES
Hours: 7:00 - 11:00 7days

WHITE PLAINS, NY (WESTCHESTER COUNTY - HPN)
Aprt Mgr: PETER SCHERRER **PH:** 914-995-4850
Field Elevation: 439 **CTAF:** 118.575 **FUEL:** 100LLA
Runway: 11/29 **Length:** 4451 **Width:** 150 **Surface:** ASPH-F
Runway: 16/34 **Length:** 6549 **Width:** 150 **Surface:** ASPH-G

Landmark Aviation – 888-359-7266
FBO Website: www.landmarkaviation.com
Affiliate: Shell
Self Service: NO
Pilot Supplies: YES
Hours: 6:00 - 11:00 7 days

FlyIn North Carolina

CARTHAGE, NC (GILLIAM - MC CONNELL AIRFIELD - 5NC3)
Aprt Mgr: S. ROLAND GILLIAM **PH:** 910-947-3599
Field Elevation: 445 **CTAF:** 0.000 **FUEL:** 100LL
Runway: 13/31 **Length:** 2538 **Width:** 36 **Surface:** ASPH-G

***** Pik N Pig BBQ - 910-947-7591
Proprietor: Janie Shepperd
Open:
> Tuesday thru Saturday: 11am - 8pm
> Sunday: Noon to 3pm

Restaurant Website: www.pik-n-pig.com
PIREP:

The airport is listed as Private so prior permission to land is required. The airport's phone number is (910) 947-3599. **Pik N Pig BBQ** is a family run restaurant right on the field, where planes line up on the grass. The BBQ stacks up with some of the best I've ever had. I love the Smoked Chicken and on one occasion was lucky enough to score some ribs which are normally only available on Saturday night.

CHARLOTTE, NC (CHARLOTTE/DOUGLAS INTL - CLT)
Aprt Mgr: JERRY ORR **PH:** 704-359-4000
Field Elevation: 748 **CTAF:** 0.000 **FUEL:** 100LLA
Runway: 05/23 **Length:** 7502 **Width:** 150 **Surface:** ASPH-CONC-G
Runway: 18L/36R **Length:** 8676 **Width:** 150 **Surface:** ASPH-CONC-G
Runway: 18R/36L **Length:** 9000 **Width:** 150 **Surface:** CONC-E
Runway: 18C/36C **Length:** 10000 **Width:** 150 **Surface:** CONC-F

Wilson Air Center – 704-359-0440
FBO Website: www.wilsonair.com
Affiliate: Shell
Self Service: NO
Pilot Supplies: YES
Hours: 24/7

*** Mr. G's - (704) 399-2542
Proprietor: George Stamoulis
Open:
> Mon - Fri: 7:00 am - 3:30 pm
> Sat: 9:00 am - 3:00 pm

PIREP:

Don't expect much from the décor – this is a true greasy spoon restaurant. Ceiling is yellow with grease and Jerry Springer is on the TV in the dining room. But you get a ton of good comfort food for your money. If you're at the main terminal you'll probably need a ride, it's a bit of a walk. It's over by the GA hangars, near the Museum, just outside the airport fence next to the National Guard facility. This is a popular spot with airport employees.

HICKORY, NC (HICKORY RGNL - HKY)
Aprt Mgr: TERRY CLARK **PH:** 828-323-7408
Field Elevation: 1190 **CTAF:** 128.150 **FUEL:** 100LLA
Runway: 01/19 **Length:** 4400 **Width:** 150 **Surface:** ASPH-G
Runway: 06/24 **Length:** 6400 **Width:** 150 **Surface:** ASPH-G

Hickory Regional – 828-327-0147
Affiliate: Shell
Self Service: YES
Pilot Supplies: YES
Hours: 7:00 - 7:00 7 days

*** Crosswind Cafe - 828-324-7800
Proprietor: Teresa Rozzelle
Open:
Monday - Friday: 8am – 3pm
Saturday: 8am – 2pm
Restaurant Website: www.crosswindcafe.com
Restaurant Email: Teresa@CrosswindCafe.com
PIREP:
It has a real chef and a nice menu. Friendly folks, reasonable prices.

RAEFORD, NC (P K AIRPARK - 5W4)
Aprt Mgr: GENE THACKER **PH:** 910-875-3261
Field Elevation: 304 **CTAF:** 123.000 **FUEL:** 100LLA+
Runway: 04/22 **Length:** 3402 **Width:** 60 **Surface:** ASPH-F

✈ Raeford Aviation – 910-875-3261
Affiliate: UNK
Self Service: NO
Pilot Supplies: YES
Hours: 9:00 - 7:00 7 days

*** PK's Aviator's Pub and Grill - (910) 904-6761
Proprietor: Thomas Wolfe
Open:
Mon - Sun: Breakfast, Lunch, Dinner
PIREP:

Super Hamburgers! Outstanding BBQ! They serve breakfast, lunch and dinner along with a great bar, pool tables and skydiving. The best part is, they are dirt cheap.

Be careful of MOA's and restricted airspace around Ft. Bragg and Pope AFB on the way in. We asked Fayette ATC to vector us in. They were tremendous. Call before you go to make sure the credit card machine for gas is working.

RALEIGH/DURHAM, NC (RALEIGH-DURHAM INTL - RDU)
Aprt Mgr: MICHAEL LANDGUTH **PH:** 919-840-7702
Field Elevation: 435 **CTAF:** 0.000 **FUEL:** 100LLA
Runway: 14/32 **Length:** 3570 **Width:** 100 **Surface:** ASPH-G
Runway: 05R/23L **Length:** 7500 **Width:** 150 **Surface:** ASPH-G
Runway: 05L/23R **Length:** 10000 **Width:** 150 **Surface:** CONC-G

Landmark Aviation – 919-840-2200
FBO Website: www.landmarkaviation.com
Affiliate: Shell
Self Service: NO
Pilot Supplies: YES
Hours: 24/7

TAC Air – 919-840-4400
FBO Website: www.tacair.com
Affiliate: Avfuel
Self Service: NO
Pilot Supplies: YES
Hours: 24/7

RUTHERFORDTON, NC (RUTHERFORD CO - FQD)
Aprt Mgr: AMY THOMAS **PH:** 828-287-0800
Field Elevation: 1077 **CTAF:** 122.800 **FUEL:** 100LLA1+
Runway: 01/19 **Length:** 5000 **Width:** 100 **Surface:** ASPH-G

Rutherford Co Air – 828-287-0800
Affiliate: UNK
Self Service: NO
Pilot Supplies: YES
Hours: 9:00 6:00 7 days

*** 57 Alpha Cafe - (828) 286-1677
Proprietor: Ron Mc Kinney
Open:
Tuesday – Sunday: 11:00 am - 2:00 pm
Restaurant Website: www.57alpha.com

PIREP:
Live Music On The Patio on Saturdays, April thru October. The food is fresh, and the surroundings are friendly and uplifting. Try this if you enjoy a day away from the rat race. This is a small place with very limited seating indoors but has picnic tables outside. Its banana pudding is legendary in the area.

SMITHFIELD, NC (JOHNSTON COUNTY - JNX)
Aprt Mgr: RAY BLACKMON **PH:** 919-934-0992
Field Elevation: 164 **CTAF:** 122.800 **FUEL:** 100LLA1+
Runway: 03/21 **Length:** 5500 **Width:** 100 **Surface:** ASPH-G

*** Low and Slow Smokehouse - (919) 578-6479
Open:
>Mon – Thur: 11:00 am - 9:00 pm
>Fri – Sat: 8:00am – 9:00pm
>Sun: 8:00am – 8:00pm

Restaurant Website: www.lowandslowsmokehouse.com
PIREP:
Great airport with lots of planes. Food is very good with a variety of BBQ, brisket, chicken and burgers. 3rd floor with an outside eating area with a great view of the runway and tie down area. Lots of locals so you know the food is worth the trip.

Hit this place on the weekends for a GREAT breakfast.

FlyIn North Dakota

FARGO, ND (HECTOR INTL - FAR)
Aprt Mgr: SHAWN DOBBERSTEIN **PH:** 701-241-1501
Field Elevation: 901 **CTAF:** 0.000 **FUEL:** 100LLA
Runway: 13/31 **Length:** 3801 **Width:** 150 **Surface:** ASPH-CONC-G
Runway: 09/27 **Length:** 6302 **Width:** 100 **Surface:** CONC-G
Runway: 18/36 **Length:** 9001 **Width:** 150 **Surface:** CONC-G

Fargo Jet Center – 701-373-8800
FBO Website: www.fargojet.com
Affiliate: Avfuel
Self Service: NO
Pilot Supplies: YES
Hours: 24/7

** Skydine Restaurant - (701) 356-2124
Proprietor: Candie Valadez
Open:
        Mon-Fri : 5:00am to Last Departure
        Sat-Sun: 6:00am to Last Departure
Restaurant Website: www.fargoairport.com/tenants.html
Restaurant Email: fargoairport@marlinsfamilyrestaurant.com
PIREP:
This restaurant is located in the scheduled service passenger service. It is what you would expect it to be; a place to hang out during a flight delay and a place to pick-up "grab and go food". The best that can be said is the ambiance and the food are serviceable.

GRAND FORKS, ND (GRAND FORKS INTL - GFK)
Aprt Mgr: PATRICK DAME **PH:** 701-795-6981
Field Elevation: 845 **CTAF:** 118.400 **FUEL:** 100LLA
Runway: 17R/35L **Length:** 7351 **Width:** 150 **Surface:** ASPH-F
Runway: 09R/27L **Length:** 3300 **Width:** 60 **Surface:** CONC
Runway: 17L/35R **Length:** 3901 **Width:** 75 **Surface:** CONC-F
Runway: 09L/27R **Length:** 4206 **Width:** 100 **Surface:** CONC-G

AvFlight – 701-772-5504
FBO Website: www.avflight.com
Affiliate: Avfuel
Self Service: NO
Pilot Supplies: YES
Hours: 4:00 - 10:00 7 days

** Red River Valley Grill and Market - (701) 738-4630
Proprietor: Oakwells Stores
Open:
Mon - Sun: 5:00 am - 6:00 pm
Restaurant Website: www.gfkairport.com
PIREP:
If you're stuck at the airport and you're hungry, as in starving, this place will suffice. It is in the main passenger terminal and will require a trip through security.

FlyIn Ohio

CARROLLTON, OH (CARROLL COUNTY-TOLSON - TSO)
Aprt Mgr: ALAN MILLER **PH:** 330-627-5501
Field Elevation: 1163 **CTAF:** 122.700 **FUEL:** 100LLA
Runway: 07/25 **Length:** 4297 **Width:** 75 **Surface:** ASPH-G

✈ **Carroll County Airport** – 330-627-5250
Affiliate: Phillips 66
Self Service: YES
Pilot Supplies: YES
Hours: 24/7

*** **Carroll County Airport Restaurant - (330) 627-5250**
Proprietor: Lisa McCord
Manager: Rhonda Vincent
Open:
> Mon - Sun: 7:00am - 7:00pm
Restaurant Email: am332904@gmail.com
PIREP:
Great home cooked food, nice folks, and a good view of airplanes. Lisa McCord does everything from scratch. The food is **WONDERFUL**. Her specialty is a wide variety of homemade pies *(try the mint Oreo)*. This is a Pies Place!

CINCINNATI, OH (LUNKEN FIELD - LUK)
Aprt Mgr: FRED ANDERTON **PH:** 513-352-6340
Field Elevation: 483 **CTAF:** 118.700 **FUEL:** 100LLA+
Runway: 03L/21R **Length:** 3802 **Width:** 100 **Surface:** ASPH-F
Runway: 07/25 **Length:** 5128 **Width:** 100 **Surface:** ASPH-F
Runway: 03R/21L **Length:** 6101 **Width:** 150 **Surface:** ASPH-F

Landmark Aviation – 513-871-8600
Affiliate: UNK
Self Service: NO
Pilot Supplies: YES
Hours: 5:00-12:00 7 days

COLUMBUS, OH (BOLTON FIELD - TZR)
Aprt Mgr: CHARLIE GOODWIN **PH:** 614-851-9900
Field Elevation: 905 **CTAF:** 128.100 **FUEL:** 100LLA1+
Runway: 04/22 **Length:** 5500 **Width:** 100 **Surface:** ASPH-F

Capital City Jet Center – 877-403-1200

FBO Website: www.capitalcityjet.com
Affiliate: Avfuel
Self Service: NO
Pilot Supplies: YES
Hours: 7:00 - 9:00 7 days

*** JP's Ribs - 614-878-7422
Proprietor: The Makar Family
Open:

> Mon: 11:00am - 3:00pm
> Tues-Fri: 11:00am - 8:00pm
> Sat-Sun: 12:00am - 8:00pm

Restaurant Website: www.jpsbbq.com
PIREP:
Come for the Ribs, you'll be glad you did. Stay for the fun. This is the only place I've found that has horseshoes, volleyball and putt-putt plus a HUGE outdoor patio.

COLUMBUS, OH (OHIO STATE UNIVERSITY - OSU)
Airport Mgr: DOUGLAS E. HAMMON **PH:** 614-292-5460
Field Elevation: 906 **CTAF:** 118.800 **FUEL:** 100LLA1+
Runway: 09L/27R **Length:** 2994 **Width:** 100 **Surface:** ASPH-F
Runway: 14/32 **Length:** 3049 **Width:** 100 **Surface:** ASPH-F
Runway: 05/23 **Length:** 3562 **Width:** 100 **Surface:** ASPH-F
Runway: 09R/27L **Length:** 5004 **Width:** 100 **Surface:** ASPH-F

**** Jack & Benny's Barnstormer Diner - 614-292-5699
Proprietor: Geno Garcia
Open:

> **Mon – Fri:** 7:00am - 3:00pm
> **Sat & Sun:** 8:00am - 3:00pm

Restaurant Website: www.jackandbennys.com
PIREP:
Come for breakfast and come hungry. Try the **"Gut Buster"**. The name is a dead giveaway of the experience. Eggs and breakfast meats stacked on top of a potato pancake and hash browns covered with cheese and smothered with country gravy. The ramp fee is waived for single-engine aircraft when you eat at the restaurant.

COLUMBUS, OH (PORT COLUMBUS INTL - CMH)
Aprt Mgr: "ELAINE ROBERTS, A.A.E." **PH:** 614-239-4000
Field Elevation: 815 **CTAF:** 0.000 **FUEL:** 100 A1+
Runway: 10L/28R **Length:** 8000 **Width:** 150 **Surface:** ASPH-G
Runway: 10R/28L **Length:** 10125 **Width:** 150 **Surface:** ASPH-G

Lane Aviation – 800-848-6263

FBO Website: www.laneaviation.com
Affiliate: Phillips 66
Self Service: NO
Pilot Supplies: YES
Hours: 24/7

Landmark Aviation – 614-238-3900
FBO Website: www.landmarkaviation.com
Affiliate: UNK
Self Service: NO
Pilot Supplies: YES
Hours: 6:00 - 11:00 7 days

***** 94th Aero Squadron - 614-237-8887
Proprietor: Chad Pew
Manager: Tom Kanbybowicz
Open:

Monday - Thursday: 4:00pm -9:00pm
Friday - Saturday: 4:00pm - 10:00pm
Sunday Brunch: 10:00am - 2:30pm
Sunday Dinner: 3:00pm - 8:00pm

Restaurant Website: www.the94thaerocolumbus.com/
PIREP:
The **94th Aero Squadron** has been a tradition in central Ohio for nearly 30 years. It is a great place to enjoy a sizzling steak dinner while watching the arriving and departing traffic just outside the huge windows of this 1914 French farmhouse replica. It sits immediately off of runway 10R/28L Either FBO will be pleased to give you a ride over and pick you up when you're ready.

MOUNT VICTORY, OH (ELLIOTTS LANDING - O74)
Aprt Mgr: EDWARD ELLIOTT II **PH:** 937-354-2851
Field Elevation: 1045 **CTAF:** 122.900 **FUEL:**
Runway: 15/33 **Length:** 2750 **Width:** 110 **Surface:** TURF-F

**** Plaza Inn - (937) 354-2851
Proprietor: Joan Wagner and Ed Elliot
Open:

Monday - Sunday: Breakfast, Lunch & Dinner

Restaurant Website: www.plazainn.net
Restaurant Email: plazainn@plazainn.net
PIREP:
The strip is 2,800 feet of turf. It can be bumpy, but it's usually mowed. Tie-down areas are available on the ramp BUT you must bring your own tie downs. There is no fuel at this airport, which is good and bad.

Good because you don't have to buy any and bad because you're in a pickle if you need it.

The restaurant is a treat. Get your mouth set for home cooking. The Plaza Inn has been in business since 1959 and has grown from 42 to 250 seats so they must be doing something right. I like this spot a bunch because I like family restaurants, and this is a great example. They offer a menu and a buffet. Think BBQ.

NEW PHILADELPHIA, OH (HARRY CLEVER FIELD - PHD)
Airport Manager: ERIC HUBBARD **PH:** 330-339-6078
Field Elevation: 894 **CTAF: 122.800 FUEL: 100LLA+**
Runway: 14/32 **Length:** 3951 **Width:** 100 **Surface:** ASPH-G
Runway: 11/29 **Length:** 1907 **Width:** 70 **Surface:** TURF-F

* Magoo's Pizza Pasta and More - (330) 365-1466
Proprietor: Calvin Schwartz
Open:
                Tue - Sat: 4pm – 10pm
Restaurant Website: www.facebook.com/maggoospizza
Restaurant Email: maggoosppm@aol.com
PIREP:
I've been here once. It is now open for dinner only no lunch. The food is simply OK. The service is someplace south of awful.

PORT CLINTON, OH (CARL R KELLER FIELD - PCW)
Aprt Mgr: JACK STABLES **PH:** 419-734-6297
Field Elevation: 590 **CTAF:** 122.800 **FUEL:** 100LLA
Runway: 09/27 **Length:** 5646 **Width:** 100 **Surface:** ASPH-E
Runway: 18/36 **Length:** 4001 **Width:** 75 **Surface:** ASPH-F

Erie Ottawa Int'l Airport – 419-734-6297
Affiliate: Phillips 66
Self Service: YES
Pilot Supplies: YES
Hours: 7:00 - 6:00 7 days

***** Tin Goose Diner - (419) 732-0236
Proprietor: Joan Wagner and Ed Elliot
Open: CURENTLY CLOSED
PIREP:
Scheduled to re-open in the late spring of 2023.

This diner is authentic, built by the Jerry O'Mahony Diner Company of Elizabeth, New Jersey, in the 1950's. It was originally operated as the Sunrise Diner in Jim Thorpe, Pennsylvania. The food is wonderful

John Purner

diner food straight out of the '50s. Want a malt? This is the place to get it. All proceeds from this diner help fund the operation of the Liberty Aviation Museum.

Liberty Aviation Museum - (419) 732-0234
Open: CURRENTLY CLOSED
Restaurant Website: www.libertyaviationmuseum.org
Restaurant Email: info@libertyaviationmuseum.org
PIREP:
Hoping to reopen in the late spring of 2023.

One reason to come to the **Tin Goose Diner** is its connection with the **Liberty Aviation Museum**. Here you'll find a few (*very few*) examples from *The Golden Age of Aviation* and they are all wonderfully presented. They also have a PT Boat and some other WWII gear.

PORTSMOUTH, OH (GREATER PORTSMOUTH RGNL - PMH)
Aprt Mgr: PAUL BROGDON **PH:** 740-820-2700
Field Elevation: 663 **CTAF:** 122.800 **FUEL:** 100LLA1+
Runway: 18/36 **Length:** 5001 **Width:** 100 **Surface:** ASPH-G

*** Skyline Family Restaurant – (740) 820-2203
Proprietor: Robert Montgomery
Manager: Beverly
Open:
　　　Monday - Sunday: 7am – 8pm
PIREP:
The restaurant is in the terminal with parking right out front. Home Style Cooking, Breakfast served all day. If you're there for lunch give the meatloaf sandwich a try. It's my favorite.

URBANA, OH (GRIMES FIELD - I74)
Aprt Mgr: CAROL HALL **PH:** 937-652-4319
Field Elevation: 1068 **CTAF:** 122.700 **FUEL:** 100LLA
Runway: 02/20 **Length:** 4400 **Width:** 100 **Surface:** ASPH-G

Grimes Field – 937-652-4319
FBO Website: www.urbanaohio.com
Affiliate: Phillips 66
Self Service: YES
Pilot Supplies: YES
Hours: 24/7

*** Airport Cafe - 937-484-2010
Open:
　　　Tue - Sat: 7am – 8:30pm

160

Sun: 8am-2:30pm
PIREP:
This is another example of a Midwestern on-airport family restaurant. They are all good and this one certainly measures up with some of the best. They claim to have the *"Best Pies and the Skies"*. I can't argue with that assessment.

While here you'll want to visit the museum and see the B-17 they are restoring.

Champaign Aviation Museum - (937) 652-4710
Open:
Tue- Sat: 10am to 4pm
Museum Website: www.champaignaviationmuseum.org
PIREP:
Open to the public with **FREE** admission. They have a B-17 which is undergoing restoration and a few very nice WWII era Warbirds.

FlyIn Oklahoma

AFTON, OK (GRAND LAKE RGNL - 3O9)
Aprt Mgr: DUANE MAYNARD **PH:** 918-257-2400
Field Elevation: 792 **CTAF:** 122.700 **FUEL:** 100LLA
Runway: 17/35 **Length:** 3925 **Width:** 60 **Surface:** CONC-G

✈ **Grand Lake Regional** – 918-257-8602
Self Service: YES
Pilot Supplies: YES
Hours: 24/7

ARDMORE, OK (ARDMORE MUNI - ADM)
Aprt Mgr: CHRIS BRYANT **PH:** 580-389-5238
Field Elevation: 777 **CTAF:** 118.500 **FUEL:** 100LLA
Runway: 17/35 **Length:** 5350 **Width:** 100 **Surface:** ASPH-G
Runway: 13/31 **Length:** 9001 **Width:** 150 **Surface:** CONC-E

Lakeland Aviation – 937-652-4319
FBO Website: www.lakelandaviation.com
Affiliate: Phillips 66
Self Service: NO
Pilot Supplies: YES
Hours: M-F 7:00 - 7:00 Sat & Sun 8:00 - 5:00

Small Business Aviation – 580-362-6977
Affiliate: Avfuel
Self Service: YES
Pilot Supplies: YES
Hours: M-F 7:00 - 7:00 Sat & Sun Call out

***** **Jake's Joint** – (580) 389-5040
Proprietor: Jerry Allan King-Echevarria - JAKE
Open:
        Mon – Fri: 11am to 2pm
Restaurant Website: www.jakesjointrestaurant.com
Restaurant Email: lcore@kingaerospace.com
PIREP:
This place is perfect with one BIG exception. It is my personal favorite flyin restaurant in this part of the galaxy.

First for the good news, all food is prepared by a chef who is a graduate of the Culinary Institute of America. All desserts are home made, and many are **JAKE's** favorite recipes from his home and ranch. When you order an "alcoholic drink" at **JAKE'S JOINT** it is going to be **JAKE's** very own Puerto Rican Bacardi Superior Rum in a tall glass with two limes and diet coke. The best thing on the menu changes every day. It's **JAKE'S Blue Plate Special** which comes with your choice of two sides, yeast rolls and dessert and a drink for ten bucks. **JAKE** hopes that you enjoy your meal but it's to his standards and no one else's! Needless to say that is why the place is called **JAKE'S JOINT** where the food is truly **"Food Fit for a King!"**

So, what's the problem? Easy, it is not open on the weekends. That's too bad for this is the best fly-in restaurant in America.

ENID, OK (ENID WOODRING RGNL - WDG)
Aprt Mgr: DAN OHNESORGE **PH:** 580-234-5476
Field Elevation: 1167 **CTAF:** 118.900 **FUEL:** 100LLA
Runway: 13/31 **Length:** 3149 **Width:** 108 **Surface:** ASPH-G
Runway: 17/35 **Length:** 6249 **Width:** 100 **Surface:** CONC-G

City of Enid – 800-259-5476
Affiliate: Phillips 66
Self Service: YES
Pilot Supplies: YES
Hours: 6 – 6 7days

*** The Barnstormer - (580) 234-9913
Restaurant Website: www.flyenid.com/barnstormers.php
Open:
Mon – Fri: 8am- 2pm
Sat – Sun: CLOSED
PIREP:
The Barnstormer has an expansive circular floor to ceiling glass window that overlooks the airport. Through it you'll see young Air Force pilots in training doing touch and goes as you eat some of the best and most artery clogging food you've ever had. Even the club sandwich is grilled! I love this place. It is covered with model airplanes and populated by hangar flying pilots.

NORMAN, OK (UNIVERSITY OF OKLAHOMA - OUN)
Aprt Mgr: WALT STRONG **PH:** 405-325-7233
Field Elevation: 1182 **CTAF:** 118.000 **FUEL:** 100LLA
Runway: 03/21 **Length:** 4748 **Width:** 100 **Surface:** ASPH-G
Runway: 17/35 **Length:** 5199 **Width:** 100 **Surface:** ASPH-G

Cruise Aviation – 405-360-3900
Affiliate: Phillips 66
Self Service: NO
Pilot Supplies: YES
Hours: 7:00 -10:00 7 days

OKLAHOMA CITY, OK (WILEY POST - PWA)
Aprt Mgr: TIM WHITMAN **PH:** 405-789-4061
Field Elevation: 1300 **CTAF:** 126.900 **FUEL:** 100LLA
Runway: 17R/35L **Length:** 5002 **Width:** 75 **Surface:** CONC-G
Runway: 13/31 **Length:** 4214 **Width:** 100 **Surface:** CONC-G
Runway: 17L/35R **Length:** 7199 **Width:** 150 **Surface:** CONC-G

Atlantic Aviation – 405-787-4040
FBO Website: www.atlanticaviation.com
Affiliate: UNK
Self Service: NO
Pilot Supplies: YES
Hours: 4:00 - 12:00 7 days

Valair Aviation – 405-516-3338
FBO Website: www.valairaviation.com
Affiliate: Phillips 66
Self Service: NO
Pilot Supplies: YES
Hours: 24 hours 7 days

**** Annie Okie's Runway Cafe - (405) 787-7732
Open:

> Mon – Sat: 7am-3pm.
> Sun: 8am-3pm.

Restaurant Website:
PIREP:
You can keep an eye on your airplane from the restaurant atrium. The food is excellent especially the omelets and the burgers. This place really fills up on the weekends.

Do not pass up the cinnamon rolls. Just don't!

PONCA CITY, OK (PONCA CITY RGNL - PNC)
Aprt Mgr: DON NUZUM **PH:** 580-767-0470
Field Elevation: 1008 **CTAF:** 123.000 **FUEL:** 100LLA
Runway: 17/35 **Length:** 7201 **Width:** 150 **Surface:** CONC-F

PNC Fuel – 580-767-0470
FBO Website: www.poncacityok.gov

Affiliate: Phillips 66
Self Service: YES
Pilot Supplies: YES
Hours: 7:00 - 7:00 7 days

*** Enrique's Mexican Restaurant - (580) 762-5507
Proprietor: Michael Avila
Open:
> Mon – Fri: 11am- 2pm
> Mon – Fri: 4:30pm-9pm
> Sat: 11am – 9 pm
> Sun: CLOSED

Restaurant Email: michael.avila@yahoo.com
PIREP:
I love Mexican food and I love flying put the two together and I'm good to go. Enrique's has been serving some of the best Mexican food I have ever eaten since 1982 and doing it from the present runway location. Enrique's was a five-peat on the **$100 Hamburger Best of the Best.**

They survived the COVID crisis and deserve your business.

TULSA, OK (TULSA INTL - TUL)
Airport Manager: JEFF MULDER **PH:** 918-838-5000
Field Elevation: 678 **CTAF:** 0.000 **FUEL:** 100LLA A1 B
Runway: 18R/36L **Length:** 6101 **Width:** 150 **Surface:** ASPH-F
Runway: 08/26 **Length:** 7376 **Width:** 150 **Surface:** CONC-G
Runway: 18L/36R **Length:** 10000 **Width:** 200 **Surface:** CONC-G

***** Evelyn's Soul Food Café – 918-835-1212
Proprietor: Wanda J
Open:
> Mon – Fri: 7:30am - 3pm

Restaurant Website: evelynsoulfood.com
PIREP:
Why five stars? This is the only flyin genuine Soul Food restaurant in the world and the food and service deserve five stars. Okra And Tomatoes? You bet! That's reason number one. Reason number two is a list of daily Specials at around $10 or less that will make your mouth water. It's a meat and two kinda' place. Monday starts the week with Meatloaf and gravy for $8.99. Here's reason number three: All the dessert you can eat for $2.99 and dessert is the best peach cobbler you've ever had.

FlyIn Oregon

John Purner

BEND, OR (BEND MUNI - BDN)
     Aprt Mgr: GARY JUDD **PH:** 541-389-0258
     Field Elevation: 3460 **CTAF:** 123.000 **FUEL:** 100LLA
     Runway: 16/34 **Length:** 5200 **Width:** 75 **Surface:** ASPH-E

Professional Air – 541-388-0019
FBO Website: www.professionalair.com
Affiliate: Phillips 66
Self Service: YES
Pilot Supplies: YES
Hours: 24/7

*** CJ's at the Airport – 541-317-4153
Open:
     Mon - Sun: 8:00 am – 2:00 pm
Restaurant Website: www.cjsattheairport.com/
PIREP:
Not everyone can cook and egg and few have the courage to attempt French Toast. At CJ's they can do both very well. I've come here for lunch too. When you do jump on **CJ'S BURGER$.** Here's how the menu describes it. Grass fed beef, crispy bacon, gouda, caramelized onions, dijonnaise, brioche bun.

'Nuff said about the food.

Flying here is the fun part. No matter your route, it's a beautiful trip. Enjoy!

INDEPENDENCE, OR (INDEPENDENCE STATE - 7S5)
     Aprt Mgr: STATE AIRPORTS MANAGER **PH:** 503-378-8689
     Field Elevation: 180 **CTAF:** 122.800 **FUEL:** 100LL80
     Runway: 16/34 **Length:** 3142 **Width:** 60 **Surface:** ASPH-G

*** The Starduster Café – (503) 838-1781
Open:
     Mon - Sun: 6 am – 3 pm
PIREP:
The airport includes approximately150 airpark homes and the Starduster Café. This is a neighborhood any pilot would want to call home. The cafe opens early and stays open for the mid-afternoon lunch crowd. In warmer weather, it's nice to sit on the outside deck and watch airplanes take off and land. The food is good, the portions generous, the service faithful and the prices humble.

MC MINNVILLE, OR (MC MINNVILLE MUNI - MMV)
Field Elevation: 163 **CTAF:** 123.000 **FUEL:** 100LLA
Runway: 17/35 **Length:** 4340 **Width:** 75 **Surface:** ASPH-E
Runway: 04/22 **Length:** 5420 **Width:** 150 **Surface:** ASPH-G

**** The Spruce Goose – (503) 434-4180
Open:
> Mon – Fri 10am – 5pm
> Sat – Sun 9am – 5pm

Restaurant Website: www.evergreenmuseum.org/
PIREP:
Let's face it; no one comes here for the food. They come here because the **Evergreen Aviation and Space Museum** is here and it provides a home for the Spruce Goose. What pilot doesn't want to see it? While you're here, the hungries will hit 'ya and they've got an answer for that. *The Liberty Belle Café* and *Cosmo Café* both serve the unique and special flavors of local farms. The food is actually very good.

The Aviation Museum houses the *Liberty Belle Café*, which is open Weekdays – 10am to 5pm and Weekends – 9am to 5pm. The Space Museum hosts the Cosmo Café, which is open seasonally and on Saturdays only.

SALEM, OR (MCNARY FLD - SLE)
Aprt Mgr: JOHN PASKELL **PH:** 503-588-6314
Field Elevation: 214 **CTAF:** 119.100 **FUEL:** 100LLA
Runway: 16/34 **Length:** 5145 **Width:** 100 **Surface:** ASPH-G
Runway: 13/31 **Length:** 5811 **Width:** 150 **Surface:** ASPH-G

Salem Air Center – 503-364-0111
Affiliate: UNK
Self Service: YES
Pilot Supplies: YES
Hours: Mon - Fri 7:00 - 7:00 Sat & Sun 7:00 - 5:00

**** Flight Deck Restaurant and Lounge - (503) 581-5721
Proprietor: Natalie Frajola and Barry Bowers
Open:
> Mon - Fri: 11:00 am - 9:00 pm
> Sat - Sun: 8:00 am - 9:00 pm

Restaurant Website: www. flightdeckrestaurant.com
Restaurant Email: dine@flightdeckrestaurant.com
PIREP:
The Flight Deck Restaurant offers a spectacular view of the Cascade Mountains as well as landing and departing aircraft. The food is

167

extraordinary; you'll certainly not be disappointed whether you order a steak, a burger or anything in between. Their clam chowder has won statewide awards (there is a large plaque on the wall by the cash register.) It is much better than any of the "famous" chowder places you find along the coast. The Willamette Valley of Oregon is known for flavorful berries. **The Flight Deck** chef makes good use of them in a triple berry cobbler that must not be missed.

TILLAMOOK, OR (TILLAMOOK - TMK)
Aprt Mgr: COLBY LOVITT **PH:** 503-842-2413
Field Elevation: 36 **CTAF:** 122.800 **FUEL:** 100LLA
Runway: 01/19 **Length:** 2910 **Width:** 75 **Surface:** ASPH-G
Runway: 13/31 **Length:** 5001 **Width:** 100 **Surface:** ASPH-G

Port of Tillamook Bay – 503-842-7152
Affiliate: UNK
Self Service: YES
Pilot Supplies: YES
Hours: 24/7

*** Fat Head BBQ and Catering - (503) 815-1786
Open:
Wed - Sun 11:00am – 4:00pm
Restaurant Website: fatheadbbq.com/
Restaurant Email: FatHeadBBQ2021@gmail.com
PIREP:
Fat Head BBQ and Catering is inside the **Tillamook Air Museum**. The good news is that you can taxi to the museum's ramp. Fat Head BBQ is a counter service only restaurant. They use smoke to create unique spins on classics. Don't be surprised if they run out of certain products.

First come, first serve.

Tillamook Air Museum - (503) 842-1130
Museum Curator: Christian Gurling
Open:
Mon - Sun: 9:00 am - 5:00 pm
Restaurant Website: www.tillamookair.com
Restaurant Email: info@tillamookair.com
PIREP:
The Tillamook Air Museum is one of the world's premiere air museums. Its collection is displayed inside the largest wooden structure in the world. Many of its airplanes are flyable and rides can be purchased in them. As you would imagine the collection includes many WWII era warbirds including a B-17. What is unusual is the mix of

modern era fighters including an F-14. The hangar that houses the collection was built in WWII as a home for eight K Class blimps.

FlyIn Pennsylvania

BALLY, PA (BUTTER VALLEY GOLF PORT - 7N8)
    Aprt Mgr: JOHN L. GEHMAN **PH:** 610-845-2491
    Field Elevation: 500 **CTAF:** 122.800 **FUEL:**
    Runway: 16/34 **Length:** 2420 **Width:** 85 **Surface:** ASPH-TURF-G

** Runway Grill - 610-845-2491
Grill Manager: Connie Babb
Open:
    Seasonal Closed: November 1 thru April 1
    Daily: 11:30 am – 2:30 pm
Restaurant Website: buttervalley.com/runway-grill/
Restaurant Email: connie@buttervalley.com
PIREP:
Located in the club house of the Butter Valley Golfport. The Runway is a fun destination. You can watch planes land and golfers finish their round from behind the massive windows. It's a breakfast and burger kinda' place that offers tasty food and friendly service for golfers and pilots.

**** Butter Valley Golf Club- 610-845-2491
Proprietor: John Gehman
Open:
    Seasonal
    Daily
Restaurant Website: www.buttervalley.com
Restaurant Email: connie@buttervalley.com
PIREP: I love golf and I love airplanes and I hate pretension. This place was built for me. It's beautiful rolling terrain, without condos or other nearby buildings, provides the same natural feeling that you experienced on golf courses decades ago. It's the perfect place to "Renew the Spirit" with family and friends. That experience begins when you line up for landing. The strip is in the center of the golf course. It is rolling and short at just 2,500 feet. Half is asphalt and half is turf. When you tiedown, a golf cart will appear to drive you to the club house.

BUTLER, PA (BUTLER COUNTY/K W SCHOLTER FIELD - BTP)
    Aprt Mgr: JOHN L. GEHMAN **PH:** 724-586-6665
    Field Elevation: 500 **CTAF:** 122.800 **FUEL:**
    Runway: 16/34 **Length:** 2420 **Width:** 85 **Surface:** ASPH-TURF-G

AirQuest Aviation – 724-586-6023

FBO Website: www.airquestaviation.com
Affiliate: Avfuel
Self Service: NO
Pilot Supplies: YES
Hours: Mon - Fri 7:00 - 7:00   Sat & Sun 8:00 - 6:00

**** Serventi's on the Runway - 724-481-1213
Open:

> Wed — Thur 2 p.m. — 8 p.m.
> Fri — Sat, 2 p.m. — 9 p.m.
> Sun — 12 p.m. — 8 p.m.

Restaurant Website: www.serventisontherunway.com/index.html
PIREP:

Serventi's has stood the test of time since opening in 1954. It provides tasty, authentic Italian food with excellent service. You'll be seated behind large panoramic windows with an excellent runway view. It's still a family-owned restaurant.

I had their terrific Spaghetti and Meatballs followed by Spumoni Citrus Italian Ice Cream.

Great meal. I'll be back!

COATESVILLE, PA (CHESTER COUNTY G O CARLSON - MQS)
Aprt Mgr: GARY L HUDSON **PH:** 610-383-6057
Field Elevation: 660 **CTAF:** 122.700 **FUEL:** 100LLA
Runway: 11/29 **Length:** 5400 **Width:** 100 **Surface:** ASPH-G

Landmark Aviation – 610-384-9000
FBO Website: www.landmarkaviation.com
Affiliate: UNK
Self Service: NO
Pilot Supplies: YES
Hours: 24/7

DUBOIS, PA (DUBOIS RGNL - DUJ)
Aprt Mgr: ROBERT W. SHAFFER **PH:** 814-328-5311
Field Elevation: 1817 **CTAF:** 123.000 **FUEL:** 100LLA
Runway: 07/25 **Length:** 5503 **Width:** 100 **Surface:** ASPH-TRTD-G

County Authority – 814-328-5311
Affiliate: UNK
Self Service: YES
Pilot Supplies: YES
Hours: Mon- Fri 5:00 - 10:00 Sat & Sun 6:00 - 8:00

John Purner

*** The Flight Deck Restaurant & Lounge - (814) 328-5281
Proprietor: Patrick Doksa
Open:

Wed – Sat: 3:00 pm - 9:00 pm
Sun: 12:00 pm - 6:00 pm

Restaurant Website: flight-deck.business.site
Restaurant Email: theflightdeck@windstream.net

PIREP:
You know an airport restaurant has good food when there are more locals than pilots. **The Flight Deck Restaurant & Lounge** is such a place. Thursday is Steak Night. You can grab any steak you like at a price you won't believe. My personal favorite is NY Strip for just $9.95. They also offer a Filet Mignon for just $16.00. Great steak with hard to beat prices!

ERWINNA, PA (VANSANT - 9N1)
Aprt Mgr: GEORGE TAYLOR **PH:** 610-847-8494
Field Elevation: 390 **CTAF:** 122.800 **FUEL:** 100LL
Runway: 05G/23G **Length:** 1340 **Width:** 200 **Surface:** TURF-G
Runway: 07/25 **Length:** 3058 **Width:** 120 **Surface:** TURF-G

*** Airport Grille – (610) 847-1119
Proprietor: Bar and Dannie
Open:

Seasonal:
Sat & Sun: Lunch

Restaurant Website: www.vansantairport.com
Restaurant Email: BarAndDannie@866mustfly.com
PIREP:
On weekends during the flying season Linda is there with her grill serving up hot dogs, hamburgers and veggie burgers. She usually has chips, cookies, fruit and an assortment of drinks available. Don't come here for the food. This stop is all about the planes and the airport. They offer hotdogs and burgers and chips and drinks. Don't expect much and you won't be disappointed.

Van Sant Historic Airfield – (610) 847-1119
Proprietor: Bar and Dannie
Open:

Summer: Wednesday thru Sunday 9:00 to 6:00.
Winter: Wednesday thru Sunday 8:30 to 4:00

Website: www.vansantairport.com
Email: BarAndDannie@866mustfly.com
PIREP:

172

This is what an aviation museum is supposed to be. There are plenty of old airplanes to see and even touch and plenty of folks who love them around to tell you about each of them. That gets you to first base. Seeing them all fly from this gorgeous turf strip is clearly a triple. Here's the home run. You can buy a ride in any or all of them and if you really catch the bug you can be instructed in how to fly them. Can you imagine landing a Stearman or a J3 Cub? How about going for a sightseeing tour over historic and beautiful Bucks County in a 1928 Travel Air? That's what this place is all about. It's a time machine that you get to step into not merely peer through the looking glass.

FRANKLIN, PA (VENANGO RGNL - FKL)
Aprt Mgr: GEORGE TAYLOR **PH:** 610-847-8494
Field Elevation: 390 **CTAF:** 122.800 **FUEL:** 100LL
Runway: 05G/23G **Length:** 1340 **Width:** 200 **Surface:** TURF-G
Runway: 07/25 **Length:** 3058 **Width:** 120 **Surface:** TURF-G

Venango Regional – 814-432-5333
FBO Website: www.flyfranklin.org
Affiliate: Phillips 66
Self Service: NO
Pilot Supplies: YES
Hours: Mon - Fri 6:00 - 11:00 Sat 6:00 - 10:00 Sun 7:00 -11:00

***** Primo Barone's Restaurant - (814) 432-2588
Proprietor: Giuseppe Barone
Open:
> Tue - Sun: 4:00 pm - 9:00 pm

Restaurant Email: gbarone21@yahoo.com
PIREP:
Primo Barone's Restaurant & Lounge consistently delivers gourmet food expertly prepared. They have a lively piano bar nightly and a jazz combo on Friday nights. Can you think of another airport restaurant that offers Baked Alaska? I use one word to define **Primo's** – **OUTSTANDING!**

HONESDALE, PA (CHERRY RIDGE - N30)
Aprt Mgr: BILL MOTT **PH:** 570-253-5181
Field Elevation: 1357 **CTAF:** 122.800 **FUEL:** 100LL
Runway: 18/36 **Length:** 2986 **Width:** 50 **Surface:** ASPH-F

** Cherry Ridge Airport Café - (570) 253-5517
Proprietor: Marty Lane
Open:
> Mon & Thurs: 8am-3pm
> Tue & Wed: Closed

Fri, Sat, & Sun: 7am-3pm

Restaurant Email: www.cherryridgeairportrestaurant.com/
Restaurant Email: kids3143@ptd.net
PIREP:
The cafe features a spot for pilots to park their planes in front of the café. The view of the runway and pond is unobstructed. The food is OK. I enjoy coming here for breakfast more than lunch.

Here's the latest from the proprietor. Read carefully:

"Due to staffing issues we will remain open with Reservations Required, and there is no outdoor dining until staffing situation changes. Sorry for any inconvenience and thank you for your support and understanding."

DEFINITELY CALL FIRST!!!!

LANCASTER, PA (LANCASTER - LNS)
Aprt Mgr: DAVID F EBERLY **PH:** 717-569-1221
Field Elevation: 403 **CTAF:** 120.900 **FUEL:** 100LLA
Runway: 13/31 **Length:** 4101 **Width:** 100 **Surface:** ASPH-G
Runway: 08/26 **Length:** 6934 **Width:** 150 **Surface:** ASPH-G

Alliance Aviation– 717-735-9507
FBO Website: www.flyfranklin.org
Affiliate: UNK
Self Service: NO
Pilot Supplies: YES
Hours: 7 days 7:00 - 8:00

**** Fiorentino's Bar and Grill - (717) 569-6732
Proprietor: Robert and Rose Billas
Open:
Sun - Thurs: 11 am to 11 pm
Fri - Sat: 11 am to 2 am
Restaurant Website: fiorentinos.net
Restaurant Email: rob@fiorentinos.net
PIREP:
Fiorentino's Bar and Grill is a pleasant break from the normal airport burger joints. It is a nice Italian restaurant which happens to be located on an airport. Hence you can get a really good lunch or dinner with a runway view. Off airport it would be worth three stars because it's on the runway, it deserves four.

Here's the plus: They a great deck which they have named the Flight Deck. Friday and Saturday nights, it rocks with hot music and cold adult beverages. Its fun!

LATROBE, PA (ARNOLD PALMER RGNL - LBE)
Aprt Mgr: GABE MONZO **PH:** 724-539-8100
Field Elevation: 1199 **CTAF:** 125.000 **FUEL:** 100LLA
Runway: 03/21 **Length:** 3609 **Width:** 75 **Surface:** ASPH-G
Runway: 05/23 **Length:** 8222 **Width:** 100 **Surface:** ASPH-G

Vee Neal Aviation – 724-539-4533
FBO Website: www.veeneal.com
Affiliate: Phillips 66
Self Service: NO
Pilot Supplies: YES
Hours: 7 days 6:00 - 10:00

***** DeNunzio's Italian Chophouse - (724) 539-3980
Proprietor: Amy Templeton
Open:
> Sunday: 10:30am - 9pm
> Monday: 11am - 9pm

Tues. – Thurs: 11am - 10pmFri & Sat: 11am - 11pm
Restaurant Website: denunziosrestaurant.com/DeNunzios_Latrobe
Restaurant Email: denunzio@wpa.net
PIREP: I love coming to Latrobe. It is **PILOT** Arnold Palmer's boyhood home. He was the world's greatest golfer and was also darn good pilot. Airplanes and golf are my greatest passions so a trip to Latrobe is way up on my bucket list.

DeNunzio's is in the terminal building and is easily accessed via the FBO next door. The ambiance is impressive while remaining invitingly casual. The food is very, very good and the service stellar. It is a great place to fly your significant other for a birthday dinner. Plan to come on a weekend evening and enjoy the live entertainment.

MONONGAHELA, PA (ROSTRAVER - FWQ)
Aprt Mgr: GABE MONZO **PH:** 724-379-6980
Field Elevation: 1228 **CTAF:** 122.800 **FUEL:** 100LLA
Runway: 08/26 **Length:** 4002 **Width:** 75 **Surface:** ASPH-G

*** Eagle's Landing - (724) 379-8830
Proprietor: Bobbi Lawson
Open:

Tue – Fri: 9:00am - 8:00pmSat: 8:00am - 8:00pmSun: 8:00am - 7:00pm

PIREP:

This is good cross-country fuel stop. 100LL prices are typically low. The service at the restaurant is fast, the food is good, and the runway view is nice. Not bad.

READING, PA (READING RGNL/CARL A SPAATZ FIELD - RDG)

Aprt Mgr: TERRY P. SROKA **PH:** 610-372-4666
Field Elevation: 344 **CTAF:** 119.900 **FUEL:** 100LLA
Runway: 18/36 **Length:** 5151 **Width:** 150 **Surface:** ASPH-F
Runway: 13/31 **Length:** 6350 **Width:** 150 **Surface:** ASPH-G

Millenium Aviation – 610-372-4728
FBO Website: www.majets.com
Affiliate: Phillips 66
Self Service: NO
Pilot Supplies: YES
Hours: 6:00 - 9:00 m-sat 8:00 - 8:00 sun

Reading Jet Center – 610-373-3000
FBO Website: www.veeneal.com
Affiliate: UNK
Self Service: NO
Pilot Supplies: YES
Hours: M-F 6:00 - 8:00 Sat & Sun 8:00 - 5:00

*** Klinger's at the Airport - 484-869-2914
Open: Daily 11 am to 9 pm CLOSED Monday
Restaurant Website: www.klingerspubs.com/klingers-at-the-airport
PIREP:

The restaurant is in the terminal building. You'll have a great view of runway 13/31. Make certain to write down or memorize the door code on the entrance to the terminal. You won't be able to get back out to your airplane if you don't.

ST MARYS, PA (ST MARYS MUNI - OYM)

Airport Manager: ALAN MCPHERSON **PH:** 814-781-6101
Field Elevation: 1934 **CTAF:** 122.700 **FUEL:** 100LLA
Runway: 10/28 **Length:** 4300 **Width:** 75 **Surface:** ASPH-F

*** West Wind – 814-781-1552
Open:

Tue – Fri: 11am – 9pm Sat – Sun: 8am – 9pm
PIREP:

The scenery is hard to beat as it's surrounded by beautiful Alleghany Mountains as you're flying in. Surprisingly, this is the place to have a great steak. While you're waiting for the chef to burn you some serious cow jump on a plate of the loaded tater tots. You'll thank me!

STATE COLLEGE, PA (UNIVERSITY PARK - UNV)
Aprt Mgr: GABE MONZO **PH:** 724-379-6980
Aprt Mgr: BRYAN RODGERS **PH:** 814-865-5511
Field Elevation: 1239 **CTAF:** 128.475 **FUEL:** 100LLA
Runway: 06/24 **Length:** 6701 **Width:** 150 **Surface:** ASPH-G

** Irving's at the Airport- (814) 238-6320
Open: Daily: Breakfast & Lunch
PIREP:
In the main terminal, and hence a 5 minute walk (around the outside of the airport fence) from the GA tiedown area. But close enough to be called on the ramp. Irving's is a mix of a cafe, a bar, and a gift shop. It is outside security, so easy to get to. A basic airport restaurant, good stopover if needed - clean, terminal has good restrooms, and restaurant sells Nittany Lions bling, if that's your thing. No view of the ramp, feels generic small commercial airport in Anywhere USA, but worth a spot on the list. They put anything you can imagine on Breakfast Bagel and their smoothies are really good.

WILLIAMSPORT, PA (WILLIAMSPORT RGNL - IPT)
Aprt Mgr: THOMAS J. HART **PH:** 570-368-2444
Field Elevation: 528 **CTAF:** 119.100 **FUEL:** 100LLA
Runway: 12/30 **Length:** 4280 **Width:** 150 **Surface:** ASPH-G
Runway: 09/27 **Length:** 6824 **Width:** 150 **Surface:** ASPH-G

Energy Aviation – 800-872-3599 **Affiliate:** UNK **Self Service:** NO
Pilot Supplies: YES
Hours: 7 days 6:00 - 9:00

FlyIn Rhode Island

BLOCK ISLAND, RI (BLOCK ISLAND STATE - BID)
Aprt Mgr: MARK HELMBOLDT **PH:** 401-466-5511
Field Elevation: 108 **CTAF:** 123.000 **FUEL:**
Runway: 10/28 **Length:** 2502 **Width:** 100 **Surface:** ASPH-E

**** Bethany's Airport Diner - (401) 466-3100
Proprietor: Bethany Campbell
  Open: Mon – Sun: 6:30am - 3:00pm
Restaurant Website: blockisland.stateairportri.com
PIREP:
A word to the wise; this airport doesn't sell fuel. There is no landing fee charged for an up to two-hour stop at **Bethany's.** A flight to Block Island is a doable adventure. When you get back to your homeport, you'll feel that you have been somewhere special because you have. This is my favorite breakfast stop in New England. The food is more than good. It's amazing. The ambiance is *"Wings"* which wasn't filmed here but it could have been!

FlyIn South Carolina

GREENVILLE, SC (GREENVILLE DOWNTOWN - GMU)
    Aprt Mgr: JOE FRASHER **PH:** 864-242-4777
    Field Elevation: 1048 **CTAF:** 119.900 **FUEL:** 100LLA
    Runway: 01/19 **Length:** 5393 **Width:** 100 **Surface:** ASPH-E
    Runway: 10/28 **Length:** 3998 **Width:** 80 **Surface:** ASPH-G

Greenville Jet Center – 864-232-7100
Affiliate: UNK
Self Service: YES
Pilot Supplies: YES
Hours: Mon - Fri 6:00- 9:00 Sat & Sun 7:00 - 8:00

*** Runway Cafe - 864-991-8488
Open:
        Sun – Tues: 11am - 2:30pm
        Wed –Thu: 11am - 2:30pm ; 5:00pm-8:30pm
Fri – Sat: 11am - 8:30pm
Restaurant Website: runwaycafegmu.com/
PIREP:
I am a big fan of the airport and I like the view from the restaurant. The food is a cut above average. I don't come here often but I do feel its worthy of a look if you're in the area.

FlyIn South Dakota

ABERDEEN, SD (ABERDEEN RGNL - ABR)
Aprt Mgr: MICHAEL WILSON **PH:** 605-626-7020
Field Elevation: 1302 **CTAF:** 122.700 **FUEL:** 100LLA MOGAS
Runway: 17/35 **Length:** 5500 **Width:** 100 **Surface:** ASPH-F
Runway: 13/31 **Length:** 6901 **Width:** 100 **Surface:** CONC-G

Aberdeen Flying Service – 605-225-1384
FBO Website: www.aberdeenflyingservice.com
Affiliate: Phillips 66
Self Service: YES
Pilot Supplies: YES
Hours: 7:30 - 6:00 7 days

Quest Aviation – 605-225-8008
Affiliate: UNK
Self Service: NO
Pilot Supplies: YES
Hours: M-F 6:00 - 8:00 Sat & Sun 7:00 - 7:00

*** Airport Cafe and Lounge - (605) 225-7210
Proprietor: Ron Erickson
Open:
Mon - Sat: 5:30am - 1:30pm Sun: 6:30am - 1:30pm
Restaurant Website: airportcafesd.com/
PIREP:
Aberdeen is home to some of the best pheasant hunting in the US. If
you're up this way you'll be pleased with the friendly service. The food
is very basic but quite good.

HURON, SD (HURON RGNL - HON)
Aprt Mgr: LARRY COOPER **PH:** 605-353-8516
Field Elevation: 1289 **CTAF:** 123.600 **FUEL:** 100LLA
Runway: 17/35 **Length:** 5000 **Width:** 75 **Surface:** CONC-G
Runway: 12/30 **Length:** 7201 **Width:** 100 **Surface:** CONC-G

Skyways – 605-352-9262
FBO Website: www.skywaysltd.com
Affiliate: Avfuel **Self Service:** NO
Pilot Supplies: YES
Hours: 7:30 - 6:00 7 days

★★★★★ **Ryan's Hangar Restaurant & Ace Lounge** - (605) 352-1639
Proprietor: Ryan Hofer
Open:
Mon - Sun: 4pm – 10pm
PIREP:
Ryan's is a **GREAT** find with one huge problem. First the good news. The food is excellent, the service amazing and the ambiance over-the-top.

The spacious Dining Room provides a panoramic view of the runway. The atmosphere is casual and relaxed, crisp white table clothes and dimmed lighting set the mood for a very enjoyable dinner. Steaks, ribs and seafood followed by the best three layer carrot cake in the country. All prepared to perfection. I have never had anything but an exceptional meal here.

What's the bad news? They don't offer lunch, only dinner. It is one of the best dinners you'll ever have at an airport restaurant, but I really wish they'd do lunch at least one day a week.

RAPID CITY, SD (RAPID CITY RGNL - RAP)
Aprt Mgr: CAMERON HUMPHRES **PH:** 605-394-4195
Field Elevation: 3204 **CTAF:** 125.850 **FUEL:** 100LLA
Runway: 05/23 **Length:** 3601 **Width:** 75 **Surface:** ASPH-G
Runway: 14/32 **Length:** 8701 **Width:** 150 **Surface:** CONC-G

West Jet Air Center – 605-393-2500
FBO Website: www.westjetair.com
Affiliate: Phillips 66
Self Service: NO
Pilot Supplies: YES
Hours: 24/7

*** **Airport Restaurant** – (605) 393-8000
Proprietor: Airhost, Inc.
Open:
Mon - Sun: 5am –
Restaurant Website:
　　　www.rapairport.com/at-the-airport/dining-shopping
PIREP:
The FBO will run you over to the terminal or you can walk the short distance. This is standard commercial airport faire. The good news is one of the two restaurants is before security so you can get in and get out with no TSA hassle. **The Airport Restaurant** has two locations on

the second level of the terminal building: the first location is across from the gift shop, **just prior to the security concourse** and the second location is beyond the screening checkpoint across from gate 3.

The restaurant hours are from 5:00 a.m. until the last flight departs. A complete line of pastries along with breakfast sandwiches will be offered in conjunction with popular salads and a variety of deli sandwich selections, freshly prepared daily. A hot breakfast and daily luncheon feature will be available during the appropriate meal hours at the pre-screening location. breakfast and daily luncheon feature will be available during the appropriate meal hours at the pre-screening location.

SIOUX FALLS, SD (JOE FOSS FIELD - FSD)
Aprt Mgr: DANIEL J. LETTELLIER **PH:** 605-336-0762
Field Elevation: 1430 **CTAF:** 118.300 **FUEL:** 100LLA
Runway: 09/27 **Length:** 3151 **Width:** 75 **Surface:** CONC-F
Runway: 15/33 **Length:** 8000 **Width:** 150 **Surface:** CONC-F
Runway: 03/21 **Length:** 8999 **Width:** 150 **Surface:** CONC-F

** Marlin's & Subway
Open:
>Daily: 8am – 6pm

Restaurant Website: sfairport.com/at-the-airport/dining-shopping
PIREP:
Inside the terminal before security. Pretty standard commercial airport stop. The food works if you're hungry but is certainly is not a destination. The names and the tenants change from time to time, but it really doesn't make any difference. They're all the same aren't they?

FlyIn Tennessee

BRISTOL/JOHNSON, TN (TRI-CITIES RGNL TN/VA - TRI)
Aprt Mgr: MR. PATRICK WILSON **PH:** 423-325-6001
Field Elevation: 1519 **CTAF:** 119.500 **FUEL:** 100LLA
Runway: 09/27 **Length:** 4442 **Width:** 150 **Surface:** ASPH-F
Runway: 05/23 **Length:** 8000 **Width:** 150 **Surface:** ASPH-F

Tri City Aviation – 423-325-6261
FBO Website: www.tricityaviation.com
Affiliate: Phillips 66
Self Service: NO
Pilot Supplies: YES
Hours: 24/7

*** Tailwind Restaurant and Lounge - (423) 212-4095
Open:
> Sun - Friday 5am – 7pm Sat: 5am – 6pm

PIREP:
Tailwind Restaurant and Lounge and **Tailwind Express** are both in the main terminal. **Tailwind Express** is on the lower concourse level. It serves snacks and coffee from 5:00 am until the last flight departs. **Tailwind Restaurant and Lounge** on the other hand is a full service sit down and enjoy yourself restaurant. It includes a full service bar for the road warrior who's been stuck in a center seat for the last two hours to unwind and reconnect with his inner self. The FBO will run you over. The TSA is not much of a hassle in this terminal so you can get in and get out fairly easily. I don't think it's worth the fuel to proclaim this as a destination but if you happen to be here and are hungry.

FlyIn Texas

AMARILLO, TX (RICK HUSBAND AMARILLO INTL - AMA)
Aprt Mgr: PATRICK RHODES **PH:** 806-335-1671
Field Elevation: 3607 **CTAF:** 118.300 **FUEL:** 100LLA1+ B
Runway: 13/31 **Length:** 7901 **Width:** 150 **Surface:** CONC-G
Runway: 04/22 **Length:** 13502 **Width:** 200 **Surface:** CONC-G

Tac Air – 806-335-3551
FBO Website: www.tacair.com
Affiliate: Phillips 66
Self Service: YES
Pilot Supplies: YES
Hours: 24/7

**** English Field House Restaurant - (806) 335-2996
Proprietor: Jose Vasquez
Open:
> Mon – Sun: 8am – 3pm

PIREP:
English Field House Restaurant is immediately adjacent to TAC Air and overlooks runway 4/22. They offer Mexican food and pretty much everything else including spaghetti and ribeye steak and breakfast of course. All served by a friendly staff that seems happy to see you.

ANGLETON, TX (TEXAS GULF COAST RGNL - LBX)
Aprt Mgr: PATRICK RHODES **PH:** 806-335-1671
Field Elevation: 3607 **CTAF:** 118.300 **FUEL:** 100LLA1+ B
Runway: 13/31 **Length:** 7901 **Width:** 150 **Surface:** CONC-G
Runway: 04/22 **Length:** 13502 **Width:** 200 **Surface:** CONC-G

Texas Gulf Regional Air – 979-849-5755
FBO Website: www.flylbx.com
Affiliate: UNK
Self Service: YES
Pilot Supplies: YES
Hours: Mon- Friday 6:30- 6:30 Sat & Sun 8:00 - 6:30

*** Runway Cafe – (979) 849 5160
Restaurant Website: www.runwaycafeangleton.com
Open:
> Tue – Sun: 11:00 - 8:00 Fri – Sat: 11:00 - 9:00

PIREP:
The food, service and ambiance are very standard for a ramp side café. Worth a stop? I think so but not a long trip at this time. Here's the thing. You can get something here you wouldn't expect to find in an airport restaurant, seafood, really good seafood. Try the fried shrimp. You won't be disappointed.

COLLEGE STATION, TX (EASTERWOOD FIELD - CLL)
Aprt Mgr: JOHN H. HAPP **PH:** 979-845-5103
Field Elevation: 320 **CTAF:** 118.500 **FUEL:** 100LLA
Runway: 16/34 **Length:** 7000 **Width:** 150 **Surface:** ASPH-CONC-E
Runway: 10/28 **Length:** 5159 **Width:** 150 **Surface:** ASPH-E
Runway: 04/22 **Length:** 5149 **Width:** 150 **Surface:** CONC-G

*** Gate 12 Bar and Grill - (979) 775-9925
Manager: Rudy Rivera
Open:
　　　　　Mon - Th 11AM- 9PM Fri Sat 11Am - 10PM Sun 11Am - 8PM
Restaurant Website: gate12barandgrill.com
PIREP:
Gate 12 Bar & Grill is a relaxed elegance, full-service steakhouse located in the General Aviation Building at Easterwood airport. It affords views of the runways. There is a full bar with a large selection of bourbons, whiskeys, scotches. What to eat? Steaks of course, some of the best you've ever eaten..

The is my favorite stop in central Texas. It will soon be yours as well.

DALHART, TX (DALHART MUNI - DHT)
Aprt Mgr: GREG DUGGAN **PH:** 806-244-5511
Field Elevation: 3991 **CTAF:** 122.950 **FUEL:** 100LLA1
Runway: 03/21 **Length:** 5437 **Width:** 75 **Surface:** ASPH-G
Runway: 17/35 **Length:** 6400 **Width:** 75 **Surface:** ASPH-G

*** The Red Baron Restaurant - (806) 244-6050
Manager: Rudy Rivera
Open:
　　　　　Daily: 6:30AM - 2:00PM
Restaurant Website: www.deltacharlies.com
PIREP:
The Red Baron Restaurant is located at Dalhart Municipal Airport (KDHT- Larsen Aviation FBO). They offer a family-oriented atmosphere and serve comfort food favorites such as hand-breaded Chicken Fried Steak. Great ramp views. The prices are fair, the food delicious and the service friendly. Well worth the stop.

185

John Purner

DALLAS, TX (DALLAS EXECUTIVE - RBD)
    Aprt Mgr: LANA FURRA **PH:** 214-670-7612
    Field Elevation: 660 **CTAF:** 127.250 **FUEL:** 100LLA
    Runway: 17/35 **Length:** 3800 **Width:** 150 **Surface:** ASPH-CONC-G
    Runway: 13/31 **Length:** 6451 **Width:** 150 **Surface:** ASPH-CONC-G

Ambassador Jet Center – 214-623-8800
FBO Website: www.ambassadorjetcenter.com
Affiliate: UNK
Self Service: NO
Pilot Supplies: YES
Hours: 7 days 6:00 - 10:00

Jet Center Dallas – 214-339-3992
FBO Website: www.jetcenterdallas.com
Affiliate: Avfuel
Self Service: YES
Pilot Supplies: YES
Hours: 24/7

**** Delta Charlie's - 214-623-9944
Proprietor: Mark and Dirk Kelcher
Open:
Tue – Sun: 8:00 am - 10:00 pm
Restaurant Website: www.deltacharlies.com
PIREP:
This is a very nice to upscale restaurant with an excellent mid-field view of the usually active runway. The menu items are impressive, but the prices are reasonable. When I am lucky enough to be around for breakfast I jump on the homemade cinnamon rolls; nothing beats fresh from the oven. They combine a wonderful dinner with a sightseeing flight for their non-pilot diners. This is a great place to come on date night.

DRYDEN, TX (CHANDLER RANCH)
    Aprt Mgr: JOE CHANDLER **PH:** 713-703-6615
    Field Elevation: 2610 **CTAF: FUEL:**
    Runway: 15/33 **Length:** 3300 **Width:** 50 **Surface:** ASPH-CONC-G

**** Chandler Ranch – 713-703-6615
Proprietor: Joe Chandler
Open:
    Everyday 9 a.m. – 6 p.m.

186

Restaurant Website: www.chandlerranch.com
PIREP:
Chandler Ranch has been privately owned for over 100 years. The land sits at the confluence of Independence Creek and the Pecos River. It's an arid region, but the Chandler Ranch is blessed to have numerous springs, which feed several ponds on the ranch, in addition to the beautiful creek and the river, its eastern border. My husband's grandfather, Joe B. Chandler, established a guest ranch, including a golf course, in the 1950s. It was a thriving business for many years but was eventually closed to the public due to Mr. Chandler's declining health. Joe A. Chandler began to rebuild the guest ranch in 2014 and opened back up to the public in 2015. We now have 3 fully and expertly renovated cabins with modern luxuries, a full-time country cook and managerial staff to assist our guests, canoes and kayaks for floating down the Pecos, ponds stocked for fishing. The original game room and spring-fed swimming pool have also been restored.

FORT WORTH, TX (HICKS AIRFIELD - T67)
Aprt Mgr: DON BROWNING **PH:** 817-296-0189
Field Elevation: 855 **CTAF:** 123.050 **FUEL:** 100LL
Runway: 14/32 **Length:** 3740 **Width:** 60 **Surface:** ASPH-G

*** Beacon Cafe & Country Store - 817-439-1041
Proprietor: Christie and Gene Bingham
Open:
Tue – Sun: 7:00 am - 2:00 pm
Restaurant Website: www.thebeaconcafe.com
PIREP:
It's a friendly, unpretentious airport cafe with an unexceptional but well executed regional menu. You can tell the food is good because the place fills up with locals particularly for breakfast when they offer everything from Migas to Blueberry pancakes. For lunch I go with the B.L.T. because it is made with really good tomatoes, a half-pound of bacon and a generous slathering of mayonnaise. When I'm really hungry I add a Greek Salad. I like this place. You will too.

FREDERICKSBURG, TX (GILLESPIE COUNTY - T82)
Aprt Mgr: DON BROWNING **PH:** 817-296-0189
Field Elevation: 855 **CTAF:** 123.050 **FUEL:** 100LL
Runway: 14/32 **Length:** 3740 **Width:** 60 **Surface:** ASPH-G

Fredericksburg FB – 830-997-3313
Affiliate: UNK
Self Service: YES
Pilot Supplies: YES
Hours: 7 days 8:00 - 6:00 Self Serve 24/7

*** The Airport Diner (830) 997-4999
Proprietor: Steven Claypole
Open:
> Wed –Thurs: 11am till 2pm
> Fri: 8am till 2pm
> Sat: 8am till 4pm
> Sun: 8am till 2pm

Restaurant Website: www.hangarhotel.com/diner.htm
Restaurant Email: garrett@hangarhotel.com
PIREP:

The Airport Diner is a classic 1940's diner, located next door to the **Hangar Hotel** and immediately adjacent to the Gillespie County Airport aircraft parking ramp. You get a great view of the airport from the booths. The menu offers the standard airport restaurant selections, the difference is the quality. The malts are prepared with ice-cream that is made especially for **The Airport Diner**. While the malts are good don't pass on the hand battered onion rings. If its breakfast you're after; know that the biscuits are homemade.

The Hangar Hotel (830) 997-9990
Proprietor: Steven Claypole
Open:
> **24 hours a day / 7 days a week**

Restaurant Website: www.hangarhotel.com
Hotel Email: kelly@hangarhotel.com
PIREP:

Hotels at GA airports are about ass rare as hen's teeth. The $100 Hamburger knows about a few but far too few. What is even rarer is an aviation themed hotel at a GA airport. **The Hangar Hotel** is a trip back in time. It was uniquely designed with an exterior appearance of a WWII hangar. It is a stylish adult environment featuring airplane memorabilia and the romance of the 1940's all wrapped in a blanket of luxury. While all of that is good, the geography makes it even better. This is the Texas Hill Country. There is no better place to be on earth. Don't miss this experience.

GALVESTON, TX (SCHOLES INTL - GLS)
Aprt Mgr: HUD HOPKINS **PH:** 409-741-4609
Field Elevation: 6 **CTAF:** 120.575 **FUEL:** 100LLA
Runway: 13/31 **Length:** 6000 **Width:** 150 **Surface:** ASPH-CONC-G
Runway: 17/35 **Length:** 6001 **Width:** 150 **Surface:** CONC-G

Galveston Aviation Services – 409-744-9000
FBO Website: www.galvestonaviationservices.com
Affiliate: Avfuel

Self Service: YES
Pilot Supplies: YES
Hours: M-F 6:00 - 8:00   Sat& Sun 8:00 - 5:00

***** Shearn's Seafood and Prime Steaks - (409) 683-4554
Chef: Urs Schmid
Open:
Tues – Sat: Dinner
Restaurant Website: www.moodygardenshotel.com/shearns
PIREP:
Call the FBO on approach and let them know you'll need the hotel shuttle. It'll be there when you land. There was a time when you could walk to the hotel but the gate has been removed. **Shearn's Seafood and Prime Steaks** is in the Moody Gardens Hotel which is part of the Moody Garden's Complex that abuts the airport. It is one of only 11 Houston/Galveston area restaurants to receive AAA's Four Diamond Award of Excellence and has done so each year since 2004.

It is Galveston's finest restaurant unsurpassed in cuisine and service with an upscale ambiance. Dressy Casual attire required. No jeans, shorts, swimwear, cutoffs, tank tops or hats allowed in the dining area. Collared shirts and sandals are acceptable. It's pricey but not atmospheric. I come here for special occasions and have never been disappointed. The views are spectacular. Normally we have dinner, spend the night, take in the museum and play a round of golf. They'll even run you over to the beach which is only three blocks away.

*** The Terrace Restaurant - (979) 233-0205
Open:
Daily: Breakfast, Lunch and Dinner
PIREP:
Call the FBO on approach and let them know you'll need the hotel shuttle. It'll be there when you land. **The Terrace Restaurant** is located in the lobby level. It is a casual venue that provides pretty standard hotel coffee shop faire. The food is more than OK but less than wonderful. The service is friendly and the pricing fair.

The Moody Gardens Hotel - (409) 683-4000
Open:
Daily
Restaurant Website: www.moodygardenshotel.com
PIREP: It is right on the airport and three blocks away from the beach. If that's not enough it sits in the middle of a 240 acre family entertainment venue which includes a pretty darn good golf course. It is a nice hotel that deserves its superior rating. Rooms go for $150 to $250 a night depending on the season. It is a large hotel with 400 plus

rooms but not mammoth. I like the place and have RONed here more than once. They've got a good SPA which I'm not much into but my wife is. While she SPAs I golf. Life is filled with trade-offs.

Moody Gardens (800) 582-4673
Open:
> 10:00am - 6:00pm

Restaurant Website: www.moodygardens.com
PIREP:

Moody Gardens is one of the top 10 attractions in the state of Texas. It bills itself as an educational destination utilizing nature in the advancement of rehabilitation, conservation, recreation, and research. That means that have a lot of animals for you in see in habitants that are hopefully more upscale than your local zoon. With that the combine guest experiences that include a lazy river and an 1800 replica paddle wheel steam boat. The focal point of the 240 acre park is a glass pyramid that contains many creatures and much plant and aquatic life. To my taste the whole place other the hotel and the golf course is thread bear. It was once nice but they simply are doing the maintenance. Have a look at the website and form your own opinion. Here's the good news. It is an airport located animal based theme park similar to Seaword. It is a good trip!

The Moody Gardens Golf Course - (409) 683-4000
Open:
> 7 Days a Week

Restaurant Website: www.moodygardensgolf.com
PIREP: This is a Jacobsen Hardy designed links golf course which says it's challenging but not enough to leave you in tears. The Houston Chronicle rates it as the most scenic course in the Houston Metro area. A round will set you back about $65. I should point out that this is a public course. Originally it was the Galveston Municipal Golf Course. It needed work, a lot of work. So the Moody's stepped in with $16,000,000 to take care of it. The deal resulted in a name change but it is still a public course. I've played it a few times in the winter but never in August. It gets really hot on the Texas Coast in late summer and the mosquitoes are the size of Cessna 150s.

GRAND PRAIRIE, TX (GRAND PRAIRIE MUNI - GPM)
> **Aprt Mgr:** RANDY BYERS **PH:** 972-237-7591
> **Field Elevation:** 588 **CTAF:** 128.550 **FUEL:** 100LLA
> **Runway:** 17/35 **Length:** 4001 **Width:** 75 **Surface:** CONC-G

Aviator Air Center – 972-988-8609
Affiliate: Avfuel
Self Service: NO

Pilot Supplies: YES
Hours: Mon - Sat 7:00 - 8:00 Sunday 7:00 - 7:00

HOUSTON, TX (LONE STAR EXECUTIVE - CXO)
Aprt Mgr: SCOTT SMITH **PH:** 936-788-8311
Field Elevation: 245 **CTAF:** 124.125 **FUEL:** 100LLA
Runway: 01/19 **Length:** 5000 **Width:** 100 **Surface:** CONC-G
Runway: 14/32 **Length:** 6000 **Width:** 150 **Surface:** CONC-G

Galaxy FBO – 936-494-4252
FBO Website: www.galaxyfbo.com
Affiliate: Phillips 66
Self Service: NO
Pilot Supplies: YES
Hours: 7 days 7:00- 9:00

General Aviation – 936-760-1717
Affiliate: UNK
Self Service: NO
Pilot Supplies: YES
Hours: 7:00 - 8:30 7 days

Wings Aviation – 936-441-9555
Affiliate: UNK
Self Service: NO
Pilot Supplies: YES
Hours: 7:00 - 9:00 7 days

***** Black Walnut Café - (936) 202-2824**
Proprietor: George Pallottas
Open:
          Mon - Sun: 7am to 3pm
Restaurant Website: blackwalnutcafe.com
PIREP:
The Black Walnut Café is located inside Galaxy FBO
(www.galaxyfbo.com). It is on the third floor and provides an amazing
airport view from its expansive floor to ceiling windows and the
comfortable deck. The ambiance is contemporary casual. The food is
expertly prepared from premium ingredients enthusiastically presented
by a professional wait staff. I ordered the Pot Roast Grilled Cheese
sandwich for its uniqueness and was rewarded by its quality.

HOUSTON, TX (DAVID WAYNE HOOKS MEMORIAL - DWH)
Aprt Mgr: ROGER SCHMIDT **PH:** 281-376-5436

Field Elevation: 152 **CTAF:** 118.400 **FUEL:** 100LLA
Runway: 17R/35L **Length:** 7009 **Width:** 100 **Surface:** ASPH-F
Runway: 17L/35R **Length:** 3987 **Width:** 35 **Surface:** ASPH-P

Tomball Jet Center – 281-251-2800
FBO Website: www.tomballjetcenter.com
Affiliate: Phillips 66
Self Service: NO
Pilot Supplies: YES
Hours: 6:00 - 10:00 7 days

Gill Aviation – 281-376-5436
FBO Website: www.hooksaiport.com
Affiliate: Phillips 66
Self Service: YES
Pilot Supplies: YES
Hours: 6:00 - 10:00 7 days

*** The Aviator's Grille - (281) 370-6279
Proprietor: Jim and Rory Duffy
Open:
> Tues - Friday: 7am - 2:30pm
> Sat, Sun, and Mon: 11am - 2:30pm

PIREP:
Hooks is a small towered airport with a high-speed cut-off from the main runway (17R – 35L). I like that. It is also interesting that they have the only man-made water landing runway I have ever seen or heard of. **The Aviator's Grille** has been a Houston flying community fixture since 1995. I have eaten here more times than I can count on all my fingers and toes and have always looked forward to my next visit. It is a supper Texas friendly place.

LUFKIN, TX (ANGELINA COUNTY - LFK)
Aprt Mgr: RANDY CARSWELL **PH:** 936-634-7511
Field Elevation: 296 **CTAF:** 123.000 **FUEL:** 100LLA+
Runway: 15/33 **Length:** 4309 **Width:** 100 **Surface:** ASPH-G
Runway: 07/25 **Length:** 5398 **Width:** 100 **Surface:** ASPH-G

*** Airport Diner Restaurant
Website: www.angelinacounty.net/airport/
Open:
> Daily: Breakfast & Lunch

PIREP:

I used to go here regularly when I lived in Houston but haven't stopped by in a couple of years. The report below is from a respected Burger Subscriber:

"Don't forget about this little stop. I give it a 5 because there just isn't anything bad about it. There are only 9 tables. The view looks right out onto the ramp. Great burgers and breakfast. Usually have a special of the day like a chicken fried chicken sandwich. Good prices, full or self serve fuel, long runways, plenty of ramp space and easy in/out. Published approaches in class echo to the surface. About as GA friendly as it gets."

SAN ANGELO, TX (SAN ANGELO RGNL/MATHIS FIELD - SJT)
Aprt Mgr: LUIS E. ELGUEZABAL **PH:** 325-659-6409
Field Elevation: 1919 **CTAF:** 118.300 **FUEL:** 100LLA B+
Runway: 09/27 **Length:** 4402 **Width:** 75 **Surface:** ASPH-G
Runway: 03/21 **Length:** 5939 **Width:** 150 **Surface:** ASPH-G
Runway: 18/36 **Length:** 8049 **Width:** 150 **Surface:** ASPH-G

Ranger Aviation – 800-326-5758
FBO Website: www.rangeraviation.com
Affiliate: Avfuel
Self Service: NO
Pilot Supplies: YES
Hours: 6:00 - 10:00 7 days

Skyline Aviation – 325-944-8858
FBO Website: www.flyskyline.com
Affiliate: Phillips 66
Self Service: NO
Pilot Supplies: YES
Hours: 7:00 - 7:00 7 days

*** Mathis Field Cafe - (325) 942-1172
Proprietor: Rose and Sam Ng
Open:
Tue - Sat: 11:00am - 7:00pm
PIREP:
This is a highly improbable find for an airport in West Texas. It is a small café located inside the terminal serving Chinese cuisine. Yes, they have some American dishes as well but you should come here for the Chinese. It's a welcome break from burgers and chicken fried steak. The food is good. Last time I was through here I ate light and just had a couple of egg rolls (homemade) and the Spicy Chicken Noodle Soup. They don't do breakfast. Maybe the Chinese don't eat breakfast.

SAN ANTONIO, TX (STINSON MUNI - SSF)
Aprt Mgr: MORRIS MARTIN **PH:** 210-932-4357
Field Elevation: 577 **CTAF:** 118.200 **FUEL:** 100LLA
Runway: 14/32 **Length:** 4128 **Width:** 100 **Surface:** ASPH-G
Runway: 09/27 **Length:** 5000 **Width:** 100 **Surface:** ASPH-G

**** The Big Bib BBQ – (210) 272-0525
Open:

Mon. – Sat: 11 AM to 2PM
Restaurant Website: www.thebigbib.com
PIREP:

Stinson Muni is a shrine to many Texan's. In 2016, The Big Bib was approached by the San Antonio International Airport concerning a restaurant space located within the Stinson Municipal Airport on the South side of San Antonio and that location became The Big Bib's second brick and mortar restaurant. To eat BBQ right underneath the tower at Stinson is worth the trip. The BBQ is award winning, so the food is also worth the trip. The pricing is more than fair, and the service is close to be welcomed home after a long absence. The long line to order confirms that your flight is worth it. Go once and you'll have to go twice!!!

SAN MARCOS, TX (SAN MARCOS MUNI - HYI)
Aprt Mgr: TEXAS AVIATION PARTNERS **PH:** 512-216-6039
Field Elevation: 597 **CTAF:** 126.825 **FUEL:** 100LLA
Runway: 17/35 **Length:** 5213 **Width:** 100 **Surface:** ASPH-G
Runway: 13/31 **Length:** 5603 **Width:** 150 **Surface:** ASPH-G
Runway: 08/26 **Length:** 6330 **Width:** 100 **Surface:** ASPH-G

Berry Aviation – 800-229-2379
FBO Website: www.berryaviation.com
Affiliate: Avfuel
Self Service: YES
Pilot Supplies: YES
Hours: 6:00 - 9:00 7 days

STEPHENVILLE, TX (CLARK FIELD MUNI - SEP)
Aprt Mgr: BILL SMITH **PH:** 254-965-2795
Field Elevation: 1321 **CTAF:** 122.800 **FUEL:** 100LLA
Runway: 14/32 **Length:** 4209 **Width:** 75 **Surface:** ASPH-G

***** The Hard Eight - 254 968 5552
Proprietor: Chad Decker
Open:

Mon - Thur: 10:30am – 9 pm
Fri - Sat: 10:30am – 10 pm

Sun: 10:30am – 8 pm
Restaurant Website: www.hardeightbbq.com/
PIREP:
I'm strictly a brisket guy. **The Hard Eight** does brisket right. Maybe that's why they've been on the annual **$100 Hamburger Best of the Best** list more than once. I also love flying into Stephenville and spending a good part of the day there. Order whatever food you like but don't forget the pecan pie. Drink only Dr. Pepper as they get the good stuff from the original Dr. Pepper Bottling Company in nearby Dublin.

Yes, it is a short walk from the terminal to the Hard 8 and yes it is slightly off the airport and yes they no longer have the golf carts so you could drive yourself over but heck this BBQ is worth bending the rules a little bit. On the ramp? No, it's not but its close enough and the food makes it worth including. 'Nuff said!

TYLER, TX (TYLER POUNDS RGNL - TYR)
Aprt Mgr: DAVIS DICKSON **PH:** 903-531-2343
Field Elevation: 544 **CTAF:** 120.100 **FUEL:** 100LLA
Runway: 17/35 **Length:** 4850 **Width:** 150 **Surface:** ASPH-G
Runway: 13/31 **Length:** 5200 **Width:** 150 **Surface:** ASPH-G
Runway: 04/22 **Length:** 7200 **Width:** 150 **Surface:** ASPH-G

Jet Center of Tyler – 903-597-1334
FBO Website: www.jetcenteroftyler.com
Affiliate: Phillips 66
Self Service: NO
Pilot Supplies: YES
Hours: M-F 5:00 - 10:00 Sat&Sun 5:00 - 8:00

*** SkyLine Cafe - 903-593-7455
Open:
Mon – Fri: 8am – 2pm
Sat: 8am – 2pm
Sun: 11am – 2pm
Restaurant Website: www.skylinecafe.orgRestaurant
Email: skylinecafe@rocketmail.com
PIREP:
Park at the Jet Center and walk into the **Skyline's** front door. They are located right inside the terminal building. The menu item I like the best is the 8oz **SkyLine** burger. It is made from Angus beef and comes out juicy and flavorful. This is a very good breakfast or lunch stop whenever you're in east Texas.

UVALDE, TX (GARNER FIELD - UVA)
Aprt Mgr: WILL CAIN **PH:** 830-279-0877

195

Field Elevation: 942 **CTAF:** 122.800 **FUEL:** 100LLA
Runway: 15/33 **Length:** 5256 **Width:** 100 **Surface:** ASPH-G

**** Hangar 6 Air Café - (830) 900-3113
Open:
>Mon – Tues 8:00am – 3:00pm
>Wed – Sat 8:00am – 9:00pm
>Sun 9:00am – 3:00pm

Restaurant Website: hangar6aircafe.com
Restaurant Email: info@hangar6aircafe.com
PIREP:
Buy $100 worth of fuel and any burger on the menu is yours for free. Now that's a new twist on the $100 Hamburger. I like it! Why doesn't every restaurant reward pilots who fly in?

Great decor. Plenty of tables inside and out, as well as counter service. Playground for kids. Extensive menu in a beautiful hard-bound booklet that includes the history of Garner Field. I'm going back!!!

VICTORIA, TX (VICTORIA RGNL - VCT)
Aprt Mgr: JASON MILEWSKI **PH:** 361-578-2704
Field Elevation: 115 **CTAF:** 126.075 **FUEL:** 100LLA
Runway: 06/24 **Length:** 4200 **Width:** 75 **Surface:** ASPH-F
Runway: 17/35 **Length:** 4908 **Width:** 75 **Surface:** ASPH-G
Runway: 12L/30R **Length:** 9111 **Width:** 150 **Surface:** ASPH-G
Runway: 12R/30L **Length:** 4643 **Width:** 150 **Surface:** CONC-P

Victoria Jet Center – 361-578-1221
Affiliate: UNK
Self Service: YES
Pilot Supplies: YES
Hours: Mon - Sat 6:00 - 9:00 Sun 6:00 - 6:00

*** The Sky Restaurant – (361) 576-5335
Proprietor: Loc Phan
Open:
>Mon – Fri: 11am – 10pm
>Sat: 4pm – 10pm

Restaurant Website: www.theskygrill.com
Restaurant Email: locphan@theskygrill.com
PIREP:
Sky serves wonderful seafood and steaks for lunch and dinner every day of the week except Sunday. Like so many airports in this part of Texas, VCT was a military airfield dedicated to pilot training during WWII. That means more than one runaway. In this case, there is also

an ILS approach. Airlines come here but only twice a day so commercial traffic isn't a problem.

Sky is located in what was once the Officer's Club. It is roomy and nicely decorated. I come here for the fried oyster. They are freshly shucked and perfectly prepared. You'll find many choices on the menu to make you smile whether you're here for lunch or dinner. The prices are moderate.

FlyIn Utah

OGDEN, UT (OGDEN-HINCKLEY - OGD)
    Aprt Mgr: ROYAL ECCLES **PH:** 801-629-8251
    Field Elevation: 4473 **CTAF:** 118.700 **FUEL:** 100 A1+
    Runway: 03/21 **Length:** 8103 **Width:** 150 **Surface:** ASPH-E
    Runway: 16/34 **Length:** 5195 **Width:** 100 **Surface:** ASPH-F
    Runway: 07/25 **Length:** 3618 **Width:** 150 **Surface:** ASPH-P

Kemp Jet Services – 801-627-0040
FBO Website: www.kempjet.com
Affiliate: Avfuel
Self Service: NO
Pilot Supplies: YES
Hours: 7 days 7:00-8:00

Mountain Valley Aviation – 801-394-3400
FBO Website: www.mountainvalleyaviation.com
Affiliate: Ascent
Self Service: YES
Pilot Supplies: YES
Hours: 7 days 7:00-8:00

CB Jet Center – 801-621-0326
Affiliate: UNK
Self Service: NO
Pilot Supplies: YES
Hours: 7:00 - 8:00 M/F

*** Doolittle's Deli – **(801) 627-3200**
Open: Mon – Fri: 7:00am – 3:00pm
Restaurant Website: doolittlesdeli.com
Restaurant Email: doolittlesdeli@live.com
PIREP:
Call first as Doolittle's has been opening and closing like a jumping frog during the COVID crisis. Post lockdowns they have experienced staffing issues.

Doolittle's Deli serves Soups, Salads, Sandwiches, Pizzas, Pastas and Calzones. It is a deli-styled restaurant located in the building which houses Kemp Jet Services, at the end of runway 16. Everything on the menu is made fresh daily including the potato chips and NOTHING comes out of a box. They are mostly known for their fried pizza and calzones. You read correctly - fried pizza! **Rickenbacker's Bistro** is right upstairs.

Three ski resorts are within 30 minutes of the airport. The Dinosaur Park is about 8 miles away. The Hill AFB Aerospace Museum is just 3 miles. My favorite is the Union Station Museum which is loaded with trains, Browning firearms and automobiles. It too is within 5 miles.

FlyIn Vermont

BURLINGTON, VT (BURLINGTON INTL - BTV)
Aprt Mgr: ROBERT MCEWING **PH:** 802-863-2874
Field Elevation: 335 **CTAF:** 118.300 **FUEL:** 100LLA
Runway: 15/33 **Length:** 8320 **Width:** 150 **Surface:** ASPH-CONC-G
Runway: 01/19 **Length:** 3611 **Width:** 75 **Surface:** ASPH-G

Heritage Aviation – 877-326-5288
Affiliate: Phillips 66 **Self Service:** NO
Pilot Supplies: YES
Hours: 7 days 5:00 - 10:00

*** Skinny Pancake – (802) 752-6761
Proprietor: Jonny and Benjy Adler
Open:
> Mon- Sun: 4:30am – 7pm

Restaurant Website:
www.skinnypancake.com/locations/burlington-international-airport
PIREP:
Out with the old in with the new. In 2013 **FOUR** new restaurants opened in the terminals of the Burlington International Airport. Skinny Pancake is a crepe restaurant. It serves a **WIDE** variety of sweet and savory crepes. All of them made from locally grown ingredients. There are more items on the menu including a really good burger. There is a Skinny Pancake in the North Terminal and another in the South terminal. Each are on the wrong side of the security gate. If you are willing to deal with the TSA you'll be well pleased with the Skinny Pancake experience. If not you can enjoy a stop at their sister shop, **The Chubby Muffin** which is outside security just across from the ticket counters in both terminals. Don't expect much, it is merely a kiosk.

---

* The Chubby Muffin – (802) 497-0653
Proprietor: Jonny and Benjy Adler
Open:
> Mon- Sun: 4:30am – 7:00pm

PIREP:
The Chubby Muffin is a sister-company to the **Skinny Pancake**, the 'Robin' to the Skinny Pancake's 'Batman' and is located on BTV's first level, across from the United and US Airways ticket counters. Don't expect much, it is merely a kiosk.

RUTLAND, VT (RUTLAND - SOUTHERN VERMONT RGNL - RUT)
Aprt Mgr: DAVE CARMAN **PH:** 802-786-8881

Field Elevation: 787 **CTAF:** 122.800 **FUEL:** 100LLA
Runway: 13/31 **Length:** 3170 **Width:** 75 **Surface:** ASPH-G
Runway: 01/19 **Length:** 5003 **Width:** 100 **Surface:** ASPH-G

*** The Hangar Cafe – (802) 770-1855
Open:
Tue - Thur: 7AM-6PM,
Fri - Sat: 7AM-8PM
Sun: 7AM-3PM
Restaurant Website: flyrutlandvt.com/hangar-cafe/
Restaurant Email: thehangarcafe@yahoo.com
PIREP:
Good food, ample parking on the tarmac out front, and friendly staff. The restaurant is upstairs in the Terminal building. The views of the mountains and the airfield are amazing. Worth a stop.

VERGENNES, VT (BASIN HARBOR - B06)
Aprt Mgr: ROBERT BEACH, JR. **PH:** 802-475-2311
Field Elevation: 132 **CTAF:** 122.800 **FUEL:**
Runway: 02/20 **Length:** 3000 **Width:** 90 **Surface:** TURF-G

**** The Red Mill Restaurant – (802) 475-2317
Open:
Mon - Fri: 11:30am – 9pm
Sat – Sun: 11:30am – 10pm
Restaurant Website: www.basinharbor.com/dining/
Restaurant Email: info@basinharbor.com
PIREP:
The Basin Harbor Resort on the shores of Lake Champlain is a gorgeous stop whether you're coming for lunch or longer. The 3,200-foot grass airstrip is one of the best I've seen in New England, but it has no landing lights or avgas and you must bring your own tie-downs.

The Red Mill Restaurant a renovated 1940 sawmill sits right on the resorts runway. Everything on the Lunch and dinner menu looks good. I've been here only twice for lunch and opted for the Fried Chicken & Waffles both times. It comes with a Cherry Compote and real Vermont Maple syrup (no surprise there). It is a very nice dish.

***** The Basin Harbor Resort – (802) 475.2311
Open:
Daily
Restaurant Website: www.basinharbor.com
Restaurant Email: info@basinharbor.com
PIREP:

John Purner

The Basin Harbor Resort on the shores of Lake Champlain is a gorgeous. The 3,200-foot grass airstrip is one of the best I've seen in New England, but it has no landing lights or avgas and you must bring your own tie-downs. It is an old time New England resort. The accommodations are superb, the staff is friendly and well trained, the food is fabulous and the wine list is first rate. You can golf, swim, boat, hike or just relax. A weekend here is expensive and worth it.

FlyIn Virginia

ALTON, VA (VAUGHAN - 00VA)
Aprt Mgr: RONNIE D. VAUGHAN **PH:** 434-753-1260
Field Elevation: 551 **CTAF:** 0.000 **FUEL:**
Runway: 01/19 **Length:** 1300 **Width:** 100 **Surface:** TURF

*** Fireside Express Grill - 540-856-2121 x 259
Proprietor: Rob Schwartz
Open:

Seasonal:
Closes for winter: October 27
April 27 re-opens:
Sat – Sun: 8am – 5pm

Restaurant Website: www.bryceresort.com
PIREP:
The Bryce Resort operates year-round. It is wise to call first to check on runway conditions, especially in the winter. The pilots' lounge at the airport has been renovated and pilots are welcome to use it. Please enter the VFR Xpdr code to open the door. The adjacent library has a Wi-Fi connection. **The Fireside Express Grill** of the Bryce Resort is a short distance (200 yards?) from the airstrip and overlooks the golf course's 1st and 10th tees. It offers pizza, burgers, specialty sandwiches, coffee, soda and beer.

*** Restaurant @ Bryce Resort- 540-856-2121 x 245
Proprietor: Rob Schwartz
Open:

Fri - Sat: 5pm – 9pm
Sun: 9am -12pm (Brunch)

Restaurant Website: www.bryceresort.com
PIREP:
The Bryce Resort operates year-round. It is wise to call first to check on runway conditions, especially in the winter. The pilots' lounge at the airport has been renovated and pilots are welcome to use it. Please enter the VFR Xpdr code to open the door. The adjacent library has a Wi-Fi connection. **The Restaurant @ Bryce Resort** is more upscale than **The Fireside Express Grill** and is open year-round for dinner. Count on good steaks and god wine with decent service.

**** The Bryce Resort- 540-856-2121
Proprietor: Rob Schwartz
Open:

Daily

Resort Website: www.bryceresort.com
PIREP:
The Bryce Resort operates year round and is all about activities. You
don't come to sit around.

Here's a partial list of what you can **DO**:

Golf
Ski
Mountain BikeHike
Zip Line

In the summer they have grass skiing, which I have never done and
summer tubing which is very, very fun. Oddly, they do not have a
lodge or any housing on the resort property there are nearby hotels, RV
parks and camping facilities. With a little luck you can rent a house on
the property.

FREDERICKSBURG, VA (SHANNON - EZF)
Aprt Mgr: MS BILLIE S. TOOMBS **PH:** 540-373-4431
Field Elevation: 85 **CTAF:** 122.800 **FUEL:** 100LLA
Runway: 06/24 **Length:** 2999 **Width:** 100 **Surface:** ASPH-G
Runway: 15/33 **Length:** 1500 **Width:** 150 **Surface:** TURF-G

** Robin's Nest Café – (540) 373-4441
Open:
Daily: 9 AM to 5 PM
Restaurant Website: www.shannonezf.com
PIREP:
I haven't visited this restaurant. The report below is provided a friend
and fellow Burger Subscriber.

"**Robin's Nest Café** is in the Main Terminal at Shannon Airport, which
has been completely renovated. The Cafe is a 1950's style diner and is
very clean. The seating area indoors is open and spacious with a view
of the runway. There is also a patio area for serving, weather
permitting. The staff is very friendly. The menu consists of a few
sandwiches (panini's, sub sandwiches, hot dogs and hamburgers), an
assortment of snack foods and very good milk shakes. There is also a
pilot shop with T-shirts and other items. Gas prices are typically the
lowest in the area. No parking fees for day only parking."

MARTINSVILLE, VA (BLUE RIDGE - MTV)
Aprt Mgr: JASON DAVIS **PH:** 276-957-2291
Field Elevation: 941 **CTAF:** 122.700 **FUEL:** 100LLA
Runway: 12/30 **Length:** 5002 **Width:** 100 **Surface:** ASPH-G

Blue

Blue Ridge Airport – 276-957-2291
Affiliate: UNK
Self Service: YES
Pilot Supplies: YES
Hours: 24/7 LL self serve 8:00 - 5:00 7 days for JetA

** Simply Suzanne's Café – (276) 957-1142
Open:
Tue - Sun: 11:00 am – 4:00 pm
Restaurant Website: www.flyblueridge.com
Restaurant Email: flyblueridge@yahoo.com
PIREP:
Simply Suzanne's Café offers lunch. It has an outside patio available where you can eat and watch arriving and departing aircrafts. The dining room has large windows if you prefer to eat inside and still enjoy the view. This is not one of my favorite stops but it is an OK place with decent food and a friendly environment.

RICHMOND, VA (CHESTERFIELD COUNTY - FCI)
Aprt Mgr: TOM TRUDEAU **PH:** 804-743-0771
Field Elevation: 236 **CTAF:** 123.050 **FUEL:** 100LLA
Runway: 15/33 **Length:** 5500 **Width:** 100 **Surface:** ASPH-G

Dominion Av Service – 804-271-7793
Affiliate: UNK
Self Service: YES
Pilot Supplies: YES
Hours: 6:00 - 9:00 7 days

**** King's Korner Restaurant – (804) 743-9333
Proprietor: Debbie Cromie
Open:
Lunch Wed - Sat: 11am – 2pm
Dinner Thur - Sat: 5pm – 9pm
Brunch Sunday : 10:00am – 3:00pm
Restaurant Website: www.kingskornercatering.com
Restaurant Email: debbiec@kingskornercatering.com
PIREP:
The food isn't just good, its great and the view is wonderful. The service is all you can eat buffet style. I try to get here on Wednesday when they have Country Fried Steak on the buffet. I love this place and you will too. The King family understands food and service. An adult trip through the lunch buffet line goes for $13.95 plus $3.00 for your drink. It is an amazing value.

John Purner

SALUDA, VA (HUMMEL FIELD - W75)
Aprt Mgr: MARCIA JONES **PH:** 804-758-4330
Field Elevation: 30 **CTAF:** 123.000 **FUEL:** 100LL
Runway: 01/19 **Length:** 2270 **Width:** 45 **Surface:** ASPH-G

**** Eckhard's – (804) 758.4060
Open:

      Wed – Sat: 4:30pm - 9:00pm
      Sun: 3:30pm - 8:00pm

Restaurant Website: www.eckhards.com/
PIREP:

Eckhard's is currently closed for remodeling and expansion. Phone ahead to check on the reopening date.

An unexpectedly good discovery in an unlikely location! Excellent German and Italian food, with an amazing selection of German beers. Reservations strongly suggested. I really like the Wiener Schnitzel. For dessert try the Bread Pudding. This is one of few places that can actually deliver it with a decent hot Bourbon sauce.

Taxi into the grass parking area at the approach end of Runway 1, and you're a 30-yard walk from the front door. Tie down points, but no ropes, on the small concrete pads. W75 also has self-service 24 hour fuel and pilot-controlled runway lighting, a great small airport. Watch out for the trees on approach and departure.

SUFFOLK, VA (SUFFOLK EXECUTIVE - SFQ)
Aprt Mgr: KENT MARSHALL **PH:** 757-514-4411
Field Elevation: 70 **CTAF: 122.700 FUEL:** 100LLA MOGAS
Runway: 07/25 **Length:** 4706 **Width:** 100 **Surface:** ASPH-F
Runway: 04/22 **Length:** 5009 **Width:** 100 **Surface:** ASPH-G

Dominion Av Service – 804-271-7793
Affiliate: UNK
Self Service: YES
Pilot Supplies: YES
Hours: 6:00 - 9:00 7 days

**** Suffolk BBQ Company – (757) 514-4416
Open:

      Mon - Sun: 8:00am – 2:30pm

Restaurant Website: www.suffolkbbqcoairport.com
PIREP:

Here's what one of our subscribers had to say. I've look forward to visiting soon:

"Food wise the ribs are superb, and the burgers are excellent. The fries are hand cut and excellent. My wife has declared their banana pudding to be the best she's ever had.

Convenience wise its first rate, located right on the ramp, and with tie down spaces right out front. The tie down ropes were even in good condition.

There was a Zenith CH605 and an RV-7A there when we arrived as well as a steady stream of walk in local customers, so people are coming for the food not just the airport location.

Aviators abound and airplane talk between tables was the norm. KSFQ is not as active as it used to be, but it's still an active GA airport with a strong home builder presence.

Not surprisingly, there was a short (5 minute) for a table given the COVID 19 limitations. Also, not surprisingly they ran out of ribs not long after we ordered. while we were there (12:30pm). If you want ribs arrive early - or maybe call ahead and see if they will save you a rack."

WILLIAMSBURG, VA (WILLIAMSBURG-JAMESTOWN - JGG)
Aprt Mgr: "DON W. BROADY, JR." **PH:** 757-229-9256
Field Elevation: 49 **CTAF:** 122.800 **FUEL:** 100LLA
Runway: 13/31 **Length:** 3204 **Width:** 60 **Surface:** ASPH-G

*** Charly's Airport Restaurant - (757) 258-0034
Proprietor: Jean Waltrip
Open:
          Daily: 11:00am - 3:00pm
Restaurant Website: www.charlysairportrestaurant.com
PIREP:
Charly's was once really great and actually made it to the annual **$100 Hamburger Best of the Best** list. It has slipped in both service and food. Hence the three star rating rather than the five of better times. That said, they still have a wonderful deck just off the runway. It is a great place to come and "hangar fly" if only over a coke or a cup of coffee. Don't expect perfection and you'll enjoy your visit.

FlyIn Washington

ARLINGTON, WA (ARLINGTON MUNI - AWO)
Aprt Mgr: ROBERT PUTNAM **PH:** 360-403-3470
Field Elevation: 142 **CTAF:** 122.700 **FUEL:** 100LLA
Runway: 11/29 **Length:** 3498 **Width:** 75 **Surface:** ASPH-G
Runway: 16/34 **Length:** 5332 **Width:** 100 **Surface:** ASPH-G

**** Ellie's at the Airport - (360) 435-4777
Proprietor: Tom and Kathy Dacy
Open:
> Sun – Fri: 8am - 2pm
> Sat –Sun: 7am - 3pm

PIREP:
I love this place. The food is awesome, at least breakfast is. I 've never stopped in for lunch.

The pattern is active, and the view is great from the patio. Come early and bring an extra load of patience with you as Ellie's is popular with the locals and the wait can be long. Trust me it's worth the wait.

Its north of the busy Seattle airspace. That's a big plus.

BREMERTON, WA (BREMERTON NATIONAL - PWT)
Aprt Mgr: FRED SALISBURY **PH:** 360-674-2381
Field Elevation: 444 **CTAF:** 123.050 **FUEL:** 100LLA
Runway: 01/19 **Length:** 6000 **Width:** 150 **Surface:** ASPH-G

Avian Flight Center – 866-263-2359
Affiliate: UNK
Self Service: YES
Pilot Supplies: YES
Hours: 8-5 7 days

Amelia's Hangar Restaurant and Lounge
Open: COMING SOON
Restaurant Website: www.ameliashangarrestaurant.com/
PIREP:
The Airport Diner closed some time ago and is sorely missed. Fortunately, a new spot is soon to open. Construction is underway. Check www.100dollarhamburger.com to know when it happens.

BURLINGTON/MOUNT VERNON, WA (SKAGIT RGNL - BVS)
Aprt Mgr: SARA K. YOUNG PH: 360-757-0011
Field Elevation: 144 CTAF: 123.075 FUEL: 100LLA
Runway: 04/22 Length: 3000 Width: 60 Surface: ASPH-G
Runway: 10/28 Length: 5477 Width: 100 Surface: ASPH-G

Corporate Air Service – 360-757-7757
Affiliate: Phillips 66
Self Service: YES
Pilot Supplies: YES
Hours: M-F 7:00 - 7:00 Sat/Sun 7:00 - 5:00

Heritage Flight Museum – (360) 733-4422
Proprietor: Maj. Gen. William A. Anders
Open:
> **Grand Opening:** Saturday, 26 April 2014
> **Hours:** TBD

Fly Days:
> 12pm - 4pm the third Saturday of the month.
> Weather permitting

Museum Website: www.heritageflight.org
Museum Email: admin@heritageflight.org
PIREP:
The Heritage Flight Museum is dedicated to the preservation and flying of historic military aircraft. The collection includes a selection of flying World War II, Korean and Vietnam era aircraft and memorabilia and artifacts from the same periods. Many of the aircraft are flyable and are demonstrated in flight on the third Saturday of each month. Admission to the museum is 'by donation' – $8/adult, $5/child over 5 years.

Flyers Restaurant and Brew Pub – 360-675-5858
Open:
> Wed - Sat: 11:30am-9pm Sun: 11:30am-7pm

Restaurant Website: www.eatatflyers.com
PIREP:
The food is good and well worth the trip. Please call before flying in as they are struggling with their re-opening from COVID due to staff shortages and supply chain issues.

Come on one of the museums Fly Days if you can arrange it.

EVERETT, WA (SNOHOMISH COUNTY (PAINE FLD) - PAE)
Aprt Mgr: DAVID T WAGGONER PH: 425-388-5125
Field Elevation: 606 CTAF: 132.950 FUEL: 100LLA
Runway: 16R/34L Length: 9010 Width: 150 Surface: ASPH-

CONC-G
Runway: 16L/34R **Length:** 3000 **Width:** 75 **Surface:** ASPH-F
Runway: 11/29 **Length:** 4514 **Width:** 75 **Surface:** ASPH-G

Castle & Cooke Aviation – 425-355-6600
FBO Website: www.castlecookeaviation.com
Affiliate: UNK
Self Service: YES
Pilot Supplies: YES
Hours: 7 days 6:00 - 11:00

** Café at the Future of Flight - (360) 756-0086
Proprietor: Future of Flight
Open:
> Thur - Mon: 9:30am – 5:00pm

Restaurant Website: www.boeingfutureofflight.com/cafe
Museum Website: www.futureofflight.org
Museum Email: info@futureofflight.org
PIREP:
No tickets for the museum are required to dine in the Café. **The Café at the Future of Flight** offers a wide range of tasty and healthy menu items, including snacks, beverages, sandwiches, soups and salads. However; coming here for the food, which is mediocre at best and not visiting the museum or touring the Boeing factory is a huge mistake.

Future of Flight & Boeing Tour - (360) 756-0086
Proprietor: Boeing Aircraft Company
Open:
> Seven days a week: 8:30 am - 5 pm

Museum Website:
www.boeing.com/boeing/commercial/tours/index.page
Museum Website: www.futureofflight.org
Museum Email: info@futureofflight.org
PIREP:
Either FBO at Paine Field can provide ground transportation to get you over to Future Flight. There is no longer an entrance into the facility from the ramp. **The Future of Flight Aviation Center** is a unique learning and interpretive facility. The 73,000-square-foot facility includes an Aviation Gallery with interactive exhibits and displays, 9,000-square-foot rooftop observation deck overlooking Paine Field, Boeing Tour Center and a125-seat café. One of Seattle's favorite aviation attractions and is where the Boeing Factory Tour begins. The center offers the only opportunity to tour a commercial jet assembly plant in North America. The Future of Flight & Boeing Tour are made possible through the collaboration of the Boeing Company, Future of Flight Foundation. You will go behind the scenes at Boeing—in the

world's largest building to watch the very same commercial jets you are often a passenger on being assembled.

PORT TOWNSEND, WA (JEFFERSON COUNTY INTL - 0S9)
Aprt Mgr: LARRY CROCKETT **PH:** 360-385-2323
Field Elevation: 108 **CTAF:** 123.000 **FUEL:** 100LL
Runway: 09/27 **Length:** 3000 **Width:** 75 **Surface:** ASPH-G

Tailspin Tommy's – 360-385-1308
FBO Website: www.tailspintommy.com
Affiliate: UNK
Self Service: YES
Pilot Supplies: YES
Hours: 24/7

***** **Spruce Goose Cafe - (360) 385-3185**
Proprietor: Christine Pray
Open:
          Mon – Sun: 7am to 4pm
Restaurant Website: www.sprucegoosecafe.com
PIREP:
I like this place. It is best for two things: pies, which are homemade and daily lunch special which are awesome. You park on the ramp right by the front door. Here's what a good friend of *The Burger* has to say, *"The burgers are fab, the Reuben sandwich sublime, and the pie is spoken of in hushed, reverent tones."*

SEATTLE, WA (BOEING FIELD/KING COUNTY INTL - BFI)
Aprt Mgr: ROBERT I. BURKE AAE **PH:** 206-296-7380
Field Elevation: 21 **CTAF:** 0.000 **FUEL:** 100LLA
Runway: 13L/31R **Length:** 3710 **Width:** 100 **Surface:** ASPH-G
Runway: 13R/31L **Length:** 10000 **Width:** 200 **Surface:** ASPH-G

Clay Lacy Aviation – 206-762-6000
FBO Website: www.claylacy.com
Affiliate: Avfuel
Self Service: NO
Pilot Supplies: YES
Hours: 24/7

Landmark Aviation – 800-341-4102
FBO Website: www.landmarkaviation.com
Affiliate: UNK
Self Service: NO
Pilot Supplies: YES
Hours: 24/7

Aero Flight – 206-762-6376
Affiliate: UNK
Self Service: NO
Pilot Supplies: YES
Hours: 24/7

*** Wings Café at the Museum of Flight - (206) 764-5720
Proprietor: Museum of Flight
Open:

Mon – Sun: 10am - 5pm
1st Thurs of the Month: 10am - 9pm

Restaurant Website: www.museumofflight.org/wings-cafe
PIREP:

Wings Café is open during Museum hours but does not require admission. On nice days, you can sit out on the deck and watch the airshow that is Boeing Field's B taxiway and long runway. First, and foremost, **Wings Café** does not have burgers....what they do have are some nice salads, a few hot entrees and usually a tasty soup.

The Museum of Flight - (206) 764-5720
Proprietor: Museum of Flight
Open:

Mon – Sun: 10am - 5pm

Restaurant Website: www.museumofflight.org
PIREP:

This is the **largest** and **best** individually funded aviation museum in the world. Its permanent exhibit includes over 150 aircraft. Temporary exhibits are rotated constantly. I was fortunate to catch the late 2013 exhibit titled "In Search of Amelia Earhart". It included a viewing of the museum newly acquired Lockheed Model 10-E Electra which is sister ship of what our girl flew on her fateful circumnavigation attempt. For itinerant parking at the **Museum of Flight**, call 206-764-5710. There is a $5.00 fee for parking 12 hours or less. If you are ever in this part of the world don't miss this.

*** CAVU Cafe - (206) 764.4929
Open:

Mon – Sat: 7am – 6pm
Sat: 11am – 9pm (April – September)

Restaurant Website: www.cavucafe.com
Restaurant Email: cavucafe@gmail.com
PIREP:

The Cavu Cafe is in the main-terminal building. Great selection of Italian-style sandwiches at reasonable prices. I normally go with the Panini paired with a side Caesar.

SNOHOMISH, WA (HARVEY FIELD - S43)

Aprt Mgr: K HARVEY **PH:** 360-568-1541
Field Elevation: 22 **CTAF:** 123.000 **FUEL:** 100 A
Runway: 15L/33R **Length:** 2671 **Width:** 36 **Surface:** ASPH-G
Runway: 15R/33L **Length:** 2430 **Width:** 100 **Surface:** TURF-E

**** The Buzz Inn Steakhouse- (360) 568-3970
Proprietor: Laurie Klick
Open:

Mon – Sun: 8am – 8pm
Restaurant Website: www.buzzinnsteakhouse.com
Restaurant Email: snohomish@buzzinnsteakhouse.com
PIREP:
The Buzz Inn Steakhouse at Harvey field is part of a steak house chain that has been in this are for thirty years. The food is very good though the service was spotty in the past. On my last visit they were really on top of things. I haven't had breakfast here only lunch. For me, that means the Chicken Fried Steak Burger and a bowl of Billy's Chili. The view from the outside deck is hard to beat, especially when the drop zone is active.

SPOKANE, WA (FELTS FIELD - SFF)

Aprt Mgr: RYAN SHEEHAN **PH:** 509-455-6455
Field Elevation: 1957 **CTAF:** 132.500 **FUEL:** 100LLA1+
Runway: 03R/21L **Length:** 2650 **Width:** 75 **Surface:** ASPH-G
Runway: 03L/21R **Length:** 4499 **Width:** 150 **Surface:** CONC-G

Western Aviation – 509-534-7371
FBO Website: www.westernaviation.net
Affiliate: Phillips 66
Self Service: YES
Pilot Supplies: YES
Hours: 7 days 8:00-5:00

**** Skyway Cafe - (509) 534-5986
Proprietor: John & Sandy Melter
Open:

Mon – Sat: 6:00am - 2:00pm
Sun: 7:00am - 3:00pm
Restaurant Website: www.skywaycafe.com
Restaurant Email: Skywaycafe@windwireless.net
PIREP:
The Skyway Cafe may be the crown jewel for Spokane. Great food, great atmosphere, great service, great folks. It is located on the ramp and has a great view of the runway which is usually very active.

John Purner

Everything is made from scratch. For me, it's the Chicken Fried Steak at lunch and the cinnamon rolls at breakfast. The place is a hangout for EAA and 99 types, so come prepared to hangar fly.

TACOMA, WA (TACOMA NARROWS - TIW)
Aprt Mgr: DEB WALLACE **PH:** 253-798-7109
Field Elevation: 294 **CTAF:** 118.500 **FUEL:** 100LLA
Runway: 17/35 **Length:** 5002 **Width:** 150 **Surface:** ASPH-G

**** The Hub – (253) 853-1585
Open:
>Mon-Sun: 11am-9pm

Restaurant Website: www.thehubgigharbor.com/
PIREP:
Located beneath the control tower at the Tacoma Narrows Airport. The restaurant is on the Tacoma Narrows Airport tarmac, with views of the airstrip, just steps away from Tacoma Narrows Aviation.

They serve Harmon Brewing Company micro-brews in a family friendly atmosphere.

FlyIn West Virginia

FAIRMONT, WV (FAIRMONT MUNI-FRANKMAN FIELD - 4G7)
Aprt Mgr: DONNIE TUCKER **PH:** 304-366-1300
Field Elevation: 1029 **CTAF:** 122.800 **FUEL:** 100LL
Runway: 05/23 **Length:** 3194 **Width:** 75 **Surface:** ASPH-G

*** DJ's Diner – (304) 366-8110
Proprietor: DJ Rundle
Open:

Mon - Thu: 7:00am - 10:00pm
Fri - Sat: 7:00am - noon
Sun: 7:00am - 10:00pm

Restaurant Email: jeff@thejinglehouse.com
PIREP:
It is a real diner with a real juke box and a group of servers called the Pink Ladies. I like everything from their slogan "Break the Chain – **EAT LOCAL**" to their meatloaf. I really like this place and so will you. It's the real deal and is located a short *(less than a 100 yards)* walk from the FBO.

** Comfort Inn & Suites - (304) 367-1370
Open:

Daily

Motel Website:
www.comfortinn.com/hotel-fairmont-west_virginia-WV010#listpos
PIREP:
It is located new to **DJ's Diner**. Arrive late in the day, have dinner at **DJ's**, fill-up at the FBO's 24 hour self-service pump, RON at the **Comfort Inn & Suites,** have breakfast at **DJ's** and you're good to go. You could eat breakfast at the **Comfort Inn** as it's included in the price of your room but it isn't even close when it comes to good. Free Wi-Fi, an exercise room and a pool round out the offering. It's a long way from a bad hotel but it is also a long way from a great hotel.

HUNTINGTON, WV (TRI-STATE - HTS)
Aprt Mgr: JERRY BRIENZA **PH:** 304-453-6165
Field Elevation: 828 **CTAF:** 0.000 **FUEL:** 100LLA
Runway: 12/30 **Length:** 7016 **Width:** 150 **Surface:** ASPH-G

Tri State Airport – 304-453-6165
Affiliate: UNK
Self Service: NO
Pilot Supplies: YES

Hours: 24/7

*** Gino's Pizzeria & Pub - (304) 453-2768
Proprietor: Rick Duncan
Open:
>   Mon – Sun: 7am - 10pm

PIREP:

Gino's Pizzeria & Pub is in the main terminal, an easy walk from the FBO. Fortunately, it is outside the security zone so no problems with TSA. It is a relaxing and cozy environment to grab drink or a bite to eat. They offer a full bar with an extensive menu of wine and beer selections. Also served is **Gino's** legendary pizza, pub style sandwiches, chicken wings and other appetizers. There is a landing fee, even for small singles, which is waived with a fuel purchase.

*** Tudor's Biscuit World - (304) 453-2768
Proprietor: Rick Duncan
Open:
>   Mon – Sun: 7am - 10pm

PIREP:

Tudor's Biscuit World is in the main terminal, an easy walk from the FBO. Fortunately it is outside the security zone so no problems with TSA. It offers a wide variety of breakfast and lunch selections. Breakfast items include made-from-scratch biscuits with your favorite breakfast meats and toppings such as sliced or melted cheese, egg, fried apples and hash browns just to name a few. For those with a more hearty appetite, breakfast platters are also available including the popular biscuits and gravy and Super Breakfast. **Tudor's** lunch menu features a large selection of made-to-order sandwiches including pulled pork BBQ, 1/3 pound hamburgers and **Tudor's** famous hot dogs. There is a landing fee, even for small singles, which is waived with a fuel purchase.

MORGANTOWN, WV (MORGANTOWN MUNI - MGW)
Aprt Mgr: "MICHAEL CLOW, A.A.E." **PH:** 304-291-7461
Field Elevation: 1248 **CTAF:** 125.100 **FUEL:** 100LLA
Runway: 18/36 **Length:** 5199 **Width:** 150 **Surface:** ASPH-G

Morgantown Muni – 304-296-2359
Affiliate: UNK
Self Service: NO
Pilot Supplies: YES
Hours: 5:00 - midnight 7 days

**** Ali Baba - 304.292.4701
Proprietor: Mike & D'zeneta Rothenback

216

Open:
> Mon - Thu: 11:00 am - 8:00 pm
> Fri - Sat: 11:00 am - 9:00 pm

Restaurant Website: alibabaexpress.com

PIREP:
I come here for two dishes, Tabbouleh and the Gyro. Imagine for a moment how good a restaurant with a Middle Eastern menu would have to be to succeed in WV. Now imagine that the restaurant is at the airport not in the city center. That's a tough fact set. Now imagine that the restaurant has been here for 35 years. This place is good.

PARKERSBURG, WV (MID-OHIO VALLEY RGNL - PKB)
Aprt Mgr: TERRY H. MOORE **PH:** 304-464-5113
Field Elevation: 859 **CTAF:** 123.700 **FUEL:** 100LLA
Runway: 10/28 **Length:** 4002 **Width:** 150 **Surface:** ASPH-G
Runway: 03/21 **Length:** 7240 **Width:** 150 **Surface:** ASPH-G

**** Jerry's Fly Away Kitchen - 304-464-5100
Open:
> Tue – Sat: 9:00am – 7:00pm
> Sun: 11:00am – 2:00pm

PIREP:
Jerry's is the latest restaurant at this airport. They seem to come and go. Here's the good news. Looks like Jerry's is here to stay because he has gained local support. The "Sunday Crowd? Comes here. That says a lot.

I tend to judge airport restaurants by their burgers and their homemade pies. Jerry wins on both counts. He makes his burgers from scratch, no frozen machine formed patties here. The pies? Worth the trip, yes sir, worth the trip.

Always a special on the board.

John Purner

FlyIn Wisconsin

EAU CLAIRE, WI (CHIPPEWA VALLEY RGNL - EAU)
Aprt Mgr: CHARITY SPEICH **PH:** 715-839-4900
Field Elevation: 913 **CTAF:** 118.575 **FUEL:** 100LLA
Runway: 14/32 **Length:** 5000 **Width:** 100 **Surface:** ASPH-CONC-G
Runway: 04/22 **Length:** 8101 **Width:** 150 **Surface:** CONC-TRTD-G

Hawthorne Global Aviation – 715-835-3181
Affiliate: Shell
Self Service: NO
Pilot Supplies: YES
Hours: 5:00 - 10:00 7 days

*** Hangar 54 – (715) 598.1880
Open:
>Mon - Thurs 11 AM - 9 PM
>Fri - Sat 11 AM - 11 PM

PIREP:
According to owner Bob Adrian who was a Naval Air A&P, **Hangar 54** was one of the hangars at Pearl Harbor that survived the bombings and had been used as a Navy training center. I really like this place. It is slightly upscale but not so much so as to be off putting to a tired and hungry pilot. The burgers are terrific. What makes them so good is that all of the meat is freshly ground on site.

Great place!

JANESVILLE, WI (SOUTHERN WISCONSIN RGNL - JVL)
Aprt Mgr: RON BURDICK **PH:** 608-757-5768
Field Elevation: 808 **CTAF:** 118.800 **FUEL:** 100LLA
Runway: 18/36 **Length:** 5003 **Width:** 75 **Surface:** ASPH-F
Runway: 04/22 **Length:** 6700 **Width:** 150 **Surface:** ASPH-F
Runway: 14/32 **Length:** 7301 **Width:** 150 **Surface:** CONC-F

Janesville Jet – 608-758-1037
Affiliate: Phillips 66
Self Service: YES
Pilot Supplies: YES
Hours: 8-5 7 days

*** Bessie's Diner – (608) 201-1669
Open:
>6AM til 3PM Daily

218

Restaurant Website: www.bessiesdiner.com/
PIREP:
Bessie's Diner is named after Beloit native Bessie Raiche, the first American woman to fly solo in an airplane. She accomplished that in 1910 without benefit of flight instruction and in an airplane she and her husband had built. If this diner is half as good as Bessie it deserves a try.

*** Cursing Stone Pub - (608) 741-1100
Proprietor: Tom Ellis
Open:
Mon - Sun: 11am - 3:00 pm
Restaurant Website: www.gleneringolf.com/cursing-stone
Restaurant Email: info@gleneringolf.com
PIREP: Irish Pub faire. Its good you won't be disappointed.

Glen Erin Golf Club - (608) 741-1100
Proprietor: Tom Ellis
Open: Mon - Sun: Sunrise to Sunset
Restaurant Website: gleneringolf.com
Restaurant Email: info@gleneringolf.com
PIREP: Glen Erin is literally part of the aviation landscape. Rental clubs are available. Call a head for taxi instructions.

LAND O' LAKES, WI (KINGS LAND O' LAKES - LNL)
Aprt Mgr: RANDY RUTH **PH:** 715-547-3337
Field Elevation: 1705 **CTAF:** 122.800 **FUEL:** 100LLMOGAS
Runway: 14/32 **Length:** 4001 **Width:** 75 **Surface:** ASPH-G
Runway: 05/23 **Length:** 2577 **Width:** 130 **Surface:** TURF-F

Land O'Lakes Airport – 715-547-3337
Affiliate: UNK
Self Service: YES
Pilot Supplies: YES
Hours: 24/7 self service only

*** Gateway Lodge Restaurant and Lounge - (715) 547-3321
Proprietor: Christina and Keith Williams
Open:
Tue - Sat: 5:00 pm - 9:00 pm
Restaurant Website: www.gateway-lodge.com
Restaurant Email: gateway@gateway-lodge.com
PIREP:
Adjacent to the **Gateway Lodge** is the Land O' Lakes Municipal Airport. **Gateway Lodge Restaurant and Lounge** is located in the lodge. Landing before and departing after dinner is no big deal as the

runway is 4,000 feet of lighted asphalt with GPS and NDB approaches for 14/32. Fuel is available 24/7 from the self-service pump. The dinner menu is varied and worthwhile. I have enjoyed the Great Lakes Perch.

Gateway Lodge - (715) 547-3321
Proprietor: Christina and Keith Williams
Open:
Year Round
Restaurant Website: www.gateway-lodge.com
Restaurant Email: gateway@gateway-lodge.com
PIREP:
The **Gateway Lodge Restaurant** has 72 customized and newly renovated suites and studios, an indoor pool, a steaming hot tub and a redwood sauna. The historic lodge is a convenient gateway to a number of area recreational opportunities, from trap shooting and golfing to waterfall chasing, skiing and shopping, it's all within reach. There is a first rate Gun Club on the property as well as bike, ATV and snowmobile trails.

LONE ROCK, WI (TRI-COUNTY RGNL - LNR)
Aprt Mgr: MARC HIGGS **PH:** 608-583-2600
Field Elevation: 717 **CTAF:** 123.000 **FUEL:** 100LLA
Runway: 18/36 **Length:** 1850 **Width:** 60 **Surface:** ASPH-G
Runway: 09/27 **Length:** 5000 **Width:** 75 **Surface:** ASPH-G

Tri- County Regional – 608-583-2600
Affiliate: Phillips 66
Self Service: YES
Pilot Supplies: YES
Hours: M-F 8:00 - 4:00

MADISON, WI (DANE COUNTY RGNL-TRUAX FIELD - MSN)
Aprt Mgr: "BRADLEY S. LIVINGSTON, AAE" **PH:** 608-246-3380
Field Elevation: 887 **CTAF:** 119.300 **FUEL:** 100LLA
Runway: 14/32 **Length:** 5846 **Width:** 150 **Surface:** CONC-G
Runway: 03/21 **Length:** 7200 **Width:** 150 **Surface:** CONC-G
Runway: 18/36 **Length:** 9006 **Width:** 150 **Surface:** CONC-G

Wisconsin Aviation – 608-268-5000
Affiliate: UNK
Self Service: NO
Pilot Supplies: YES
Hours: 24/7

*** Pat O'Malley's Jet Room - (608) 268-5010

Proprietor: Nick and Megan Tarczynskis
Open:
>Mon - Sat: 7:00 am - 2:00 pm
>Sun: 8:00 am - 2:00 pm

Restaurant Website: www.jetroomrestaurant.com
Restaurant Email: info@jetroomrestaurant.com
PIREP:
Located within Wisconsin Aviation's building. They offer great views from floor to ceiling windows that run the length of the restaurant. The coffee is good, the seating is fast and the ambiance is all airport. Nick runs one of only two restaurants' I know of that offers a Burger that costs a hundred bucks. The burger comes with a scenic airplane ride over Madison, which is one of America's most beautiful cities.

MOSINEE, WI (CENTRAL WISCONSIN - CWA)
>**Aprt Mgr:** TONY YARON **PH:** 715-693-2147
>**Field Elevation:** 1277 **CTAF:** 119.750 **FUEL:** 100LLA
>**Runway:** 17/35 **Length:** 6501 **Width:** 150 **Surface:** CONC-F
>**Runway:** 08/26 **Length:** 7648 **Width:** 150 **Surface:** CONC-G

Central Wisconsin Aviation – 715-693-6111
Affiliate: Phillips 66
Self Service: NO
Pilot Supplies: YES
Hours: 5:00 - 10:00 7 days

** The Blind Rooster – (404) 373-4007
Open:
>Mon-Sun: 4:45am – 5:45pm

Restaurant Website: www.fly-cwa.org
Restaurant Email: julrick@fly-cwa.org
PIREP:
The **Blind Rooster** is located in the concourse area of the terminal just past the security checkpoint. It is about a two-minute walk from the FBO to the terminal. You go here if you are hungry, it is not to be confused in anyway with the term "destination restaurant". I once had the three-cheese grilled sandwich here. It was actually pretty good.

OSHKOSH, WI (WITTMAN RGNL - OSH)
>**Aprt Mgr:** PETER MOLL **PH:** 920-236-4930
>**Field Elevation:** 808 **CTAF:** 118.500 **FUEL:** 100LLA+
>**Runway:** 13/31 **Length:** 3061 **Width:** 75 **Surface:** ASPH-F
>**Runway:** 04/22 **Length:** 3697 **Width:** 75 **Surface:** ASPH-F
>**Runway:** 09/27 **Length:** 6179 **Width:** 150 **Surface:** CONC-G
>**Runway:** 18/36 **Length:** 8002 **Width:** 150 **Surface:** CONC-G

Basler Flight Service – 920-236-7827
Affiliate: UNK
Self Service: YES
Pilot Supplies: YES
Hours: M-F 7:00 - 7:00 Sat - Sun 8:00 - 5:00

EAA AirVenture Museum - (920) 426-4800
Proprietor: Ron Twellman
Open:
              Mon-Sun: 10am - 5pm
Restaurant Website: www.airventuremuseum.org
Restaurant Email: museum@eaa.org
PIREP:
The EAA AirVenture Museum, has become one of the world's most extensive aviation attractions, and a year-round family destination. It is located on the site of the world's largest aviation event, EAA AirVenture.

The collection of historic artifacts began in 1962 when Steve Wittman donated his famous air racer "Bonzo". It now comprises more than 20,000 aviation objects of historic importance. Included are 250 historic airplanes, the count grows almost weekly as exhibits are constantly added. Everything from a powered parachute to a B-17 Flying Fortress is maintained in airworthy condition! Some are available to give ordinary people the chance to fly in historic aircraft. Most are used to provide flight demonstrations or support special activities such as the EAA Young Eagles program.

The EAA AirVenture Museum's library contains almost 9,000 volumes. The collection covers a variety of topics including biographies, aerodynamics, history, fiction, aeronautics, air racing and homebuilding.

The library's photographic collection archives more than 100,000 images of aircraft, spacecraft and the people made and flew them. Many photos chronicle the homebuilding movement of the early 1950s. They tell the story of an emerging group of people determined to design, build and fly their own aircraft. Important photo archives donated by private collectors are curated here. Included are:

The Radtke Collection: One thousand negatives of military aircraft, civilian aircraft and famous aviators from the '30s.

The Worthington Collection: 125 plus, glass negatives donated taken by an unknown photographer.

The Zeigler Collection: Over 200 glass negatives of early German aviators of post WWI era.

The Norman Collection: Hundreds of eight by ten black and white photographs covering the golden years of aviation.

This is truly one of the great aviation museums. Do not pass up an opportunity to visit. Be warned! Timing your visit to coincide with the EEA's annual airshow is a great mistake. It becomes very crowded and is hardly "user friendly" at those times. Plan you trip for a nice spring or summer weekend. Combine you trip with a visits to The Pioneer Airport, it is right next door. Here you want to spend thoughtful time and soak-up the history that is all around you. Plan to spend time here.

Food? Yes, they have food but that's not the reason to come!

WEBSTER, WI (VOYAGER VILLAGE AIRSTRIP - 9WN2)
Aprt Mgr: STEVE JOHNSON **PH:** 715-259-3910
Field Elevation: 1020 **CTAF:** 122.900 **FUEL: N/A**
Runway: 04/22 **Length:** 3500 **Width:** 50 **Surface:** ASPH

***** The Grill at Voyager Village – (715) 259-3910
Open:
Mon: 11:00am - 9:00pm
Wed - Fri: 11:00am - 9:00pm
Sat- Sun: 8:00am - 8:00pm
Restaurant Website: www.voyagervillage.com/bar-grill/
Airport Website: www.voyagervillage.com/airstrip/
PIREP:
This is a hard to beat breakfast flyout. **Voyager Village** is a LARGE housing development in Northern Wisconsin. It's home to 5,200 acres of woodland lakes, two golf courses a paved landing strip and one really good **Grill**.

The food is excellent, the service wonderful and views unbeatable. Do yourself a favor; drop in for breakfast and a round of golf.

FlyIn Wyoming

RIVERTON, WY (RIVERTON RGNL - RIW)
Aprt Mgr: WILLIAM A. URBIGKIT **PH:** 307-856-9128
Field Elevation: 5528 **CTAF:** 122.800 **FUEL:** 100LLA
Runway: 10/28 **Length:** 8204 **Width:** 150 **Surface:** ASPH-F
Runway: 01/19 **Length:** 4800 **Width:** 75 **Surface:** ASPH-G

✈ **Jim's Aircraft** – 307-856-3599
FBO Website: www.superiorflying.com
Affiliate: Phillips 66   **Self Service:** NO
Pilot Supplies: YES
Hours:
>   Mon-Fri 8:00 -6:00
>   Sat/Sun 8:00 -4:00

THERMOPOLIS, WY (THERMOPOLIS MUNI - THP)
Aprt Mgr: TARA CHESNUT **PH:** 307-864-2488
Field Elevation: 4592 **CTAF:** 122.800 **FUEL:** 100LL
Runway: 01/19 **Length:** 4800 **Width:** 100 **Surface:** ASPH-P

JT Aviation – 307-864-2488
Affiliate: Phillips 66
Self Service: YES
Pilot Supplies: YES
Hours: 8 – 7 7 days

Legion Town and Country Club Golf Course - (307) 864-5294
Proprietors: Mike McManis
Open:
>   Seasonal

PIREP:
Legion Town and Country Club Golf Course sits right across the parking lot from the FBO. It is a 9 hole public course that's fun to play with just enough terrain roll to make you remember that you are in Wyoming. If you are in the area, be sure to stop by and play this one. It's a great little course with terrific views. The green fee ranges from $18 on the weekend to $16 during the week.

The Back of the Book

Defending the Burger Run

The $100 Hamburger Diet

Why New Aircraft Cost So Much and Why They Shouldn't

The Current Burger Fleet

The Sky High Cost of Flying

Partnerships

Flying Clubs

The Death of 02GOLF

Is it time to buy a Legacy LSA?

Summer Flight Planning

John Purner

Defending the Burger Run

A few months ago one of the major general aviation magazines allowed a guest columnist to write an article blasting owner/pilots use of their time and aircraft to make Burger Runs. He pontificated for three pages about the worthless of *The $100 Hamburger* activity. He went on and on ad nauseam about how much time and money we were wasting on this activity and that we must put our flying privilege to a higher purpose.

I boiled over it for a while; I am after all the head burgermeister! Finally, I let it go realizing that even a fine magazine can make a mistake by giving a foolish person a pulpit every now and then.

Well, it's back on my mind and I want to take a few moments to refute the notion that *$100 Hamburger* flights are useless. I actually believe they are the most important flying that 98% of general aviation pilots can and should do. Point one: **it is darn good training.** *$100 Hamburger* flights are cross-country missions to never before visited or infrequently visited airports. Staying in the pattern and shooting landing after landing at your home 'port does nothing to improve your ability to use your aircraft, your license and your ratings for the purpose they were intended - **travel!** If you don't make frequent cross country training flights, your annual vacation flight with the family aboard is going to be a real anxiety producing sweatfest for you and your passengers. Yes, they can tell when the pilot is not comfortable with what he is doing and it scares the heck out of them and should. So train and stay sharp. Your passengers will appreciate it.

Point two: **it promotes general aviation.** Introduce your non-pilot friends to the joys of personal flying. Right now, general aviation is under attack, CBS news is busy alerting the public to the danger that lurks inside every overhead 172, *"It could be piloted by a terrorist."* They are not attacking corporate aviation. Television executives like their private jets; therefore, they pose no terrorist threat and are off limits to the attacks of any muckraking reporter, your 172 is another matter.

Take as many people from your local community flying as you can, take them as far as you can and point out the utility of a single engine personal aircraft or a light twin to get you where you need to go in a hurry. Show them the advantages of general aviation over commercial aviation for trips of less than 500 miles. Think of it as a long duration *Young Eagle Flight* for an adult.

General aviation aircraft are wonderful tools in the hands of trained and practiced pilots. So train and practice. Stay sharp. The best practice is cross-country flying. The best practice flights are $100 Hamburger runs.

The $100 Hamburger Diet

The $100 Hamburger Diet is pretty simple.
It requires no will power and very little won't power. It has been scientifically proven by **ALL** researchers to work. It is sure fire. You were probably expecting to read a tongue in cheek comedy bit. This is no laughing matter. Americans are becoming as fat as if they had been shipped to a Kansas City feed lot in preparation for a trip to the Chicago slaughterhouse.

The problem of obesity has now spread to Europe. EU men are busting the scales at higher weights than American men as they blow past their traditional diets in favor of our fast food lifestyle.

We all have two appetites; one is **biological** the other is **psychological**.
Feed your body, the biological you, whenever you feel hunger pangs. When you're thirsty, drink. When you're hungry, eat. Sounds simple so far doesn't it. It is!

How much should you eat? Easy, stop when you're full. If your plate is still half full, leave it. Remember you are a human being not a human garbage can. Don't worry at all about how much is left on your plate. Eat as much as your body, the biological you, wants, listen to its signals very closely.

Rule one: When you eat, eat exclusively.

Don't eat and watch TV or drive the car or walk down the street. When you eat, sit down at a table and eat.

Rule Two: Eat slowly.
How?
Simple!

Deal with one bite at a time. Place your fork on your plate while you're chewing what's in your mouth. Don't think about the next bite. Enjoy the one in your mouth. Chew it well and take in all the flavor of the food. Now pick up your fork and take another bite. The moment you feel your body's *"I'm getting full"* signal, **STOP!**

Rule Three: What foods can you eat?

Anything that you want.
Burgers? Bring 'em on!
Pie? You bet!
Ice cream? That, too!

John Purner

Your waistline problem isn't caused by the food you eat. It is caused by the amount you eat. Take a look at your fat friends. They are becoming bulbous on a diet of grapefruit and water. Why? Because they never stop eating and they eat like there is no tomorrow!

Rule Four: Avoid Fast Food.

This doesn't mean fast food restaurants. It means fast food. Food isn't meant to be eaten quickly. Get that out of your mind. Mealtime is meant to be enjoyed. Think about mealtime as being a sit-down event. Think about food as being slow not fast!

Be guided by your biology. When your body is hungry feed it whatever it is hungry for even a Big Mac. Don't buy it at the drive through window. Park your car, walk inside, buy the burger, sit down at a table and eat it.

What about feeding the psychological you?

D O N 'T!

Food is a biological necessity and a psychological trap. If you eat because you're happy or sad or mad or glad or bored you will get **FAT**, very **FAT**. Find other things to do to have fun. **Read, fly, run, swim, talk, write, etc. etc. etc. Obesity** is a problem because we feed our egos not our bodies. Stop it!

John Purner

Reader Feedback

Great article,

The truth always speaks clearly!

Francis

Dear John,

I enjoyed your editorial on the **$100 diet**.

One thing needs to be adjusted; you cannot get fat on ***grapefruit and water***, period. I think that managing your diet by not mixing meat, milk, bread and potatoes will do much more for you in terms of losing or not gaining weight. My recommendation would be to adjust the section on "***what can you eat?***" to reflect the food selection. I recommend, *green salad, vegetables and vegetable juices*. If you eat **meat**, restrain from **milk products** for *30 minutes* and vis a versa. Limit your bread intake to 1 pc. per meal.

228

I agree with everything else you wrote.
Best regards,
Jack

John Purner

Why New Aircraft Cost So Much and Why They Shouldn't!

Walter Beech listened to the comments of a dissatisfied private aircraft owner. *"I drive to the airport in my spacious, comfortable, quiet car with all types of amenities,"* the pilot said, *"Then I climb into my airplane (which costs three times as much) and is loud, cramped and miserable!"*

In 1947, he answered them and set a new standard for private planes. The Bonanza's cabin noise faded to a hum at cruising speed, and passengers were pampered with padded seats, surrounded by all-wool fabrics and wall-to-wall carpet. Why would anyone want to fly anything else? The design criterion was simple, luxury car quality in an airplane.

A 1947 Cadillac Model 62 four door sedan was priced at $2,523 or about 1/3 of the Bonanza's $7,975 sticker. Walter Beech had truly met his customers' quality and cost expectations. The right product at the right price was his winning strategy. Fifteen hundred Bonanza's left Wichita in 1947.

Let's fast-forward twenty years. The purchase price of a 1968 Cadillac Sedan Deville had crept up to $5,785 ($30,427 in 2007 dollars). A little more than double the 1947 sticker. Beech introduced the A36, a product destined to take-on Cessna's 6 passenger variants, the 210 and 206. The Bonanza continued to be the plane every private pilot wanted, but its $40, 650 ($213,808 in 2007 dollars) price had crept to a level that only a few could afford. In twenty years, its sticker had not only risen to match the inflation rate but its relationship to a Cadillac Sedan Deville, had more than doubled. Beech now demanded seven times the value of the car their customers drove not the historic three. The sales figures showed the results. Only 184 A36's were sold during their first year, a far cry from the Model 35's introductory success. As low as the number was, it represented the most successful year the A36 would ever have. Only 2,709 A36's of all variants have been produced in 40 years; an average of just 68 per year.

The 1968 A36 had six seats and a gigantic aft door. Its *"state of the art"* avionics could take advantage of the country's newly installed ILS system and could track a VOR like a setter on point. It was not; however, a new design. It was a model 33 Bonanza with a 10-inch stretch added to the fuselage. The Model 33 was a model 35 (*the 1947 Bonanza*) with a straight tail rather than a v-tail. The A36 was merely an improvement on the 1947 Bonanza not a NEW design. Twenty years had passed and nothing much had changed. The engine had grown from 185 horses to 285 horses but it was still a pre-war pancake engine sparked by dual magnetos. The A36 did say goodbye to the carburetor of its ancestor in favor of fuel injection. Yes, the fuselage was longer but that was accomplished

230

in much the same way a Fleetwood is turned into a stretch limo, no design breakthrough required or even claimed.

Where are we today?

The Sedan Deville has been replaced by the Cadillac DTS. The base price for the 2007 model is $41,900. That's 16.6 times the 1947 price. The car is radically different as is the highway system it is designed to navigate. In 1947 no one kept a car for more than three birthdays and 30,000 miles was about all that you could expect to get out of old Bessie. It was something the writer Vance Packard called "engineered obsolescence". Cars were made to be thrown away so the car company could sell you another one. There is no similarity between a 1947 Cadillac and a 2007 Cadillac other than the name and the fact that they are both cars. You cannot look at or drive a 2007 Cadillac and KNOW that it is related to the 1947 model. No way, no how, no one! I won't even spend time listing the improvements other than this one - the 2007 Cadillac comes with a 100,000 mile / 5 year warranty. Times have changed.

Let's forget about Cadillac for a moment and look at the top luxury car in the world, the Rolls-Royce. In 1947, the first post WWII model arrived in New York. It wasn't cheap but it could be had for $19,000. Rolls has always been a pretty much one-off kind of company. You place your order down to the thread color you want on your machine's upholstery and you wait. Not much has changed. I still consider them to be the most sought after car in the world. The price matches the esteem in which we hold them and the trouble it takes to design and build one. Even today they are pretty much hand made, one-off machines. The 2007 Rolls Royce Phantom will rock you back $333,350. That is almost exactly the same rate at which its American cousin the Cadillac has price inflated - 16.6 time its 1947 price. It too is a much better car than its predecessor and is still largely hand made.

What about the model 36 Bonanza?

No one can look at a 1968 A36 and not know that it is related to a 2007 G36. As a matter of fact many, many pilots wouldn't be able to tell them apart at 50 paces. The engine has been swapped for a more powerful version of the 1930's style pancake design, the prop has sprouted another blade and the panel has gone all glass. Garmin *(the Bendix/King of the new century)* supplies Beech with its popular G-1000 just as it does most other aircraft manufacturers. What about the price? In 1947 you could have had two Bonanzas and $3,000 in change or you could have one Rolls-Royce. Today the Bonanza, which is virtually unchanged, cost almost twice as much as one Rolls-Royce. That is surely a fruit basket turnover.

Bonanza - $597,500 - FOB Wichita! *(That was true in 2007 when this article was written. Today's G36 will set you back about one mega buck. It's the same airplane all that's changed is the price.)* If the Bonanza had inflated at the same

John Purner

rate as Cadillac or Rolls Royce, today's price would be $132,385. I'll bet that if it were $132,385 you'd buy one. Unfortunately, NO currently manufactured, certified general/aviation aircraft cost anywhere near $100,000 today, other than a Light Sport Aircraft.

Inflation is not the answer to sky-high aircraft prices as they are going up at rates much, much higher than the inflation rate. There is no reason at all that aircraft prices should go up at a higher rate than automobile prices and certainly not the most luxurious automobile in the world. The Bonanza now sells for 75 times more than its 1947 price. The Cadillac and the Rolls Royce have risen by only 16.6 times. Inflation can't explain this anomaly.

What about lawsuits?

Production of general aviation aircraft was consistently in excess of 10,000 units per year during the decade of the 1970's with a peak of 17,811 aircraft during 1978. By 1983, annual production had fallen to only 2,691 units. By 1994, production had fallen to a record low of 444 aircraft.

Without mentioning:

1. an obvious oversupply of aircraft
2. lack of interest from the public
3. competition for expendable income
4. increased complexity of the aviation environment
5. higher operating costs6. failure to implement product improvement and innovation
7. abolition of the investment tax credit

The general aviation industry suggested one cause and one cause only *"soaring product liability costs."* The General Aviation Manufacturers Association (GAMA) was successful in convincing Congress that a true crisis existed, that over 100,000 jobs had been lost nationwide, and that unprecedented federal relief was required. This relief came in the form of the **General Aviation Revitalization Act of 1994**, which legislated immunity from long-term liability for general aviation aircraft manufacturers.

Russell W. Meyer, Jr., Cessna's Chairman and Chief Executive Officer promised that Cessna would restart its single engine piston aircraft production line if some type of meaningful nationwide tort reform were enacted. By the early 1990's Meyer was saying that the demand for new single engine airplanes greatly exceeded the current supply, and that there was a *"tremendous need to replace existing units and satisfy the demand of people who want to learn to fly."* In March 1995, Meyer stated that Cessna would build 2,000 single engine airplanes annually by 1998. In 2006, more than a decade after the law took effect; the entire industry manufactured just 2,208 single engine aircraft in the United

States. Cessna has seen its 172 replaced as the world's best selling airplane by the Cirrus SR22, an innovative design that provides performance figures that Cessna could only dream of prior to their acquisition of Columbia Aircraft.

Do lawsuits have an effect on product prices? Yes, they absolutely do. The affect is the same for all products. The more dangerous the product, as measured by insurance company payouts, the higher the cost of insurance for that product across the board. Consider this, it cost you, the operator of an aircraft no more to insure your aircraft than it would a car of similar value with similar policy limits. The estates of Vari-Eze and Long-Eze owners have sued Burt Rutan countless times. Mr. Rutan went to court each time he was sued and as I understand it never lost. Lawyers don't make damage awards, judges and juries do. Juries do not ordinarily make awards in the absence of provable fault and demonstrable liability. When they do, the appeals process corrects their mistake. No showing can be made that any product, aircraft included, has seen its price rise by 75 times since 1947 due to lawsuits. Cadillac and Rolls Royce have been sued more times than all of the aircraft manufacturers combined, and they don't have anything like the **General Aviation Revitalization Act of 1994** to hide behind. They make their arguments in the marketplace and when necessary in court, not in Congress. It is certain that lawyers and lawsuits were never the problem. Clearly, general aviation was not revitalized by the 1994 Act.

If neither inflation nor lawsuits is the problem, what is?

Suppose for a moment that you were to walk into a Cadillac dealer this afternoon. Sitting on the showroom floor is a brand new Caddy, which is the spitting, imagine of the 1947 model. It is 10 inches longer to accommodate two more passengers and the salesman proudly informs you that the engine produces 100 more horsepower even though it is still a straight eight, cast iron crankcase topped by an L-head just like the one built in 1947. The tailfins have been changed. Other than that, everything is the same. Ooops! I almost forgot, a CD player and a GPS have been added to the dashboard and the kids can watch a DVD in the back. In 1947 this baby would set you back $2,523 if it followed the Bonanza model it would sell for $189,225 today. That would be real sticker shock!

Here's the question - at that price how many units of this six decade old design do you think Cadillac would sell each year? What if they charged $600,000? Let's say that **ALL** of the automobile manufacturers followed this same concept. Do you think the automobile industry would be the worldwide powerhouse it is today? Do you think they would sell millions of cars every year? Of course not! Their products would be undesirable and unaffordable but for those who needed or loved cars they would also be unavoidable. That is the exact problem confronting and confounding general aviation today; dated products, high prices with a few devotees and indifference from the larger market.

The reason that production rates of GA aircraft have fallen so tragically is the high prices the airframe, engine and avionics manufacturers charge for their wares. The more they charge, the more the market contracts and the more the market contracts the more they must charge to stay in business. It is a *"death spiral"*.

The fixed cost of any business caught in a decreasing market ultimately kill it. Let's say that the combined compensation for every executive at Mooney Aircraft Company equals $1,500,000 per year. That's pretty light for a President, Vice President Sales/Marketing, Vice President Manufacturing, Vice President Finance and Vice President Engineering, you must agree. In 2006 Mooney sold just 75 airplanes. Using our $1,500,000 executive compensation example, each of those machines would be burdened by $20,000 as their share of executive compensation. Fixed costs add up pretty quickly for a low volume manufacturer, don't they? The last time the transportation industry saw this phenomenon was the buggy whip manufacturers. As the public shifted away from horses to automobiles the demand for buggy whips dropped dramatically. Their price went up, way up. Expensive buggy whips are still manufactured today, cheap ones aren't.

Overpriced and outdated piston powered aircraft are merely the symptoms of the problem. Piston engine singles do not measure-up well as travel tools when compared to private jets or airliners. Piston singles simply don't answer the four primary travel questions; reliability, comfort, speed and safety. How could they, they were designed for the travel market of sixty years ago. I don't think I have ever met anyone who travels by air that doesn't aspire to owning a private jet. It is a universal dream. Conversely, I have met very few people outside of the aviation community that express interest in owning or traveling by a single engine piston powered aircraft, most people don't. Four million dollars for a jet seems understandable to the general public but $600,000 for "one of those little airplanes" is a jaw dropper that typically evokes the *"that's insane"* comment. Not only is the general public not aspiring to ownership, they no longer understand why anyone else would. That is a market killer.

Cirrus successfully designed a marketing plan to bring some newbie's into the game. It worked for a while but has now stalled. They promoted the SR22 in non-flying magazines like the ***Robb Report*** as though it was a personal airliner and that learning to fly it was easy. Their early adopters now want to move-up after a few years of trying to make the plane they purchased perform as the message of the advertising indicated that it might. Cirrus has responded by announcing their intentions to build a jet. Time will tell if they are able to make good on that plan. I hope so. This is the same path that Beech, Cessna and Piper have all followed. A very lopsided amount of Cessna and Beech's revenue come from jet fuel burning machines. The same is true of Piper. The legacy manufacturers have all watched the market leave them as they waited for new piston engines to become available that would allow them to produce personal aircraft that could routinely fly above the weather in pressurized comfort. After sixty years of waiting they have simply given up and moved on.

The legacy manufacturers have learned another lesson. The demand for their products is inelastic above the floor price they have tested. Whether Cirrus SR22 cost $180,000 or $400,000 the demand is the same, about 60 per month - WORLDWIDE. Their total sales in units are one half of Bonanza's 1947 sales yet the population of the United States of America has more than DOUBLED! That being the case it makes perfect sense to charge $400,000 not $180,000 regardless of the manufacturing cost. Cessna has followed the same pattern. They re-entered the market with the 172R in 1996 with a sticker just south of $100,000. Today *(2007)* it is north of $230,000 *(2018 - $396,000)* and demand has not been affected in the slightest. This is a very typical niche market pattern.

What would happen if new aircraft prices dropped to $50,000? Sales would up tick but only slightly. Single engine aircraft are today seen largely as recreational objects not as transportation tools. The market for recreational flying is saturated and stagnant, there are as many people exiting the hobby, as there are new entrants.

If price won't positively affect market performance what will?

The market can expand by continuing down the recreational path and finding a way to entice more excited entrants or it can offer updated products that truly answer the requirements set down by the traveling public; reliability, comfort, speed. Safety and ease of use. The last option is very difficult to do in the absence of new low cost propulsion technology. In 1997, we were all thrilled by the announcement of the LOW cost fanjets that Williams' showed at Oshkosh. As the result of a NASA funded program they demonstrated a very small, very light weight, very powerful, low cost fan jet that would allow for the immediate development of Very Light Jets which would be powered by two of these little powerhouses. Vern Raburn bought in and started Eclipse with an announcement of a revolutionary aircraft that would fly at 350 knots at 41,000 feet while burning 20 gallons per hour and costing a mere $800,000 to purchase. Williams failed to deliver, and the revolution didn't take place. The Eclipse 500 now sells for over twice the announced price and Eclipse the company is teetering on collapse *(2019 update, it did collapse. A new organization took over in 2011. The Eclipse is still produced but the price is over $2,695,000 and climbing)*. NASA also funded diesel engine research. Diamond announced that they would come to market with a twin-engine aircraft that would cruise along at 203 knots while sipping just 10 gph of fuel at 12,000 feet. They did produce the plane and it is a good seller to flight schools because performance isn't an issue for flight schools. That's right they missed the performance numbers by a mile. We badly need a reliable low-cost propulsion system to replace the 1930's pancake engines that can't permit us to fly above the weather. So far NOTHING has come

John Purner

forward that can even match let alone beat the pancake engine. That is really sad! I think we will go electric but that is another LONG article!

Light Sport Aircraft and Part 103 Ultralights before them were supposed to expand the recreational market. Neither has. The Part 103 Ultralights apparently did not meet the minimum perception of what a *safe* aircraft must be. The Light Sport Aircraft so far are stuck in the mud with prices that are way too high for the perceived recreational benefit. The standard price for any LSA is above $130,000 and that is simply too high. Look these are two passenger play toys. You can't begin to think of them for family recreation as you can the six-sleeper sailboat that cost the same amount. Two seats equates to motorcycles, jet skis, ATV's and snow mobiles. Priced at more than seven times competitive recreational devices, LSA's are not likely to excite the interest of new entrants. At best they will shift some sales away from used aircraft and new aircraft. They will likely not expand the market at all. The 7% decline that the legacy piston powered aircraft manufacturers have experienced in the first three quarters of 2007 is almost exactly equal to the sales of LSA's.

So, where does this leave us?

It leaves those of us that love piston singles in darn good shape for a long while. There continues to be a good supply of used aircraft at affordable prices. Aftermarket vendors introduce new bells and whistles constantly. Each works their magic to bring old birds up to date. Fuel prices, though high, are manageable and **WILL** come down. Let me suggest a strategy to you. If you're in the market for another bird here's what to do. Decide what purchase price you can handle. Next consider how many years and hours you are willing to accept on your next magic carpet. Then consider the bottom line *"must have features"*, two place or four, etc. Then become an expert at using the search function on Trade-A-Plane. In minutes you'll be given a list of possibilities. Let's say that can afford $75,000. If you want a plane with at least 4 seats that was manufactured after 1967 and has fewer than 4,000 hours total time with at least 200 hours and no more than 1,000 on the engine, a quick Trade-a-plane search will show you over 6 dozen that meet your requirements. For the active owner/pilot times have never been better. Wait to buy **new** until there is truly something **new** to buy, in the meantime there are wonderful used airplanes just waiting for new owners.

The Current Burger Fleet

What does the current burger fleet look like??

On December 13th, 2004 I spent a lot of time discussing what a burger ship isn't and what a burger pilot isn't.

To summarize; a burger pilot is **not** an active commercial pilot flying a kerosene burning, cloud jumping, twin engined jet. True some of our guys are high-time, active airline pilots and some of our members do indeed fly private jets but the vast majority of us have less than 1,000 hours in our logbooks and fly less than 100 hours a year in a single engine spam can. That's a fact.

The planes we fly typically come from one of four manufacturers Cessna, Piper, Beech and Mooney. The majority fly a Cessna 172. That's not so hard to accept given the fleet size. Most of our ships were manufactured prior to 1980. Since 172s spent more than a little time in training fleets our aircraft typically have more than 6,000 hours on their airframes. Our engines are largely past mid-time. The avionics panels we fly behind are a hodge-podge, a little of this and some of that. I am not talking about the fleet mind you, but each airplane. A Narco this, a King that, some Garmin mixed in and a II Morrow way over on the other side near the co-pilot. They have been upgraded a piece at a time and components have been replaced as they wore out or broke completely. Am I right about this? Virtually all of us have a handheld GPS bolted onto our yoke. Its tiny screen provides excellent situational awareness and it's cheap. Yes, a Garmin 530 would be best but the $15,000 installed cost would equal 25% or more of the total value of most of our ships.

Autopilots are things that most of us don't have. They were not a fixture in the Skyhawk and Cherokee fleets. To add an S-TEC System 20 cost about $14,000 installed. That's a lot to spend when you have a top overhaul starring you in the face. The S-TEC would be nice but the TOP is essential. Tradeoffs are tough but they are the facts of a part-time aviator's life.

Our ships are solid VFR aircraft. They have four seats and can haul four passengers, if we're willing to leave a little fuel and a lot of baggage behind. Normally we fly with less than three people on board including the pilot. After 25 years of flying, I have only been in a single engine aircraft twice with four or more people on board. Once in a 182 and once in a 210 and sadly I can make only three trips through my fingers and toes counting the number of times I have had more than one onboard not counting an instructor. Sad but true!

Conclusion: We fly older VFR equipped Skyhawks and Cherokees and we spend a ton doing it!

John Purner

The Sky High Cost of Flying

Maybe you got your ticket last week or maybe you've had it for five decades. In either case, lining up a burger running airplane is not easy. It has to be fit for the recreational mission you're about to fly. As we've discussed before this leaves out names like Lear and Gulfstream. This mission is better suited for a Cessna, Piper, Beechcraft, Mooney or some other single engined blue fuel-burning beast.

That's what to fly but how do you get your hands on one? Fortunately the option list is fairly long and includes some more creative options than buying or renting. Those are the two extremes.

Buying is at the top of the list for convenience, control, security and oh yes, **COST!** If you own, scheduling the airplane is a snap. Drive to the airport and fire it up! It is truly ready when you are but the cost can be a killer. Through out this editorial we're going to use a mid 1970's Cessna 172 as our example, one that was manufactured between 1970 and 1975. Whether you borrow the money or cut the check you're in for $50,000, more or less.

Your bird will need a place to live. A tie-down will run you about $600 per year, a hanger will typically cost five times that amount. The annual inspection will set you back about $2,000 by the time a modest squawk list is corrected. Insurance? Yes, you'll need some and it will run you another $1,000 per year. Is that it? Insurance, tie-down, annual inspection? Certainly not! Count on spending another $1,000 a year for non-scheduled maintenance. It adds up very quickly. A magneto here, a battery there and necessary oil changes. IFR certification comes up every two years at $250 just for the check plus a new altimeter or whatever else now and then. If your ship isn't IFR certified, you'll still need to have the transponder checked. Count on $200 a year for recertifications.

So here's what we have so far:

Acquisition cost: $50,000
Fixed cost: (Insurance, tie down, annual, re-certs.): $ 3,800
Non-Scheduled Maintenance: $ 1,000

That's 50 grand to buy it and almost 5 thousand a year to own it, if you never fly it!

Let's assume you do fly it and you average 5 hours per month. Interestingly enough, that's the average time flown for an aircraft owner. The variable costs are simple to calculate; price per gallon for low lead fuel times 9 gallons per hour. Yes, you'll burn a little oil but not enough to worry about between oil changes. Let's just look at fuel and chart cost. Charts? Yes, my friend you gotta'

238

have 'em and they must be current. That is if you don't want to live in fear of discovery by the FAA or your insurance company. That's right, an out of date set of charts is all the reason required to deny a claim. Figure on $250 per year for charts. Fuel is currently averaging $3.00 per gallon across the US **(much higher today, 2019)**. You can pay a lot more and sometimes you can pay a little less. So $27 per hour for fuel times 60 hours a year equals $1,620 plus charts puts you at $1850 per year for variable operating cost.

Ooops! We almost forgot reserves. That's right. Sooner or later you are going to spend big money to replace the engine, TBO is 2000 hours, the prop TBO is also 2000 hours. The paint? Figure every ten years and the interior about the same. An engine rebuild for your Cessna will run about $12,000 or $6.00 for every one of those 2,000 hours flown. A new prop will cost about $2,000 or $1 per hour. The paint and interior will set you back about $6,000 a piece. So that's another $1,200 per year or $20 per hour you need to set aside.

Reserves total $27 per hour. You don't have to set the money aside but you will have to spend it eventually and your accountant will advise you to reserve for it. It's just a good business practice.

What about that $50,000 you put into the airplane? You could have deployed it in another fashion. If you bought Google stock with it your pile would have doubled in a year. If you bought a CD you'd pickup maybe 2 ½ percent per year. That's $1,250 my friend. Yes, older aircraft have tended to go up in value. That is not the case today. The ones that do go up do so at a lesser rate than other investments. Let's just add in $1,250 for annual lost opportunity cost and call it a day. That's $20 per hour.

A sixty-hour per year pilot is spending $157.00 per hour to fly his ship. A Cessna 172 of the same vintage can be rented at your local flight school for no more than $95.00 per hour.

Flying your own ship is a good way to go from the security and convenience point of view. There is no denying that, but at $62.00 per hour more cost, is it worth it?

Maybe.

Can any of these costs be avoided?

NO!

Some folks try to defer the maintenance and sell the bird before its time to pay the piper. That seldom works as the purchaser will certainly deduct for a shabby paint job, a high time engine, worn out avionics and a logbook that raises more questions than it answers.

John Purner

Wait a minute! If it cost you $157 per hour to operate a Cessna 172 how can the flight school rent it profitably for only $95 per hour? Aren't their costs the same?

Actually, they are higher! The flight school **MUST** perform an inspection every 100 hours of operation in addition to the annual. They also pay a ton more in insurance cost. Yes, they have administrative and management burden that a private owner doesn't carry and they generate a profit.

How the do they do it?

Lesson number one. They don't do the maintenance that you do. Take a look at the planes that are typically rented at flight schools. Not very pretty are they? They need paint, the interiors are shot and at least one item on the panel is inoperative! The engine may be well over TBO and the prop has telltale *"dressing"* marks, where the mechanic has filed out stone hits.

Lesson number two. The flight school typically is the FBO. They buy fuel and parts at huge discounts. Next the A&P is their employee so their hourly fee for his services is much reduced. But why are they willing to lose profit margins on these items? That's lesson number two, they aren't.Typically they don't own the aircraft you rent. They merely manage it under a purchase/lease back arrangement. The true owner is a relatively high-income individual who can take advantage of the depreciation available on the purchase of an aircraft. No owner ever makes money on a leaseback deal. He simply hopes to lose a little and get it all back on his income tax return. It usually doesn't work out that way and most owners are eventually unhappy with these arrangements. They leave their ship in the rental fleet hoping that they can one day sell it and break even. The FBO or flight school gets a management fee.

Lesson Number Three. They figure their cost on 1,000 hours of operation annually not 60. So that $2,000 annual adds $2.00 to hourly operating cost not $33.00. The $600 annual tie-down cost is lowered to only 60 cents per flight hour not $10. The effect of greater use on those two items alone has saved over $40 per flight hour. Lesson three simply stated is that higher usage lowers hourly operating costs.

Scheduling a rental is normally a nightmare. Trying to get a rental plane at the time you want it is tough. When you show-up to use it, sometimes the last renter is late in returning it or it is down for unscheduled maintenance. Either way you will wait or cancel.

Renting is the worst flight option!

240

Partnerships

Our December 28, 2004 Editorial points out that it cost a lot to own an aircraft all by yourself. The other truth brought out by that Editorial is that you won't fly it very much. The average owner pilot puts just 60 hours a year under his wings. A friend of mine in Texas, owns a truly beautiful ***Bellanca Super Viking***. It is his only aircraft. Last year he flew it just 4 hours!

Our study ship is a *1970ish* Cessna 172. Our thought is that an average one can be had for **$50,000**. For something that you will use so little it seems logical to consider shared ownership. Cutting the acquisition cost four ways would certainly be helpful.

Fixed ownership cost will also be divided four ways. We calculated those costs to be **$5,000** a year. Anyone who has ever owned a Piper Cherokee or a Cessna 172 will not quibble with that number. Being responsible for only 1/4th of it is very appealing. Is it not?

Operational cost will not vary. Fuel and oil cost are what they are and the burn rate won't vary. Currently a C-172 will hit your wallet for about **$27.00** per hour for consumables. That's not bad! We also discovered that reserves must be setup for the things that wear out predictably. The engine is a good example. Taken together we reasoned that reserving money to replace or repair these items was a good idea and that the total for engine, prop, avionics, interior and paint should be about **$27.00** per hour. So the cost per flight hour of **$54.00** will not vary whether you share the ownership of your ship or own it outright.

The pros of shared ownership are all financial and they are obvious, acquisition and fixed monthly cost. We all learned early in life, somewhere around kindergarten that sharing has its downside. First among these is the scheduling dilemma. The airplane won't be constantly available for you if you share it. The next are the simple control issues of any group - turf wars! Who decides? Will there be work parties? What if you don't want to or can't attend? Even worse what if you're the only guy who really wants a clean machine? What if one of the *"others"* constantly leaves cookie wrappers and coke cans in the airplane? Who decides where the maintenance will be done? What about adding an autopilot?

Sharing is tough!

At least you'll be saving money! Will you? Remember you bought an airplane with a mid-time engine. Flying alone at a 60 hour per year pace you won't need to spend for an overhaul for 15 years! At least that's what the arithmetic says. With three partners that expense will come along in just 4 years and you'll have to reach for your checkbook and so will each of your partners. Your reserves will only cover half of the rebuild cost because you only owned the plane for half of the engine's life. What if you or one of your partners can't write the check? Maybe it's not the engine that goes first maybe it's a radio. Some guys will fly with just one, so they'll vote to let it go for a while. Others like everything working perfectly!

Ooops!

When you put the group together you searched long and hard to find three guys that you felt could stand the strain of partnership. You made good choices and then the day comes when somebody has to move and sell his share. The new guy is an *"alpha dog"* creep! There goes the fun. What was once workable is now a hemorrhoid. The problem with partnerships seems to be management. There isn't any. Because of the lack of full-time professional management expenses soar and egos get bruised. Eventually the partnership evaporates, and the plane is sold.

The good news is that the one thing you worried about, **scheduling**, turns out to be a non-problem! As time goes on, frustration builds, and the ship gets used less and less. Trying to share just doesn't seem to work over the long haul. Of all the possible methods of getting into an airplane this weekend, a partnership is the worst!

****

John,

Nice job on pointing out many of the pitfalls of partnerships. I would just like to add one basic idea: If you are considering a partnership, how many partners should you have?

None?
If you own 100% of the plane, you have none of the disadvantages of a partnership, but you have 100% of the cost.

One?
If you add one partner, now you have the inconvenience of sharing the airplane, and the possible personality and budget conflicts that it takes for two people to agree on how to manage the airplane. The good news is that you save 50% of the fixed costs of ownership, and if you agree on them, you can do upgrades at 50% of the cost as well.

Two?
If you add a second partner (three owners total), then you double your headache! You now have to compromise with two people, not just one. They also need to agree with each other as well as with you. Perhaps the likelihood of conflict is

more than double. Your cost savings for adding this additional partner only brings your share from 50% to 33.3%. All that extra conflict for only 17% of additional savings!

Three?
A partnership of four owners is common but adding that fourth only reduces fixed costs from 33.3% to 25%. With that many partners, agreement may become impossible, and scheduling conflicts are inevitable...all for an additional savings of only 8%! Obviously, my point is that if you do choose to have a partnership, I would suggest that you limit it to two owners, to get most cost savings for the least amount of headache.

Ray

John Purner

Flying Clubs

For the past few weeks we've been exploring how best to get into an airplanes pilot's seat; rental, full ownership, and partnerships. All are good and each is deficient. This week we're going to take a look at *Flying Clubs*. In my mind, they fall somewhere between rental and partnerships.

Clubs seem to be divided into two groups. Those that own their aircraft and those that lease them. The difference between a club and a partnership is equity. In a partnership your equity is in the airplanes. In a club your equity is in the club not the aircraft, whether the club owns or leases the aircraft. If you are told that you are joining a flying club and that you will have equity in the aircraft then you really aren't joining a flying club, you're joining a partnership. A rose by any other name is still a rose.

Typically a flying club is formed by a person or a group of persons who own one or more aircraft and are having a hard time justifying the expense. They form a club and look for members. Typically the newly formed club will lease the aircraft from the previous owner. So many dollars a month and so many dollars per flight hour. The club charges its members an initiation fee, monthly dues and an hourly fee to use the aircraft. More often than not a lot of flight training goes on at the club by a club member who is also an instructor. The members are having a similar experience to renting from a flight school. The advantage is that the aircraft are available to be rented by a selected pool rather than the public at large.

The big benefit to the club members is a lower hourly rate for the rent of a similar or better piece of equipment than the ones available at the local flight school. Good enough!

What are the problems?

First problem is the initiation fee and the monthly dues. Normally these are reasonable, less than a thousand dollars to join and less than $100 a month to maintain the membership. The problem arises if you don't use the plane enough to offset these cost. If you're flying less than 20 hours a year, you're really financially better off renting from a flight school. Many clubs will apply the monthly dues against that month's rental fees. It is much the same for a country club's food and beverage assessment. You will spend $200 a month on food whether or not you eat it. It is a guarantee to use at least that much of the club's services. This affords the club a minimum monthly income stream to pay for tiedowns, insurance and periodic fleet maintenance, its fixed cost.

Typically, clubs rent airplanes **"dry"**. Each member establishes his own account with the local FBO. The member assures that the tanks are indeed full before departure and orders fuel on return. The tanks are always full and the fuel is always paid for. Problem number two is availability. Typically, the fleet size will be much lower than a rental operation. If you show up to use the club's plane and the last pilot left it at the maintenance hangar with a bad vacuum pump you are **Fresh Outta' Luck** unless the club has other planes and one of them is available and you are trained and cleared to fly it. I have noticed that most clubs will have a varied fleet, perhaps a 172, a 182 RG and an Aztec. All good planes, but if you are only checked out on the 172 and it is broken it does not help that the 182 and the Aztec are available.

The third problem is finance. Sooner are later the cows come home. The lower rates that club members enjoy, the low initiation fee and the low monthly dues allow enough money to do the maintenance if everything happens as it is supposed to happen. When a 2,000-hour TBO engine dies at 800 hours, things get complicated. If the plane is leased, it is a problem for the owner. If he has deep enough pockets it gets fixed quickly. If not the club has to search for another owner willing to lease them his airplane. In the meantime, members are **ground bound**! If the club owns the plane, then the members get a short course in assessments! The cost of the new engine is divided by the number of members. Each is expected to contribute. Some can't, don't or won't. The solution often is to solicit more members and to use their initiation fees to cover the short-term financial problem. What a mess! The fourth problem is management. Just like a partnership there isn't any. It is all-volunteer. Typically, the guys that want the club officer jobs are the ones that shouldn't have them.

There are good clubs out there with many happy members. They are in the minority. Most clubs aren't around long and most members have long frowny faces.

John Purner

The Death of 02 GOLF

As we passed over Lake Somerville I pointed out my parent's lake house. From 3,000 feet it was easy to spot.

Thud!

"Mr. Purner, what was that?"

"I don't know Scott, but it didn't sound good."

The silence between us grew as we both strained to detect any out of the ordinary sound and to decipher were it came from. We heard nothing. All seemed normal. I pulled off my David Clarks to see if I could hear any better. I couldn't, of course.

I saw them first then Scott asked, **"are those rain drops on the windshield?"**

"I don't think so Scott. There's not a cloud in the sky."

The tension in the cockpit was building. We both knew instinctively that something was terribly wrong but we didn't dare guess what it might be. Just on cue, the engine trembled and bucked, not bad enough to be awful but not good enough to be OK.

I started a climb. We struggled to 4,000 feet. I didn't think it would go higher as we were straining for 100 FPM vertically. **NOT GOOD!**

My panel scan began to tell the tale. The oil pressure and oil temperature gauges were both moving in the wrong direction, temperature climbing and pressure falling. At least I knew what those drops on the windshield were. Oil, and not just any oil, it had to be AeroShell 100. I liked it better when it was inside the crankcase. The drops were quickly becoming streaks and pretty wide ones at that.

"Scott, why don't you hand me the sectional. We need to find a place to land; I think we split an oil line or something. In any event we need to land to have a look."

He handed over the chart and opined that the nice oyster shell road below us leading up to somebody's farmhouse looked like a place we could land.

The chart showed the Caldwell airport to be just 8 miles ahead. Close but not close enough for a glide. The engine needed to keep running at least a little while longer. Mile by long mile we crawled to the airport during the longest four

246

minutes in the history of aviation. The vibration coming from under the cowling increased with each second. Oil now covered the windshield. I was piloting through the side windows.

"Caldwell Unicom, 8802 GOLF is inbound with a rough engine, request airport advisory.

Caldwell Unicom, 8802 GOLF request airport advisories.

Any aircraft in the pattern at Caldwell, 02 GOLF is inbound with a rough engine request airport advisories."

Wonderful!

A laryngitis epidemic had struck the Caldwell Airport.

I was on my own.

The little green book showed Caldwell's runway to be 3,252 feet of grooved asphalt. The orientation, 15/33 was almost perfect for my plight. Naturally I wanted to use 33 but what about the wind direction and speed? Without an airport advisory I was clueless.

I checked the chart again and noticed that while College Station's Easterwood Airport wasn't close enough to be a landing option it was certainly in radio range.

"Easterwood Tower, Cessna 8802 GOLF, request."

"8802 GOLF, Easterwood, say your request."

"Easterwood, 8802 GOLF is making an unscheduled landing at Caldwell with a rough engine. I am unable to get an airport advisory. Request your current conditions."

"Winds are light and variable from the south. We are using runway 16. Can I provide further assistance?"

"Negative. Thanks for the report."

The winds favored 15 but to use it I would have to fly the pattern with a dying engine. My thoughts went to the word *light*. If the winds wouldn't help me, they at least wouldn't hurt me very much. Wish the runway was longer.

"Mr. Purner are we gonna' be OK?"

John Purner

My attention went to my passenger who was my best friend's oldest boy.

Are we gonna' be OK? I silently wondered that myself. Getting back on the ground was a certainty. All airplanes eventually find their way back to Mother Earth. We would too, one way or another. If we made an off-airport landing in the rolling country below us our chances were really very good. It wasn't at all like the mountainous terrain I zipped over just a few days earlier. Our odds were good. The airport was now just two minutes away. An emergency landing at an airport was far more to my liking than flipping upside down in Farmer Brown's cotton patch.

"Caldwell area traffic, Cessna 8802 GOLF is making a straight in approach to 33 with a rough engine. We'll be a full stop."

The field elevation was listed as 391 feet. I needed to shed 3,600 feet of altitude quickly. That was easy but it met trading altitude for speed, and I didn't need or want that much of either. Coming down gradually until I was sure the landing was made and then adding full flaps and slipping down vigorously was my call.

I made a late reply to Scott's question, **"Sorry Scott I got kinda' busy. Yes, we're going to make it and we're going to be just fine. When we land, we'll need to find a phone to call your Dad to come pick us up. Would you mind hoofing it over to the office. There will likely be a pay phone just outside."**

"Yes sir, I'll do that."

"I'll be bringing us down pretty quickly so watch your ears. They'll pop some and may hurt a little."

"No problem, it'll be good to be back on the ground even with popping ears."

"Yes it will."

"OK here we go, cross your fingers and say a prayer."

"Caldwell traffic 8802 GOLF is on a 2 mile final at 3,500 feet."

I pulled the engine back to idle. It responded by smoothing out. That was welcome. As the electric motor began bringing the flaps all the way down I started a radical slip. A side benefit was I could see the runway much better out of the pilot's side window than I could through the windshield. The altimeter was spinning off 1,500 feet per minute. We might just make it. The rush of the wind was amazingly loud. Airspeed dropped to 80 mph and held steady there. The flaps were doing their job. I was becoming more optimistic. The fence was maybe a quarter of a mile away when I realized that we wouldn't make it. We were way too high. Just over the fence. I added throttle and prayed for power. **02**

GOLF responded with all she had which wasn't much. The vibration was beyond bumpy it was very, very rough. For a moment I wondered if I had lost a hunk out of the propeller.

"Scott, we're too high and will have to go around. Hang on tight!"

I released the left rudder to come out of the slip, retracted the flaps and pulled back on the yoke. We rolled out at exactly pattern altitude as we charged along the east side of the airport on a downwind for 15. **02 GOLF** was doing her best to stay in the air but had little left. The vibration was increasing. Sticking this landing was beyond important. I would have only this one last chance. The runway raced along outside my window and then disappeared. Soon I'd have to make the best and shortest downwind to base and base to final turns of my career and I would have to use techniques I had never learned, practiced or seen in person. This situation called for a carrier landing. I was no more than 300 feet to the left of the runway. There would be no base followed by base to final there would merely be an arc from downwind to short final. How would I accomplish this?

I pulled power as I entered the turn and steepened the bank all the way to 60 degrees and dropping the nose to compensate for the speed that was draining off. Out the side window I watched for the end of the strip to come into view. It did and I rolled slightly past it and quickly whipped and I do mean whipped **8802 GOLF** back to the right with both aileron and rudder. Thanks be to God, it worked! I came over the numbers just 15 feet in the air at 70 mph. You would have thought that I was good but let's call it **blessed**.

8802 GOLF touched down normally and quickly presented me with the next set of problems. **NO BRAKES!** Thank God for a steerable nose wheel. If I had been flying a Grumman Yankee or any other plane with a pivoting nose wheel, I'd be in the weeds! As it was, we simply steered down the runway until all the energy **02 GOLF** had left bled off and she rolled to a gentle stop.

Encouraged by the smoke that was curling out of the cowling, Scott and I exited quickly. There was no fire just a lot of oily, acrid smoke.

Scott moved out in the direction of the office to find a phone, I grabbed the tool kit and the fire extinguisher.

Oddly enough the cowling wasn't hot so opening her up was easy except for the smoke. My eyes began to burn but needing to know the source of our distress I resolved to bear-up. What I saw was shocking. Just above the front cylinder on the pilot's side, #3, there was a frown shaped split in the crankcase big enough to stuff your fingers into. I could look through the crank with a flashlight and see all that had once made this engine hum and all that would never do so again. Then I placed both hands on the cylinder itself and found that I could wiggle it like a small child's loose tooth. This jug was ready to come off. I don't know why it hadn't, but I was very grateful and felt truly blessed to be alive and safely on the ground. Many times, I had read accident reports about engines that had come apart in a similar fashion. They usually spit out their cylinders through the side of the cowling while inflight, occasionally the plane and crew would survive but not often.

Why had this happened? What had caused the crack?

As the smoke cleared the answer showed itself like a thief in the night. Pat's weld had given way. The split of the exhaust stack leaving #3 was again visible. Those blowtorch hot gases had worked their will on my engine. The failure point was the crankcase. So now I knew. What should work often doesn't and airplanes aren't like cars. If something breaks you can't just pull over to the side of the road and park. When something breaks on an airplane in-flight the result is seldom good. The cheap fix quickly becomes the most expensive fix. I should have bought a new exhaust manifold rather than opting to have the broken one repaired. Now I was in for a new engine, which was worth more than the aircraft that needed it.

Lesson learned.

Is it time to buy a Legacy LSA?

When the LSA rules were announced, the FAA gave us a nice surprise. Any legacy aircraft that met the 1320-pound weight restriction and operated below the 120 mph maximum speed qualified as an LSA. One hundred and thirty-one models from eight manufacturers today make up the approved list; Aeronca, Ercoupe, Interstate, Luscombe, Piper, Porterfield, Quicksilver, Taylorcraft.

Here's the link to see the whole list:
www.faa.gov/aircraft/gen_av/light_sport/media/ExistingModels.pdf

The reason to buy one is pretty simple. Flying a Legacy LSA is a hobby that will make you smile when you are flying, when you think about flying and when you remember flying! Here's the best part, you can buy one **NOW** for about the price of a Harley-Davidson Road Glide. Riding a Harley is a great hobby but is it as much fun as flying a plane? You decide.

Let me first say that I am a huge fan of **ALL** the aircraft on this list and have enjoyed flying a few of them. They're fun to fly though they are admittedly **VFR ONLY,** short flight machines. Who among us doesn't love the **Piper J-3 CUB** in all of its variants? I've flown them, ridden in them, lovingly studied them on the ground and starred at them, as they flew not so high above me.

Of all the planes I've owned, the **ERCOUPE 415C** is my all-time favorite. I loved that plane and many afternoons I find myself saddened that I don't still own it or one like it. My friend Charlie McBride owns a **Taylorcraft BC-12D**, I have shared many hours with him as a right-seater gliding low and slow above the rice fields outside Wharton, Texas. A Legacy LSA can be purchased for as little as 10% and no more than 20% of the price of a newly manufactured LSA. **CUBS** are the most sought-after aircraft in the Legacy LSA fleet and command premium prices.

So why is now the time to buy a Legacy LSA?

Two reasons.

First, the fleet size is fixed and shrinking. The average Legacy LSA is 70 years old. Each year a number of them are retired from the fleet for service issues and accidents.

Second, prices are climbing. The shrinking fleet naturally causes prices to go up and they are. Price increases are also being driven by the economy's recovery. The price of **ALL** Legacy aircraft is up sharply not just Legacy LSAs.

Legacy LSAs are fun to fly, relatively inexpensive and are a safe investment as their value is appreciating. You can buy one today, fly it for a while, sell it and make money.

Let's take a look at one possibility.

An **Ercoupe 415-CD** located outside Dallas. I found it advertised on Trade-A-Plane. A quick look at the FAA Legacy LSA list assures us that this plane qualifies though most people don't know that as the common wisdom has it that **ONLY** the **Ercoupe 415C** qualifies for LSA. The price is amazing at just $19,950 and it has great specifications: 2388 TT, 75 SMOH, new prop, cloth wings, King GPS/COM, Val 760, a transponder, dual fork nose gear and all logs since new.

I would never buy this machine as rudder pedals have been added. In my view, rudder pedals don't belong on **Ercoupes**. My point is this. You're not looking for a plane that is close to perfect; you want a plane that is **perfect**. If I don't want rudder pedals neither will a large percentage of the people I will one day seek to sell this machine too.

As I point out in my book, ***The $100 Hamburger Guide to Buying and Selling Aircraft***, you should never buy a plane today that you can't sell for a profit tomorrow and yes I literally mean sell tomorrow as in tomorrow. It isn't my mission to lose money and it shouldn't be yours either. If it takes longer than two weeks to sell your airplane at a fair price, you bought the wrong airplane, simple as that.

The next lesson is this, $19,950 is a great price for an Ercoupe that is LSA qualified. The average price for a good LSA Ercoupe today is $32,000. I'm not saying you should pay $32,000 for one I'm saying that if the asking price is substantially less than the average for its type, the seller probably knows something about it that you'll find out later. Don't waste your time trying to buy cheap. Spend your time buying value!

With an **Ercoupe** you want a 415C or 415CD, with fabric wings preferably Ceconite, no rudder pedals, approximately 2,200 hours total time, 500 SMOH or less on the engine, a dual fork nose wheel, Cleveland brakes, good glass including a bubble windshield, paint at least 8 and interior at least 8, shoulder harnesses as well as seatbelts, **ALL** log books since new, **NDH**, no corrosion, no hail damage, in annual and never missed an annual, **ALL** AD's and SB's complied with, a Nav/Com, a transponder and serviceable flight instruments.

I like **Ercoupe**s because they are one of only two legacy LSAs that have tricycle gear, which I prefer and an electrical system, which I demand. If you're a tailwheel guy and are comfortable propping your machine to get it going your options are greatly increased.

Here's the signoff. Now is the time to buy a used airplane. They are still plentiful and the prices though higher than they have been are still affordable. Interest rates are low, not as low as they have been but lower than they soon will be. Use a home equity loan if you can. The interest rate will be lower than a aircraft loan and I think you can still deduct the interest you pay on a home mortgage though I haven't yet studied the 2019 tax rules yet as I'm struggling with my 2018 return.

The final reason to go with a Legacy LSA is the medical. If you fly, it as an LSA then you don't need a medical as long as you have a pilot's license and a driver's license, you're good to go. For me that's a good thing. I no longer fly for business and don't have to keep to a schedule so daytime VFR flying works for me.

An iPAD running *ForeFlight* takes care of situational, traffic and weather. Naturally I would replace the transponder with a **Stratus ESG** and add a **Stratus 2s** for a complete ADS-B IN and OUT solution with wireless connectivity to *ForeFlight*. Better/cheaper ways may soon arrive but for now that's what I would do

How does a legacy LSA compare with a brand spanking, new LSA? Which is the better value? Great question which each owner/pilot must answer for himself.

John Purner

Summer Flight Planning

I started the website ***www.100dollarhamburger.com*** because I'm primarily a Recreational Flyer. That is why I continue to write books, fiction and non-fiction about the gift of flight. Airplanes light my fire!

Long ago I learned that I couldn't fly all the time but I could be around airplanes even when I wasn't pushing them through clouds. Each summer I head out for aviation museums, small ones and large ones, crowded famous ones and lonely obscure ones where I'm likely to be the only visitor. This year I'll go to some that I have been to before many times and three that I haven't seen in a long while.

We have reviewed several museums on the website. What follows are my write-ups on the three I'm excited about visiting this summer.

Glenn H. Curtiss Museum

Glenn Curtiss is a complicated figure. I like him for the work he did particularly for the wonderful aircraft he produced and the company he built. My all time favorite airplane is the P-40 Warhawk which emerged from his firm's design table. He personally produced over five hundred inventions in his lifetime. The distraction for me was his obsession with winning at any cost and his early infringement of the Wright Brothers' patents.

Aviation would not have gotten off the ground as quickly as it did without Curtiss. His early flying days were monumental. It was Curtiss who designed and flew the first flying boats. The world took great advantage of these designs. During World War I it was Glenn H. Curtiss who gave America the "Jenny" and it was the "Jenny" and the "barnstormers" who flew her, that really introduced America to the airplane!

This museum profiles this American life and brings together a fine collection of the things that his life touched and produced. It is worth the trip, for without Curtiss the airplane would have developed much more slowly. Next, it is worth the trip for the geography it occupies. Can there be a more beautiful place on earth than the Finger Lakes region of New York State? I think not. Your stay at the museum may be brief but you'll want to spend at least a week in the area.

https://www.glennhcurtissmuseum.org

Wright Brothers' National Memorial

Wilbur and Orville Wright made the first successful sustained powered flight in a heavier-than-air machine here. That is such a simple sentence to craft and such a difficult feat to have accomplished. From the beginning of human history, virtually every person has looked skyward and wanted to take to the air. Each has wondered what it would be like to fly. In 1932, a 60-foot granite monument was placed atop the 90-foot tall Big Kill Devil Hill to commemorate what had happened there on December 17, 1903 when man's dream was finally realized!

Start your outing at The Visitor Center. It is packed with exhibits that you'll want to see. Don't miss the program that is given by a Park Ranger in the auditorium. It is stirring.

Tour the reconstructed camp buildings; they will give you a glimpse into how harsh conditions must have been for the Wrights. There are two buildings. One served as a hangar for their aircraft, The Wright Flyer. The other was a workshop and living quarters. Each is filled with items similar to the ones used by the Wrights. You will notice a large granite boulder. Walk over to it and read the inscription. This is the spot where the Wright Flyer with Orville Wright at the controls lifted off. This is the exact spot where man's imagination of what it might be like to fly became reality. In a straight line extending from this spot you will notice four numbered markers. They indicate the distance of each of the four flights made that day. The longest is 852' from where you'll be standing. The final and longest flight of the day lasted 59 seconds and reached an altitude of 10'.

The First Flight Airstrip sits in the trees to the west of where you'll be standing. You may; of course, land here in your own aircraft. If you're a pilot you'll certainly want to do that. It is a short runway at an airport offering no services at all.

The museum and the grounds can comfortably be toured in 2 hours. You can spend the rest of the day at the beach just across the road.

https://www.nps.gov/wrbr/index.htm

Cradle of Aviation Museum

The Cradle of Aviation Museum is unique for two reasons. It is one of America's newest major aviation museums and I believe it's the most spectacular one. It sets out to tell the tale of aviation in Long Island and in doing so chronicles the history of flight, for the story of one belongs to the other. It is the only Museum in the United States other than the National Air and Space Museum where the entire story of flying is told from the early 1900's until tomorrow.

To my mind there are three major aviation achievements and only one was not directly connected to this geography. If it was the Wright Brothers' that taught man how to fly, it was most certainly Lindbergh that showed us why we should.

John Purner

On May 20, 1927 he took off from a spot near here, Roosevelt Field. The actual ground he struggled to break free of is today the asphalt covered parking lot of a shopping center. Ask one of the museum's docents for directions. You need to stand where he stood and imagine his takeoff. Lindbergh took the American imagination on a trip from Long Island to Paris. His flight taught us that aviation was about high-speed travel. The world, all of it, now belonged to each of us.

If Lindbergh gave us a reason to fly then it was Neil Armstrong who removed the boundary. Landing a ship that was manufactured near here on the moon was indeed *"one small step for man and one giant leap for mankind."* With it, he gave us the stars. Yes, Houston the Eagle had landed at Tranquility Base and in a very real way it had taken off from Long Island - *The Cradle of Aviation*.

In the span of the past 100 years aviation was called upon to defend our very freedom to dream that we might go to the stars. Many of the airplanes that went to war were built here. Grumman became simply **"the Ironworks"** to Naval aviators that flew their faithful planes. You know them, they were the ones that brought our men back aboard ship with their wings shot so full of holes that they should have crashed into the ocean but they flew on because of the way the men of Long Island designed and built them - like iron angels!

If you can come to only one museum make it this one. It isn't just about the planes and spacecraft that are displayed; it is about the place that made them. When you come here you will be over-powered by the sense of history that surrounds you. History is a combination of time, people, things and place. Here they all come alive.

Come with a sense of curiosity and leave with a sense of wonder.

https://www.cradleofaviation.org

Start now to plan a great summer of flight. I'll be waiting to hear where you went.

John Purner